CW01023999

THE TRAFALGAR CHRONICLE

Dedicated to Naval History in the Nelson Era

New Series 8

Journal
of
THE 1805 CLUB

Edited by

JUDITH E PEARSON AND JOHN A RODGAARD

In association with The 1805 Club

Seaforth
PUBLISHING

Text copyright © individual authors 2023

First published in Great Britain in 2023 by
Seaforth Publishing,
A division of Pen & Sword Books Ltd,
George House, Unit 12 & 13, Beevor Street, Off Pontefract Road,
Barnsley, South Yorkshire S71 1HN

www.seaforthpublishing.com

British Library Cataloguing in Publication Data
A catalogue record for this book is available from the British Library

ISBN 978 1 3990 3900 0 (paperback)
ISBN 978 1 3990 3901 7 (epub)
ISBN 978 1 3990 3902 4 (kindle)

All rights reserved. No part of this publication may be reproduced or transmitted in any form or by any means, electronic or mechanical, including photocopying, recording, or any information storage and retrieval system, without prior permission in writing of both the copyright owner and the above publisher.

The right of the individual contributors to be identified as the authors of this work has been asserted by them in accordance with the Copyright, Designs and Patents Act 1988.

Pen & Sword Books Limited incorporates the imprints of Atlas, Archaeology, Aviation, Discovery, Family History, Fiction, History, Maritime, Military, Military Classics, Politics, Select, Transport, True Crime, Air World, Frontline Publishing, Leo Cooper, Remember When, Seaforth Publishing, The Praetorian Press, Wharncliffe Local History, Wharncliffe Transport, Wharncliffe True Crime and White Owl.

Designed and typeset in Times New Roman by Mousemat Design
Printed and bound in the UK by CPI Group (UK) Ltd, Croydon, CR0 4YY

Contents

President's Foreword

This year's *Trafalgar Chronicle* showcases the scholarship and talent of thirteen excellent authors from six countries. For this year's theme, 'The Navies of the Georgian Era – An International Perspective', the editors received articles on the prominent navies of the Age of Sail: UK, US, India, Russia, Sweden, Denmark, the Ottoman Empire, and France. No previous issue has contained such a compilation – a tour de force in capturing the naval history of the eighteenth and nineteenth centuries.

I was particularly taken with an article by Saikat Mondal, a graduate student in Calcutta, who wrote about how the Bombay Marine trained under and supported the Royal Navy, becoming the Indian Navy. Even our most seasoned readers will learn something new from this unique piece.

This issue also salutes the 500th anniversary (in 2022) of the Royal Swedish Navy with three excerpts from *The Baltic Cauldron* – a recently published comprehensive history of the Royal Swedish Navy. Many 1805 Club members contributed to this volume and some donated funding for the translation from Swedish to English. An introduction and two excerpts come from previous *Trafalgar Chronicle* editor, Peter Hore. Additionally, in this issue and on its cover, I am pleased to see the exquisite maritime artistry of our 1805 Club member, Captain Christer Hägg, Royal Swedish Navy Rtd.

Through these theme-related articles and excerpts, readers will get a sense of how the navies of the Georgian era continuously vied with one another for naval superiority and control of the seas – sometimes in war with battles and blockades, sometimes in alliances and treaties, sometimes in diplomacy and finesse. Here, we can glimpse the foundations of today's maritime world.

As always, this issue offers excellent biographical portraits of Royal Navy officers who served with dedication, gallantry, and honour, under difficult and dangerous circumstances: Captain Charles Cunningham, Admirals Rodney and

Kempenfelt, and a new personage to many readers, Captain Sir Jacob Wheate.

It's one thing to conduct in-depth research on a single, well-defined, yet little-known topic. It's another thing to mould that research into a tale that makes for good reading. The three authors in the general interest section have done just that. Mark Barton documents the swords with which the Duke of Clarence awarded naval officers. From Professor George Bandurek we have the astonishing saga of HMS *Whiting* – a Royal Navy ship lost to privateering and piracy. Finally, what did Nelson think of pirates and privateers? Ryan Walker lets our readers know.

This issue of the *Trafalgar Chronicle* combines skilful writing on fascinating topics and a lavish selection of seventy illustrations. Again, I convey my warm congratulations and appreciation to the editors and the writers who have contributed to another fine publication of The 1805 Club!

ADMIRAL SIR JONATHON BAND GCB DL
Former First Sea Lord
President of the 1805 Club

Editors' Foreword

Disputes over territorial waters, shipping lanes, and fishing rights, the intent of ocean-based missile launches, responsibilities toward refugees afloat, and global concerns about climate change – one has only to read the daily headlines to know that the navies of the world are often at the centre of international conflict, trade, and diplomacy. The same was true of the Georgian era. Naval history is often about the interactions of navies as they extend the reach of their governments beyond their countries' shores. These are the types of stories we wanted to capture in this 2023 issue of the *Trafalgar Chronicle*. That's why we chose as our theme 'The Navies of the Georgian Era – An International Perspective'. With this theme, our readers can see how international naval history provides the back-story for the many international tensions, rivalries and alliances of today's geopolitical landscape.

The 2023 edition offers fourteen well-written articles by authors from six countries on the leading navies of the Age of Sail. This edition presents articles on the navies of England, US, India, France, Sweden, Denmark, Russia and the Ottoman Empire. This issue begins with an article by frequent contributor Dr Anthony Bruce, writing about the Royal Navy's Western Squadron's two victories over the French at Cape Finisterre in 1747. Vice Admiral George Anson led the first battle and Rear Admiral Edward Hawke led the second. Andrew will take you right into the heart of each tense engagement!

Nicholas James Kaizer, Canadian scholar and expert on single-ship actions of the War of 1812, examines the factors leading to Royal Navy defeats in the largely forgotten sloop actions of the War of 1812, and highlights their importance to the study of the Royal Navy in that war.

We like to think that the *Trafalgar Chronicle* can welcome not only articles from established naval historians, but can also serve as an incubator for those who are just entering the field. Such is the case with college student Saikat Mondal of Calcutta who provides an erudite history of the Bombay Marine, and its support to the Royal Navy in India from 1607 to 1830, when the Marine became the Indian Navy. This scholar has certainly introduced a new topic to this journal!

Next, we have Kenneth Flemming's history of the eighteenth-century Russian Navy beginning under Peter the Great and revitalised by Catherine the

Great. By the time of her death in 1796, she had transformed a deteriorating fleet into a formidable naval power that contested the Black Sea and Mediterranean during her wars against the Ottoman Empire, and eventually dominated the Baltic in her wars against Sweden. As a result of these victories on land and sea, Russia expanded its territory into Ukraine, Crimea and Moldova. Catherine's mercurial successor, Tsar Paul I, would send the Baltic and Black Sea fleets to join the Royal Navy and the Ottomans to oppose France's designs on Italy, the Dalmatian coast and the Greek Ionian Isles in 1798.

Through naval historian Andrew Venn, we learn of Saumarez's diplomacy in the Baltic; maintaining diplomatic ties with a neutral yet volatile Sweden, keeping the threat of the Russian fleet at bay, and defending against the fiery Danish gunboat threat to merchant shipping.

Andrew's article makes a perfect segue to the next section in this issue – three chapters reprinted from *The Baltic Cauldron: Two Navies and the Fight for Freedom*, a richly illustrated compilation published in 2022 to document Sweden's naval history and to commemorate the 500th anniversary of the establishment of the Royal Swedish Navy. Peter Hore opens this section with an introduction to the book itself, followed by three articles: two by himself and one by Captain Christer Hägg, RSwN, ret, a maritime artist whose work graces the cover of this issue. Both Christer and Peter are members of The 1805 Club and Peter is the former editor of the *Trafalgar Chronicle*.

In Biographical Portraits we have Andrew Field's stunning recounting of Captain Charles Cunningham's daring actions and decisions when he extricated his ship, the Fifth Rate frigate HMS *Clyde* (38), from the Nore Mutiny. Next, Dr Hilary Rubinstein documents the lives of George Brydges Rodney and Richard Kempenfelt, 'two of the most capable and cerebral British admirals of George III's reign'. She supplied genealogical research to reveal that they were cousins, although they could not have been more different in character.

The next article is about Bermuda. A few years ago, Judy and John were visiting St Peter's Church in St George, Bermuda, when they learned that the remains of Captain Sir Jacob Wheate RN had been found under the church floor in 2008. He and his ship, the Fifth Rate frigate HMS *Cerberus* (32), both met their ends in 1783 in Bermuda. Judy could not get this sad, dramatic tale off her mind and had to write about it.

Our General Interest section offers a delightful collection of three informative, highly readable articles. First Dr Mark Barton identifies, compares and contrasts thirty-five swords that the Duke of Clarence gave as awards to Royal Navy officers between 1786 and 1834. Dr George Bandurek provides a whopping good tale about HM Schooner *Whiting* – a ship that underwent several reincarnations after she was captured by a French privateer in 1812.

This Bermuda-built schooner was the subject of lengthy court proceedings in America because when she was sold to the United Provinces of Granada, her new captain engaged in piracy. As an apt follow-on to Dr Bandurek, Ryan Walker astutely analyses what Nelson thought about privateers.

On a sad note, we mourn the loss of Liam Gaul, who passed away in January 2023. We met him in 2018 when we were in Wexford, Ireland, representing the Naval Order of the US. We were there for the unveiling of a historic marker describing the US Navy's presence in Wexford in the First World War. Liam attended the event on the behalf of the Wexford Historical Society. He was the author of *Wings over Wexford*, a book about US Navy patrol aircraft flying over the Irish Sea to spot German submarines. Liam was a contributor to the 2021 *Trafalgar Chronicle*, with a biographical portrait of John Barry, Wexford's native son who became the Father of the US Navy. Fair celestial winds and following seas, Liam!

As always, we thank all our authors for their acumen as historians, and for their expertise in making maritime history memorable and rich in detail. We admire the depth of their research, their selection of illustrations, and the quality of their writing. They were all marvellously obliging and co-operative with our questions and requests for revisions and/or clarification. They made our work as editors easy and enjoyable.

Next year, 2024 will mark our fifth year as editors to this journal. We have chosen as the theme for the 2024 issue: 'Naval Intelligence in the Georgian Era'. We also want to know about events and personalities that shaped the navies of the world, 1714–1837. If you like to write and conduct historic research about all manner of things pertaining to the maritime world of the Georgian era, send us a proposal and/or get on our email list of potential contributors.

To our readers: we welcome your comments, questions, ideas, and suggestions about this issue and future issues. Please tell your friends and colleagues about the *Trafalgar Chronicle*. We are eager to see reviews! Our publisher, Seaforth Publishing, welcomes purchases from individuals, organisations, universities, institutes and libraries. The 1805 Club members receive the *Trafalgar Chronicle* as well as *Dispatches* digital newsletters and the biannual *Kedge Anchor* magazine as benefits of their membership. If you aren't a member of The 1805 Club, please join by completing an application at our website, www.1805Club.org.

JUDITH E PEARSON, PhD
BURKE, VIRGINIA

JOHN A RODGAARD, CAPTAIN USN, RET
MELBOURNE, FLORIDA

The Battles of Cape Finisterre, 1747

Anthony Bruce

In August 1746 Vice Admiral George Anson (1697–1762), the circumnavigator and Admiralty Lord, took command of the new Western Squadron, which had been created in response to the threat of a French invasion and the need to improve the navy's performance. War between the two countries had been declared shortly after Britain's failure at the Battle of Toulon in 1744, which led to the dismissal of Admiral Thomas Matthews, head of the Mediterranean Fleet. British naval operations against France (and Spain) formed part of the War of the Austrian Succession (1740–48), the wider European conflict between Prussia and Austria and their respective allies.

The Western Squadron was formed by combining the navy's previously dispersed forces in home waters and would soon form the core of Britain's future naval strategy.[1] Its principal role was to cruise off the Western Approaches (the area to the west of the English Channel) for as long as possible, with several objectives in mind. These included the protection of British merchant shipping, providing a defence against invasion and monitoring the movements of the French fleet at its main bases on the Atlantic coast – Brest, Lorient and Rochefort – with the aim of intercepting convoy departures, as well as fleets returning from overseas. This article examines the Western Squadron's two victories over the French, both off Cape Finisterre; the first led by Anson and the second by Rear Admiral Edward Hawke (1710–1781).

George, Lord Anson, commander of the Western Squadron, 1746/7. Stipple engraving by Ridley, after Joshua Reynolds. Published in *Naval Chronicle*, vol 8 (1802) by J Gold, London. (Naval History and Heritage Command, Washington, DC, NH 65992)

Anson at the first Battle of Cape Finisterre

With seventeen ships of the line under his command, Anson went in search of the French fleet, commanded by Admiral Jean-Baptiste de La Rochefoucauld de Roye, Duc d'Anville, which was expected to return from Halifax in the autumn of 1746. He was realistic about his chances of success, even though he commanded a more powerful squadron than the French: 'all schemes at sea are very uncertain. The nights are long, the winter gales blow hard, and, unless fortune favours, a good look out will not always succeed.'[2] He was right to be cautious, as he returned home empty-handed in February 1747 because the French had been forewarned of his presence.

Not long after Anson's arrival, the government learnt that the French planned to despatch two convoys, one to Canada, the other to India, and it decided that 'all the force that can be got should go to sea under the command of Vice Admiral Anson'.[3] Anson's friend, Rear Admiral Peter Warren, was appointed as his second in command and was to play a leading role in the forthcoming engagement. His instructions, dated 30 March, gave him a considerable degree of discretion: 'you are to cruise on such station or stations as you shall judge proper. … You are at liberty to send detachments from you, whenever you judge it necessary, to cruise on separate stations, for the better meeting with ships of the enemy'.[4]

On 6 April Anson left Spithead in the Second Rate *Prince George* (90) with Warren in the Third Rate *Devonshire* (66); they were joined by six more ships of the line and a bomb vessel. Five other ships that departed later were ordered to join Anson sixty miles west of Belle-Île, an island off the southern coast of Brittany. He sailed for Plymouth, where he was joined by a further eleven ships, with others expected to leave later. In total, Anson's squadron consisted of eighteen ships of the line, five frigates, three sloops and two bomb vessels.

As he approached the French coast, he despatched two ships to cruise off Brest, with orders to gather information about the presence of the French convoys. After three weeks at sea, poor weather meant that the two ships had been unable to obtain any useful intelligence, but on 20 April the Fourth Rate *Nottingham* (60) learnt that a convoy bound for Canada was anchored in Aix Roads off Rochefort. It was likely that the warships waiting there had been sent from Brest, and Anson switched his attention to Rochefort.

After consulting with Warren and his captains, Anson concluded that the convoy was likely to pass the coast of Galicia in northwest Spain and that Cape Ortegal would be the most likely location to intercept it. But it was no more than their best guess and they were aware that the French might take a different route. As Warren commented to Anson, if they encountered a southerly wind, it was 'likely they may not be able to hold their course off Spain nor you to get there',

Admiral Sir Peter Warren, second in command of the Western Squadron, 1747; a painting by
Thomas Hudson, c1751. (© National Maritime Museum, Greenwich, London, 14552)

in short 'tis all chance to which we must submit, and content ourselves with the
merit of deserving success by our diligence whether we meet with it or not.'[5]

Anson left Belle-Île without delay and sailed south across the Bay of Biscay.
He ensured that the squadron was kept ready for battle, taking the opportunity
to hold daily exercises 'in forming line and in manoeuvres of battle till then

absolutely unknown'.[6] His captains were ordered to cruise in extended order in line-ahead and line-abreast formations, while instructing his Fourth Rate ships of fifty to sixty guns 'to extend the front as look-outs, taking station at daylight as far in advance, when in line ahead, or as wide upon the beam when in line abreast, as signals could be seen'.[7] During these exercises Anson used the *Additional Fighting Instructions* he had produced before the cruise, which gave him greater flexibility when issuing orders to his captains.[8]

When he reached his new station off Cape Ortegal, Anson deployed his ships in line abreast about a mile apart, but after several days with no sign of the convoy, he became concerned that the French had taken a different route. On 2 May he despatched the Sixth Rate *Inverness* (22) and *Falcon* (10) to Rochefort for news, while sending frigates to monitor movements in other French Atlantic ports. *Falcon* returned the next day to report that the previous afternoon she had sighted a fleet of thirty-eight ships sailing westwards at a distance of some fifteen miles. By this point, it was calculated that the French were to the southwest of the squadron, and Anson issued orders to intercept them: within thirty minutes, Edward Boscawen in the Third Rate *Namur* (74) had sighted them. A general chase was signalled, and the ships were cleared for action.

By 11.00am, the French had come into view and Anson followed them in loose formation (as was permitted by the *Fighting Instructions* when pursuing an enemy). Consisting of two squadrons, the French had fewer ships and guns than the British. The first, under the command of Jacques-Pierre de Taffanel, Marquis de La Jonquière, consisted of his flagship the Third Rate *Sérieux* (64), four other warships, and twenty-four merchant vessels. The convoy was bound for Canada, where La Jonquière was to take up the post of governor-general and make another attempt to retake Cape Breton Island from the British.

The second squadron, under the command of Jacques-François Grout, Seigneur de Saint-Georges, carried reinforcements destined for India, where the French sought to extend their territorial gains following the capture of Madras in September 1746. It consisted of the Third Rate *Invincible* (74), commanded by Saint-Georges, the Fourth Rate *Jason* (52), six converted warships operated by the Compagnie des Indes, and eighteen merchantmen. The combined squadrons were due to sail southwest across the Bay of Biscay for the northwest coast of Spain, where they would pass Cape Ortegal and Cape Finisterre.

By 1.00pm, the British, who were now some seventy-two miles west of Cape Ortegal, had closed to within three miles of the French. La Jonquière ordered his nine largest ships (including his East Indiamen) to turn into the wind with shortened sail and form a line-ahead formation while the rest of the convoy sailed away to the west as quickly as possible. Anson responded by forming his squadron in line abreast, but soon afterwards he made a signal to form a line of battle ahead.

As *Devonshire* came alongside *Prince George*, Warren discussed the position with Anson. Suspecting that the French manoeuvre was designed to allow the convoy to escape overnight, he suggested an immediate pursuit without forming a line. However, despite his overwhelming superiority, Anson cautiously decided to continue forming a line of battle ahead before mounting a concentrated attack. As a result, offensive action was delayed, allowing the French merchant ships time to escape. It has been argued that Anson's caution meant that his 'performance on the day fell short of what it should have been'.[9]

It took some two hours for the British line to form, and it was not until 3.00pm that Anson ordered his leading ships to head for the centre of the French line. When Warren saw the signal, he bore away in chase rather than in succession, and several members of his van division followed. Anson immediately signalled Warren to reform the line, enabling them to strike the French centre followed by an attack on their rear. Although the reasons for these decisions were not recorded, it is likely that 'after months of practising his fleet in bearing up and attacking in good order, he may well have determined that his attack should be orderly, his squadron well in hand, and its effect as conclusive as possible.'[10]

When La Jonquière saw the British heading for his centre in great strength, he ordered a fighting retreat and sailed away to the southwest. At about 3.15pm, after the French had broken their line, Anson hoisted the signal for a general chase for the first time, abandoning the line, which had been 'sacrosanct since the time of James, Duke of York [Lord High Admiral, 1660–73]'.[11] At about 4.00pm, the Fourth Rate *Centurion* (54) was the first to engage the French, opening fire on the enemy's rear with her chase (bow) guns. She attacked the flagships *Sérieux* and *Invincible* alone at close range for fifteen minutes before three other members of the van division – *Namur*, the Fourth Rates *Defiance* (60) and *Windsor* (60) – entered the fight.

At first, the British were outnumbered as 'they came into action in a rough line ahead and were met with a heavy fire from the more closely grouped French main body, each British ship as she arrived receiving the broadsides of two ships and the shot from the chase guns of others'.[12] As the remaining members of the van division – the Fourth Rate HMS *Nottingham* (60), the Third Rate *Yarmouth* (64) and *Devonshire* – arrived, the balance began to shift in favour of the British. At this point, Anson sent *Falcon* to shadow the convoy, with orders to send signals indicating the course it was taking, and she later captured the Indiaman *Dartmouth* (18).

The French fought with courage and determination, inflicting significant damage on the British ships that joined the fight in the first hour. By 5.00pm, the majority of the British squadron had engaged the French rear and were now able to bring their greater force to bear upon them. *Devonshire* played a leading role in the battle, fighting *Sérieux* at close quarters before she surrendered with 140 crew killed or wounded. She then opened fire on *Invincible* (74), the largest ship in the French fleet, which surrendered after a second broadside from the Fourth Rate *Bristol* (50), commanded by William Montagu. When the Fourth Rate *Pembroke* (60) attempted to get between *Bristol* and *Invincible*, 'Mad' Montagu shouted at her commander, 'Run foul of me and be damned; neither you, nor any other man in the world, shall come between me and my enemy.'[13]

By 6.00pm, when the first French ships surrendered, Anson had come up in the slow-moving *Prince George*, but along with five other English ships, *Prince George* played no part in the battle. The engagement continued until 7.00pm when the French surrendered after all hope of resistance ended. Anson now turned his attention to the rest of the convoy, which had slipped away and, as the battle ended, he sent three more ships, the Third Rate *Monmouth* (64), *Yarmouth* and *Nottingham* in pursuit. They vanished as night fell, but eighteen ships were captured the following day together with the Sixth Rates *Vigilante* (22) and *Modeste* (22). The surviving merchant ships, accompanied by the Sixth Rate frigate *Émeraude* (24), reached Quebec safely towards the end of June.

The four-hour engagement had resulted in heavy casualties on both sides, with the French losing seven hundred men killed and wounded. Both La Jonquière and Saint-Georges were taken prisoner and remained in British captivity until the peace of Aix-la-Chapelle (1748). The British lost some 520 men killed and wounded. They took eighteen French ships (including six ships of the line, several frigates and part of the convoy) and prize money valued at £755,896 (nearly £132 million in 2022). Apart from their heavy losses in ships, men, guns and money, the French had incurred £1.5 million (£268 million in 2022) in abortive costs in equipping the two expeditions.[14]

The French had fought a British squadron that was significantly stronger and had been deployed skilfully, engaging at close range as Anson had demanded. They had surrendered only when there was no alternative. Although Anson did not lead his squadron in battle, he directed it effectively from a distance, and his well-trained captains had followed his orders. In explaining his success, Anson pointed to the benefits of superior British gunnery: 'my ships made a much hotter fire, and much more regular than theirs, when they had a superior number, which they had in the beginning.'[15] He might also have mentioned that, unlike the French, the English were able to fire their large cannon from the lowest gun deck.[16]

When news of the navy's first decisive victory after seven years of war reached London, the Duke of Bedford, First Lord of the Admiralty, reported that 'the King told me … this morning that I had given him the best breakfast he had had this long time; and I think I never saw him more pleased in my life.'[17] The battle was 'far reaching in its effects', as Prime Minister Henry Pelham pointed out: it represented the 'total defeat of their projects in both India and America, [and was] an event which no one could have expected, and seems reserved for the fortunate and able hand of our friend Anson.'[18] Anson received £62,991 in prize money (almost £11 million in 2022), representing two-thirds of the flag's eighth share. He was raised to the peerage as Baron Anson of Soberton, and Peter Warren was knighted.

Hawke and the second Battle of Finisterre

When Anson went back to the Admiralty, he was succeeded by Warren as head of the Western Squadron, but in August Warren was taken ill with scurvy. He was replaced by Rear Admiral Edward Hawke, who had distinguished himself at the Battle of Toulon and had gained valuable experience during service in the Mediterranean. Armed with Warren's instructions, which required him to cruise between the latitudes of Belle-Île and Ushant, keeping about a hundred miles west of Ushant, Hawke left Plymouth in the Fourth Rate *Windsor* (60) on 9 August.[19] When he arrived off Ushant, he found four ships of the line on station and during the following weeks others joined him, increasing his squadron to fourteen ships of the line.

After spending some time at his original rendezvous, where he sought information about French preparations from neutral coastal vessels, he sailed south to Cape Ortegal, close to where Anson had intercepted the French in May. Hawke's movements along the coast were intended to 'leave false trails to persuade the French to come out by the route the British wished them to choose'.[20] He hoped his presence off Cape Ortegal would discourage them from leaving the Bay of Biscay by the normal southern route and make it more likely that they would choose a northerly route, where he would lie in wait.

By late September, sufficient intelligence had been collected to indicate that a large convoy was being assembled at La Rochelle, with an escort being prepared at Brest. In preparing for the battle ahead, Hawke transferred his flag to the more powerful *Devonshire* and consulted his captains about the aggressive tactics he intended to employ. As he was likely to have a more powerful force than his opponent, he expected to raise a signal for a general chase during the engagement. He also wanted his captains to adopt an opening firing distance of fewer than 20yds – within the range of a pistol shot – and

The Right Honourable Edward Lord Hawke (1705–1781), 1793. Engraved by John Hall
from a painting by Francis Cotes RA and printed by Craven William Richards.
(Yale Center for British Art, public domain)

there is evidence that they followed this requirement, with George Rodney, for example, engaging *Neptune* very closely for two hours.[21]

On 14 October, more than two months after his departure from Plymouth, Hawke was cruising in search of the French some 140 miles to the west of Ushant and due north of Cape Finisterre when the enemy convoy was first spotted. At 7.00am, the Third Rate HMS *Edinburgh* (70) signalled that seven ships had been seen to the southwest and Hawke issued the signal for a general chase. As they sailed towards the enemy, it became clear that they faced a large convoy, although they did not yet know how many warships were present.

Three hours later, when the squadron was four miles from the enemy, Hawke raised the signal for forming a line of battle to concentrate his force, but it had dispersed during the chase and would take time to form. As Hawke approached, the French commander, Henri-François des Herbiers, Marquis de L'Estenduère, ordered his convoy of some 250 merchantmen to escape to the west, accompanied by the East Indiaman *Content* (64). Despite this precautionary measure, many of the French merchantmen were captured before they reached Martinique, their final destination in the West Indies.

L'Estenduère now had eight warships remaining, including the flagship, the Third Rate *Tonnant* (80), three 74s, two 64s and one 50-gun ship, and at 10.40am, he began forming a line of battle sailing to the southwest, close to the wind. Although he was heavily outnumbered, five of his 'ships were not only more heavily armed than the British but were much more strongly constructed and bore bigger complements.'[22] With the convoy escaping, Hawke planned to defeat the escort first before pursuing the merchantmen. At 11.00am, he again raised the signal for a general chase, putting to one side the *Fighting Instructions*, which specified that he 'should have pitted his eight strongest ships against [the French line], ship for ship, and signalled to the other six to fall back into a *corps de réserve*.'[23] He deployed the signal to close rapidly on the French and it remained in place until the end of the battle.

The opposing forces were now some three hundred miles west of Lorient and three hundred and fifty miles north of Cape Finisterre, a considerable distance from the place which gave the battle its name. At 11.30am, Hawke raised the red flag ordering the squadron to engage, and a confused action, in which they fought aggressively, followed: 'each British captain engaged whichever ship of the enemy he first came up with, fought her until a fresh ship came up from astern and then passed along the line to engage the next ahead.'[24]

The Fourth Rate *Lyon* (60), which was the first British ship in action, opened fire on the lee side of *Neptune* (58), the last of four in the French rear, as she came within 'pistol shot range'. She was to run the whole length of the French line, reaching the leading ship after about four hours' fighting. *Lyon* was soon joined by the Fourth Rate HMS *Princess Louisa* (60) and *Monmouth*, which engaged with 'great bravery'. In an unplanned manoeuvre, she was the first of three British ships to reach the windward side of the French line. This enabled the British simultaneously to attack the enemy rear on both sides, giving them a clear advantage, despite their ships being weaker individually than their opponents.

As other British ships joined the action, the Fifth Rate *Severne* (50) came under heavy fire from Hawke in *Devonshire* and was the first French ship to surrender (to be followed by *Fougueux*). He later described the action: 'in passing on to the front ship we could get near, we received many fires at a distance till we came close to the *Severne* of 50 guns, whom we soon silenced and left to be taken up by the frigates astern.'[25]

As the British squadron progressed up the French line, from rear to van, it continued to fire broadsides from both sides and by 3.15pm, all four ships in the French rear – *Neptune*, *Fougueux*, *Severne* and *Monarque* – had surrendered.

Running battles with the remaining ships in the French van – the Third Rates *Intrépide* (74), *Terrible* (74), *Trident* (64) and *Tonnant* – continued for another two hours. After engaging *Severne*, *Devonshire* had closed on *Tonnant*, but collided with the Fourth Rate HMS *Eagle* (60), commanded by Rodney, which *Neptune* had damaged. *Devonshire* was then out of action for two hours when her lower-deck guns broke away from their breechings before returning to the fight to engage *Trident*. By this point, Hawke had complained that *Kent* was 'not so closely engaged as I could have wished', and signalled to Captain Fox to come to a 'closer engagement'.[26]

As it became dark, at about 5.30pm, *Intrépide*, the leading French ship, helped *Tonnant*, which was now surrounded, to break away to the north, with Rodney in pursuit. He asked Philip Saumarez and Charles Saunders to join him, and from 7.00pm they engaged the more powerful French ships in an unequal engagement. These distinguished captains continued the fight for more than ninety minutes before both ships disappeared into the night and returned to Brest. Saumarez was killed, bringing a promising career to a premature end, and the masts and rigging of all three ships were badly 'shott all to pieces'.[27] Augustus Keppel later commented: 'Poor Saumarez died like what he was, alongside of *le Tonnant*, much regretted by the whole squadron … I enquired particularly after Rodney and Charles Saunders, and by accounts no one outdid the latter.'[28]

Further south, the action in the van had continued. From about 6.00pm, Hawke exchanged fire with *Terrible*, with *Princess Louisa* joining the fight. As *Devonshire* closed to within pistol shot of *Terrible*, she surrendered at 7.30pm, bringing the engagement to a close. Hawke described the end of the battle:

Having observed that six of the enemy's ships had struck, and it being very dark and our own ships dispersed, I thought it best to bring to for that night; and seeing a great firing along way astern of me, I was in hope to have seen more of the enemy's ships taken in the morning. But instead of that I received the melancholy account of Captain Samaurez being killed, and that the *Tonnant* had escaped, by the assistance of the *Intrepide*.[29]

On 15 October, while emergency repairs were carried out, Hawke called a meeting of his senior captains to discuss whether they should pursue the two warships that had escaped. As the meeting assembled, most of the captains objected to Captain Fox's presence because *Kent* had failed to engage closely enough. Hawke was forced to exclude him and announced that he would request a court martial to give him the opportunity to clear his name.[30] Fox was tried in November, found guilty and cashiered, but was later reinstated as a superannuated rear admiral under the new retirement scheme developed by Lord Anson.

It was agreed that four ships would be required to pursue *Tonnant* and *Intrépide*, but none of the squadron's ships was able to do so. Hawke had already decided against detaching any ships of the line to go after the convoy and also ruled out sending his frigates, as it was strongly defended by the Indiaman *Content* and several frigates. Instead, he despatched the sloop *Weazel* (16) to warn the commander-in-chief of the Leeward Islands, and she arrived there a day before the convoy. Nearly forty merchantmen were captured as a result.

The French ship *Intrépide* (74) in action against several English ships at the Second Battle of Cape Finisterre, 14 October 1747, an engraving by an unknown artist, 1747. (Naval History and Heritage Command, Washington, DC, NH61792)

Hawke spent two days rigging the French ships with jury masts before carrying them to Portsmouth. As many as four thousand French seamen had been killed or captured, compared to British losses of 170 dead and 577 wounded. Hawke's victory considerably enhanced his reputation, and soon after his return he was knighted and elected as a Member of Parliament for Portsmouth. He was to play a prominent role during the Seven Years War before winning a second decisive victory against France at the Battle of Quiberon Bay in 1759, and was created Baron Hawke in 1776.

Reflections on the successes of the two battles

The Royal Navy's successes in 1747 had fully justified the decision to create the Western Squadron a year earlier and the priority Anson gave to training had rapidly turned it into an effective fighting force. During the two battles of Cape Finisterre, Anson had displayed more caution than Hawke, but both had acted decisively, encouraged aggressive action, and were not constrained by official regulations about forming a line of battle. Both commanders had adopted a 'similar tactical sequence of chase, then line, then chase again, followed by the signal for close engagement' as they responded to the moves of their French opponents.[31]

Following their defeats at the hands of Anson and Hawke, the French did not attempt to launch a naval counter-attack in 1748. As the Duke of Newcastle, the Secretary of State for the Southern Department, pointed out:

> The marine of France will, I hope, by these two last affairs have received an almost fatal blow. Sir Peter Warren told me this morning that the King had more ships in his ports than remained now in the ports of France; that we could beat them with their own ships; and that he desired to carry the challenge.[32]

Lord Anson's own assessment of the position soon after Hawke's victory was that: 'our fleets have had pretty good success and are in excellent condition, for which reason the French will never think of trying their strength at sea nor carry on more trade than is necessary to supply their colonies.'[33]

In these unfavourable circumstances, the French focused on land operations in the Austrian Netherlands before peace preliminaries were agreed upon in April 1748; the Treaty of Aix-la-Chapelle finally ended the war in October.

George Anson's victory off Cape Finisterre, 3 May 1747, see colour plate 1

Hornet versus *Peacock*:
The Lost Historical Significance of the Single-Ship Actions of the War of 1812

Nicholas James Kaizer

The War of 1812 is chiefly known in the United Kingdom for its dramatic single-ship actions. Even in Canada and the United States, these actions hold an outsized place in the historical memory. In the historiography of the Royal Navy, however, these actions are largely dismissed as unequal contests of little note; giants such as N A M Rodger or Andrew Lambert remind readers that the Fifth Rate frigates HM Ships *Guerriere*, *Macedonian* and *Java* were defeated by heavy frigates such as the Fourth Rate USS *Constitution*, against whom they never had any real hope of success. That was also the public understanding at the time, in Britain and here in Nova Scotia, the home of the Royal Navy's North American Station. In a previous article (published in the 2022 edition of

Constitution and *Guerriere*, engraving print by Mason after Woodside, 1813.
(Naval History and Heritage Command, Washington, DC, NH 69-019-A)

the *Trafalgar Chronicle*), this author argued that this view was not reflective of the serving officers of the Royal Navy, in particular most of the officers who actually fought in these actions. However, it was nonetheless the view which has come to dominate popular imagination and historiography.[1] But this understanding also ignores most of the single-ship actions that actually occurred during this conflict. Missing from the general historical narrative are the many smaller-scale actions between sloops of war, where a very different picture emerges.

This paper will examine the factors leading to the defeats in the largely forgotten sloop actions of the War of 1812, and highlight their importance to the study of the Royal Navy in the immediate post-Nelson period. The sloop actions of the conflict reveal that the notion, apparent in modern scholarship and contemporary sources, that the British generally won evenly matched fights is not correct. Consequentially, these actions reveal a possible problem of competency amongst officers of the Royal Navy, most evident in the two most dramatic of these sloop actions: the losses of HM Sloops *Peacock* and *Epervier*.

Sloop actions of the War of 1812

The three single-ship actions involving *Constitution* and *United States* in 1812 are frequently discussed in British and American accounts of the conflict, as is the *Shannon–Chesapeake* action of 1813.[2] Much less has been written about the eight single-ship actions involving sloops of war; even at the time, they lacked the same lustre of the more dramatic frigate actions, and so quickly faded into history.[3] By ignoring these actions, however, some British academics over the past two centuries have drawn incorrect conclusions. In a previous article (published in the 2022 edition of the *Trafalgar Chronicle*), this author demonstrated that the prevailing view of the British contemporary public and modern historiography was that the single-ship actions of the War of 1812 were unimportant as, in the words of N A M Rodger, 'in the case of 18-pounder frigates in action with 24-pounder ships, the disparity in force is a sufficient explanation.'[4]

Others, such as Andrew Lambert, highlight that the actions between more evenly matched opponents – *Shannon* vs *Chesapeake*, 1813; *Phoebe* vs *Essex*, 1814; and *Endymion* vs *President*, 1815 – were all British victories. The conclusion often reached in contemporary and modern public discourse was that the British lost when they were unfairly matched and won when they faced evenly matched opponents. This conclusion is obvious enough, on face value, when considering the frigate actions – the views of contemporary naval officers aside – but it does not hold up when you consider the eight sloop actions of the conflict. Most, in fact, were American victories, and their courts martial reveal that the British defeats were the clear result of an appalling lack of leadership and preparedness on the part of the British officers.

That they have been largely forgotten in British and Canadian histories of the conflict, therefore, is not surprising. Indeed, contemporary sources on this action are difficult to come by, as no contemporary news publications in Britain or Canada printed any of the official reports or courts-martial coverage, which had been common practice even for defeats in the period. Contemporary and modern historians have had little interest in these actions, but they are not unimportant. These actions show that the Royal Navy had a larger problem in the War of 1812 than simple disparity in force (the focus of modern historiography): there was also a serious issue of competency amongst its commanders. Commander Peake of *Peacock*, and Commander Wales of *Epervier*, in particular, demonstrated a profoundly incompetent command of their ships, and their respective crews were woefully unprepared for battle when they went into action.

The first such action was the loss of HM Sloop *Alert* (16), a slow and poorly armed ex-collier that was engaged and decisively defeated by the Fifth Rate frigate USS *Essex* (36). The result of this battle was never in contention, as *Alert* was vastly outmatched by the American frigate, with sixteen 18lb carronades to *Essex*'s thirty-six 32lb carronades. The action had almost no impact on popular imagination, and was quickly overshadowed in the press by the frigate actions later in the year. Indeed, *Essex*'s captain David Porter was one of few who thought anything of the battle; the disparity in force was such that the outcome was never in doubt, but he was deeply impressed that *Alert* had fought the battle at all, given such odds.[5]

Shortly after, a badly damaged HM Sloop *Frolic* (18), a *Cruizer*-class brig sloop commanded by Captain[6] Thomas Whinyates, was captured by US Sloop *Wasp* (20), under Master Commandant Jacob Jones. *Frolic*'s encounter with *Wasp* could not have been worse timed; she had suffered extensive rigging damage in a recent gale and was in the midst of reassembling a scattered convoy when she spotted *Wasp*. They were, though, relatively well-matched ships on paper. Both carried a main battery of 32lb carronades, which meant any action would be at close range, where the Royal Navy typically was most comfortable. Early in the action, Whinyates was confident of victory, on account of what proved to be deceptively effective gunnery. His gun crews were faster than the enemy, firing three for every two broadsides, but his guns were inflicting less damage than *Wasp*'s. This was a problem, for *Frolic* was already in a poor state to begin with, and as the damage mounted, *Frolic* was left unmanageable and at the mercy of *Wasp*'s raking fire.[7]

More important was the loss of HM Sloop *Peacock* (18) in February 1813 to

Hornet and *Peacock* shown in 'John Bull in Distress', by Amos Doolittle, 1813. In one of America's earliest political cartoons, the small but mighty American hornet is assaulting Britain, represented by a mash-up of the traditional John Bull and a peacock, representing the defeated sloop. (Yale University Art Gallery, Library Transfer – Accession Number 1955.55.20, no copyright)

the US Sloop *Hornet* (20). *Hornet*'s commander, Master Commandant James Lawrence, was spoiling for a fight; recently, he had attempted to challenge another British sloop, *Bonne Citoyenne* (20), to battle, but the British captain declined.[8] His encounter with *Peacock* on 24 February 1813 then was a godsend for the ambitious American captain. It was precisely the opposite for the British commander, William Peake. Though relatively evenly matched – each carried carronades, 32pdrs on *Hornet* and 24pdrs on *Peacock* – it was immediately apparent that *Hornet*'s ship's company was better trained and commanded. *Peacock* was very quickly torn apart by *Hornet*'s heavier broadside, which was fired both faster and more accurately. Peake was killed in the cannonade, leaving her lieutenant Frederick Wright to surrender his quickly sinking sloop.

While Wright cited the larger crew of *Hornet* – not, interestingly, the heavier guns – in his defence at the resulting court martial, it was the pitiful state of gunnery which most interested the court. It was found that *Peacock*'s fire was very poor and often missed the target, therefore doing little damage to *Hornet*. One officer attributed it to the rough conditions of the waves, although the gunner attributed it to a poor gunnery training regime.[9] Under Wright, *Peacock* was well known as a tidy ship, and had been nicknamed 'the Yacht'. Because of her dedication to decoration and polish, however, her crew had not been sufficiently trained in the use of the guns, resulting in a poor performance, with deadly consequences, when she went into action with *Hornet*.[10]

The news improved following this action: HMS *Shannon* took USS *Chesapeake* off Boston, in an as evenly matched contest as naval officers could hope for. Shortly after, the brig-sloop, HMS *Pelican* (18) overwhelmed the brig USS *Argus* (18) too. Both victories were the result of excellent command and gunnery displayed by the British ships' companies.[11] In September, however, the brig USS *Enterprise* captured the British brig HMS *Boxer*.

Both were armed with 18lb carronades, and again the action was decided due to a marked disparity in the quality of command and gunnery. The British managed to only inflict minor damage on *Enterprise* and her rigging, while the Americans managed to take out *Boxer*'s officers, much of her rigging, and several guns.[12] Naval historians William James and Theodore Roosevelt (James a contemporary observer and the first and chief defender of the prevailing British historical argument) argued that *Enterprise*'s superior armament and crew size sufficiently explained her victory, and while James admitted that the Americans' guns were handled with more skill, Roosevelt asserts that the two

Enterprise versus *Boxer* off the coast of Maine, 5 September 1813, painted by Michel Corne. (Naval History and Heritage Command, Washington, DC, NH 1000/NH 1161)

forces fought with equal skill, pointing to the fact that the casualties on both sides were close to equal.[13] However, the officers overseeing *Boxer*'s court martial were of a different mind:

> The court is of the opinion that the capture of H.M. brig *Boxer*, by the U.S. vessel of war Enterprise, is to be attributed to a superiority in the enemy's force, principally in the number of men, as well as to a greater degree the skill in the direction of her fire, and the destructive effects of her first broadside.[14]

Enterprise had two more guns than *Boxer*, and otherwise the two sloops were armed with the same main battery. The court martial was not very interested in this relatively insignificant advantage in firepower. They were more concerned with the larger crew onboard *Enterprise*, which went into action with nearly double the men. In fact, other naval officers of this period argued that larger crews were of more consequence than heavier broadsides. Contemporary accounts of naval officers Captain William Tremlett, Captain Sir William Dillon and Lieutenant Henry Edward Napier all make the case that larger and better trained crews posed more significant advantages than heavier broadsides.[15] More concerning for the Royal Navy, though, was the finding that *Boxer*'s loss was in part the result of less skilful and effective gunnery, as had been the case with *Peacock*.

The most egregious example, arguably, was HMS *Epervier* (18), another *Cruizer*-class brig-sloop, commanded by Richard Wales (a nephew of the prominent Admiral John Warren).[16] *Epervier* was by no means a lucky sloop. The highlight of her career was sinking at anchor in Halifax Harbour, resting under water for some time before being raised and repaired. On 29 April 1814, whilst on route to Halifax, she encountered the American sloop of war USS *Peacock* (20), named for the unfortunate 'Yacht' captured in 1813.

Things immediately went badly wrong for Wales: several of *Epervier*'s 32lb carronades snapped from the sides as they were fired, and went careening along the deck. Their fastenings were corroded, likely due to exposure to the saltwater while the ship was submerged, and the impact of recoil caused them to snap off. With every broadside, more and more carronades came loose, threatening to crush the sailors scrambling around her deck. Men had to be diverted with every broadside to catch and restrain the guns, stretching the demoralised men to their limits as they tried to keep up with the Americans' rate of fire. *Epervier*'s morale deteriorated over the next half-hour, many men fleeing their stations and taking refuge below. The senior lieutenant, John Hackett, attempted to rally the men, but was struck in the arm by enemy shot,

Action between USS *Peacock* and HMS *Epervier*, War of 1812, by American watercolour artist Worden Wood (1880–1943). (Yale University Art Gallery – 1941.210, no copyright).

which carried his elbow joint clean off. Meanwhile, *Peacock*'s gunnery made quick work of *Epervier*'s rigging, leaving her unmanageable and subject to the waves. After the mainmast went by the board, only one carronade was left in action, and Commander Wales 'deemed it prudent to surrender', forced to be content with the fact that he had fought long enough to allow his convoy to escape.[17]

The two vessels were evenly matched on paper, but *Epervier* really did not stand a chance, and the court martial tells us why. For one thing, we learn in the court martial records that *Epervier*'s crew was wholly unprepared for action. The court had questioned Wales on the state of training of his crew, and on the cause of the carronades chaos:

Q: Have the crew generally speaking exercised in the use of the great guns?
A: They were frequently exercised, but there were many who were not so expert as I thought they ought to have been, from the time they had been exercised.

…

Q: Did the [fighting] bolts ever come out of their places in a similar manner when the guns were exercised?
A: No.[18]

According to Wales, though the guns had been exercised frequently, no defect in the carronade fastenings had been discovered. The reason soon became apparent, though, when Lieutenant Hackett admitted they had only ever fired one live round in practice:

Q: Did the same circumstance ever occur when the guns were exercised?
A: No, as we never exercised with powder and I conceived it was from the concussion of the guns.
Q: From the time of your pointing the *Epervier* until the Day of the Action was the weather frequently [unintelligible] as to have allowed your exercising with powder, and frequently at a mark?
A: After we went to sea, I think the latter end of January or the beginning of February there was so much to do from the brig being lately fitted out, that we were obliged to take every opportunity of putting the rigging in order during the first cruise when we went out the second time with convoy for Bermuda, and the West Indies during that voyage after leaving the convoy we certainly had frequent opportunities of firing at a mark although the ship now was in a bad state from the bowsprit and heel of the foremast being sprung.
Q: Were the men well acquainted with the use of the great guns?
A: They were.
Q: How often were they exercised without powder?
A: Every evening for an hour when the weather would permit.[19]

The men had drilled frequently, but almost never with live ammunition. Not only had the men received an inadequate level of gunnery drill, but the officers had not even attempted to test their gunnery equipment after the sloop had been partly submerged in Halifax Harbour.

Remarkably, all of the officers of *Epervier* – the commander, the lieutenants, and the master – blamed their loss on the poor state of the crew. *Epervier*'s ship's company was described on the whole as 'a weak crew and not bred as seamen'.[20] This bizarre defence ignores the obvious culpability of Wales and his officers as those responsible for training and leading their men. If the crew were abysmal fighters, that was surely the fault of their commanders, who had neglected to even test the ship's equipment after she had spent days under water. Indeed, a full reading of the court martial makes it clear that Commander Wales's lack of leadership was largely responsible for *Epervier*'s loss.

Despite this, the court was (publicly, at least) satisfied with Wales's conduct. They did not consider his training regime or his responsibility for training the crew when rendering their verdict, and instead judged him on his conduct in action. Since he had acted bravely and did everything in his power to fight and defend the ship, he was acquitted accordingly. The loss was blamed on the poor state of the crew and the ship, with little consideration for his role in the ship being in such a state.

Finally, in 1814, a newly built sloop USS *Wasp* (20) set off on a dramatic cruise into the heart of British territory, on which voyage she defeated two British sloops-of-war, *Reindeer* (18) and *Avon* (18), before she disappeared without a trace. As with the other battles described above, neither of these two sloops was significantly under-armed compared to *Wasp*. Indeed, aside from the loss of *Alert*, a disparity in broadside weight was not a decisive factor in any of the outcomes of the sloop actions of the War of 1812. This concurs with the prevailing views of the Royal Navy: an analysis of after-action reports, courts-martial minutes, and correspondence of contemporary serving officers highlights that even with the three frigate actions of 1812, the Royal Navy on the whole did not consider the stronger broadsides of the American heavy frigates to be a decisive factor.[21] Instead, it was the quality of gunnery that played a decisive role in most of the actions. Evidence suggests, in fact, that the Admiralty was concerned about this very thing as the war progressed.

The subject of the quality of gunnery displayed by Royal Navy crews in the single-ship actions of the War of 1812 was a not infrequent subject in public discourse, in particular in publications like the *Naval Chronicle*. The *Chronicle* was marketed, and today understood, as being published 'by and for' naval officers,[22] although many of its contributors were somewhat ill-informed of naval matters, enough so that the few naval officers who did contribute letters stand out from the rest. One such contributor was Captain William Tremlett, who wrote to the *Chronicle* to add his voice to the public discourse following the losses of 1812. Among other insights, Tremlett asserts that in general the victorious American ships had crews whose:

seamen have been more exercised in firing at a mark than ours – their government having given their commanders leave to exercise whenever they think proper, and to fire away as much ammunition as they please. By the rules of our navy, we are not allowed a sufficient quantity of powder in one year to exercise the people one month (notwithstanding we try, by every means in our power, to add to this allowance).[23]

Here, Tremlett highlights the importance of live-fire drill and effective gunnery practice, something generally lacking in British ships compared to American vessels. This was certainly the case with Peake and Wales, and their ships' logs and courts-martial testimonies attest to that. They relied on pantomime exercises, carrying out all of the moves of loading and firing a gun without actually burning any of their gunpowder supplies. This often meant that inexperienced sailors would go into action and be shocked by the noise and commotion of a gunnery duel, which hampered their morale and effectiveness in action. Confusion on board a ship, in as cramped a space as a gun deck, was not conducive to safety or efficiency.[24]

Based upon Wales's court-martial testimony, it seems he considered his general training regime sufficient. Others, however, may have resorted to pantomime drilling because, as Tremlett argued, the Admiralty did not supply their captains with enough powder to both frequently train their men and take their ships into naval combat. In fact, before 1813 Admiralty instructions on gunnery drills were often quite vague to begin with: live fire had never been explicitly required, and captains were given great leeway to avoid exercising when conditions were not 'convenient'. Officers such as Peake or Wales might neglect their gunnery drill if the weather conditions were not perfect, for example. Their ships were kept to a vastly inferior state of readiness compared to those commanded by captains of the calibre of Philip Broke, whose unique and scientific approach to gunnery training turned his frigate *Shannon* (38) into one of the most efficient fighting machines in the Royal Navy.[25] Most would have existed somewhere between the two extremes, and so the actual quality and fighting efficiency of Royal Navy crews varied considerably. Captains of the calibre of Peake and Wales, however, could not have been rare. Throughout the War of 1812 there were hundreds of ships stationed in North American waters, and dozens of sloops of war. Three of the eight that fought a single-ship sloop action with the Americans proved to be woefully unprepared for action.

The losses of 1812 prompted new directives from the Admiralty. At their request, the commander-in-chief of the North American Station, Admiral John Warren, issued a memorandum to his captains:

Their Lordships trust that all of the Officers of His Majesty's Naval Service must be convinced that upon the good discipline and the proper training of their Ships Companies to the expert management of the Guns, the preservation of the high character of the British navy most essentially depends, and that other works on which it is not unusual to employ the Men are of very trifling importance, when Compared with a due Preparation (by instruction and practice) for the effectual Services on the day of Battle.[26]

This reminded captains that success in battle depended on handling of the guns; Royal Navy captains had to take gunnery drills seriously in order to keep up a rate of fire and accuracy needed to compete with the Americans, and to that end were ordered to instil regular gunnery drills and to record exercises in the ships' logs.[27] Just as this memorandum was being issued, however, Commander Peake's *Peacock* was demonstrating exactly the problem the Admiralty was warning against, and as the war progressed, *Boxer* and *Epervier* would do the same.

Why had the Admiralty allowed such leniency when it came to gunnery drill amongst the Royal Navy – and provided insufficient stores of gunpowder – when, in their own view, the 'preservation of the high character of the British navy' depended upon the skill of their officers and crews in the 'expert management of the Guns'? Surely, many Royal Navy captains had ensured their crews were expert in the use of the guns, regardless of how lenient and hands-off the Admiralty was on the subject, but some (perhaps many) captains had not. This was not unknown, either, for *Peacock*'s reputation as 'the Yacht' was well known. The answer may lie in the calibre of the enemies that the Royal Navy stood against during the Napoleonic era.

However bad some Royal Navy ships' crews were in gunnery, and however poor their commanders were, the average performance from the French or Spanish navies was little better. Even in the close approach to the Franco-Spanish fleet at Trafalgar, where the leading ships of the British fleet suffered long bombardment from the allied fleet, arguably performed at their best, and were unable to respond in kind, they suffered little damage.[28] The substandard gunnery that could be found in some ships of the Royal Navy had not been a noticeable problem for the British. But the United States Navy was not the navy of Revolutionary nor Napoleonic France. In addition to their larger crews with more sea-training and larger ships with heavier guns, the young United States Navy took gunnery training and preparation very seriously.[29] They did not have an established reputation of victory and invincibility, but they did have lots of powder and guns to fire.

Conclusion

An analysis of the frigate actions of the War of 1812 demonstrates that the argument that 'the disparity in force is a sufficient explanation',[30] the prevailing

British historiographical view since William James, was not accepted by the majority of Royal Navy officers. Many officers believed that a British Fifth Rate frigate, with a good enough captain and crew, could conceivably engage and defeat even American heavy frigates like *Constitution*. These actions do not, however, provide evidence to suggest that the historiographical view is wrong; each of the frigates lost by the Royal Navy was in fact defeated by much more powerful opponents, whatever contemporary naval officers thought. By contrast, when British frigates engaged American frigates of equivalent force, they won. The sloop actions, however, tell a very different story. With one exception, in evenly matched contests the British sloop lost.

The examples of *Peacock*, *Boxer* and *Epervier* also suggest a problem of competency amongst crews and commanders of the Royal Navy. Here, a lack of training and preparedness, and poor command more generally, are to blame for the losses. *Peacock* was well known as a spit-and-polish ship, and the lack of attentiveness to gunnery was apparent in her quick defeat and sinking. In the case of *Boxer*, the court martial concluded explicitly that poor gunnery was the primary cause of her defeat. *Epervier*'s example is even more stark: Wales and his officers had systematically failed to train their crew in the use of the guns, and had not even tested their guns and equipment following her brief time under water. Following this, Wales and his officers sold out their own crew during the court martial, and blamed their weakness for the loss.

The War of 1812 saw the Admiralty, which had always taken a hands-off approach to gunnery drill, issue orders to highlight its importance. In the war against Napoleon and his allies, substandard commanders and their under-prepared crews had proved of little consequence. The arrival of better-trained and better-led adversaries in the United States Navy, however, demonstrated that the Royal Navy had a problem, enough for the Admiralty to take several direct and indirect policy measures to protect their ships and avoid losses.[31] Interestingly, though, this did not include any effort to hold poorly performing commanders publicly accountable for their mistakes. In any case, the sloop actions of the War of 1812 are of deep historical significance, similar to the frigate actions of the conflict. Though they had little strategic impact, and though they have been largely forgotten by history, an analysis of these actions and the captains and crews who fought them can tell us much about the culture, habits and efficiency of the Royal Navy in the early nineteenth century.

Bombay Marine, the Vanguard and Precursor of the Royal Indian Navy

Saikat Mondal

In 1498 Vasco da Gama discovered the route to Asia around the western coast of Africa via the Cape of Good Hope, thus opening the connection between the western European countries and India, with a focus on Goa. The English at first tried to connect to India via the land route through Russia along the Caspian Sea but failed miserably. The English East India Company was formed in 1600 with a royal charter giving it the sole trade monopoly with Asia. The Company faced competition from the Portuguese, who had established themselves in the Indian Ocean region. In 1607 Captain Sir William Hawkins, representative and captain of HMS *Hector*, landed in Surat and set up a factory with permission from Mughal Emperor Jahangir. To defend their seaborne trade, the English formed a fleet of small Indian craft known as ghurabs and galivats. In its early stages, the marine force consisted of ships built in England and many built in India.

The ghurabs or grabs were armed with six 9 to 12pdr guns, while the galivants were smaller craft armed with six 2 to 4pdrs.[1] The crews consisted mainly of Hindu fishermen from the Konkan Coast. In 1614 the Indian Marine emerged victorious in a battle with the Portuguese, and the East India Company was granted further trading rights.

King James I appointed Sir Thomas Roe as ambassador to the Mughal courts in 1615. In 1622 the English annexed Ormuz (or Hormuz) from the Portuguese and the Persians, which allowed Britain to pursue uninterrupted trade with Persia.

Eighteenth-century grab. (Radhakumud Mookerji, *Indian Shipping – A History of the Sea-Borne Trade and Maritime Activity of the Indians from the Earliest Times, 1912,* Read Books, 2006)

Although the 1640s saw the Dutch challenge on the Indian coast, the English maintained their dominance in the Indian region by taking some casualties in the First Anglo-Dutch war, despite temporarily losing control of the English Channel and North Sea to the Dutch. The marine acquired the name Bombay Marine in 1674 after the English East India Company acquired the island of Bombay (Mumbai) from the Portuguese as part of a dynastic marriage between King Charles II of England and the Portuguese Infanta Catherine of Braganza.[2] The Company's base of operations was moved from Surat to Bombay in 1685 to control trade more efficiently and avoid the Marathas' aggressive eye towards Surat. The Bombay Marine were tasked with anti-pirate operations and were assigned to the Southern Indian Seas. The Marine also represented the Company when conducting negotiations with the Mughal Emperor Aurangzeb. The Europeans made treaties with the Mughal emperor to conduct their trade in India, as the hinterland for obtaining their goods was located in the domains of the Mughal emperor.

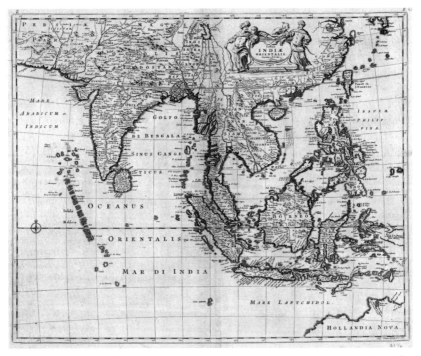

Tabula Indiae Orientalis (Map of East India) by cartographer Frederik de Wit (1610–1698), 1662.
(Norman B Leventhal Map Center, Boston Public Library)

Struggle with the Angrias

At the beginning of the eighteenth century, an admiral of Shivaji's Maratha Fleet, Kanhoji Angre, rose to prominence. His name would become legendary during this period and his achievements are engraved in gold letters in the history of the Indian Navy. Shivaji firmly believed in the philosophy of '*Jalaim Jasya, Valaim Tasya*' (he who commands the sea is all-powerful), which was put into practice by Admiral Tukoji Angre, and later by his son, Kanhoji Angre, and his descendants.

Kanhoji's fleet threatened and significantly curtailed British trade between Bombay and the southern Malabar Coast in 1706 and conquered the island of Colaba (or Kolaba)[3] from the Sidis.[4] A year later, Arab pirates operating out of Muscat jeopardised the Indian Ocean maritime trade by plundering many ships of the Company.

Kanjohi's fleet consisted of ten ghurabs with almost 400 tons of displacement which could mount fifteen to twenty guns, and fifty galivats mounting eight to twelve guns apiece. With his fleet, crewed by Arabs, Africans and Portuguese renegades, Kanhoji Angre drove the Arab pirates away from the Indian Ocean.[5]

Kanhoji then achieved control of the Konkan coast by reinforcing his fortress at Gheria (Vijaydurg). This castle was held by a specially trained garrison that had been armed and provisioned to withstand land and sea attacks as well as long periods of blockade. Kanhoji also ordered the construction of a dockyard, adjacent to the citadel, equipped to build bigger, stronger and better seagoing craft for his navy. By this time, the Portuguese had been reduced to an insignificant sea power, along with the Sidis (African Muslims) and the British, who faced a strong challenge from the Maratha fleet. The size, manoeuvrability and firepower of the Maratha fleet continued to grow, and hence the East India Company decided to build corvettes for the Bombay Marine, which, since 1715, could not counter Kanhoji's fleet. The Bombay Marine would be responsible for escorting the merchant ships of the Company, protecting them from Kanhoji's Maratha fleet.

In 1717 Angrian cruisers captured the ship *Success*, which was sailing under British colours. This incensed the Company authorities, and Charles Boone, governor of Bombay, decided to attack Gheria with a strong fleet under the command of Captain Edward Barlow. A bitter engagement followed, and the Marathas forced the Company's ships to beat a hasty retreat after inflicting severe damage on their ships and killing a large number of the Company's men. Undeterred by the near-catastrophe, Charles Boone ordered Barlow to attack Gheria's fort at Vijaydurg again. On 5 November 1718 Barlow's ships succeeded in silencing many of the fort's guns after a ship-to-shore artillery engagement. The next day, however, when British forces landed, the Maratha defenders had positioned artillery to cover the entire beachhead. The landing force suffered heavy casualties, with the handful of survivors hastily withdrawing to their ships.

In April 1720 four grabs and ten galivats of the Angrian fleet attacked the British ship *Charlotte*, captured her, and took her to Gheria. Therefore, on receiving a petition from the governor of Bombay for naval reinforcement, King George I sent a squadron of four warships under Commodore Thomas Mathews RN to support the Bombay Marine.[6] Mathews's squadron and that of the Bombay Marine were able to reduce Angrian operations against Company shipping. However, when British and Portuguese ships under Mathews's command carried out an attack against Colaba in October 1722, the Marathas successfully repulsed the attacking force which suffered severe losses – 'their strongholds were unassailable'.[7] The key to Maratha success was Kanhoji's tactic of using a large number of light, strong and fast craft, adequately armed, which surrounded the heavier vessels of the enemy and simultaneously attacked them from all sides, 'thus overwhelming the crews of the enemy ships and then boarding them and putting them out of action by scuttling them or setting them on fire.' Historian K M Panikkar, commenting on this victory, remarked that 'Kanhoji's power on the Konkan coast was unchallenged'.[8]

The superiority of the Marathas soon waned with the death of Kanhoji, who suddenly passed away in 1729. His territory and forces were divided between his two sons Sekhoji Angre and Sambhaji Angre. Soon Sekhoji was killed by his half-brother Manaji. The British quickly signed a treaty with Manaji to stabilise the northern part of the Angrian domains. The British also made a treaty of alliance with the Sidis to fight the Angres in 1733.

In the southern part of the Angrian domains, the British fought a different kind of warfare against Sambhaji. Sambhaji was far more aggressive than his northern counterpart and attacked and sank the English trading ships *Bombay*, *Bengal* and *Ockham*. Commodore George Bagwell in 1738 fought a hard battle against Sambhaji's ambush and inflicted damage on the pirates, but had to retreat.

According to the Bombay Diary, a sort of ledger[9] of the East India Company, 1742/3, the strength of the Bombay Marine in 1742 was as follows: one ship of forty-four guns, four of twenty-eight guns, four of eighteen guns, six bomb ketches, and twenty large galivats, employing nearly a hundred officers and from 1,700 to 2,000 men. As the officers made frequent complaints of favouritism, it was resolved that promotion should be regulated according to dates of commission, and thus the seniority system was introduced into the service.[10]

In 1749 Captain William James, who commanded *Guardian* (28), *Bombay*

(28), and a bomb ketch, *Drake*, led a highly successful convoy defence against an Angrian fleet. Captain James then launched a counter-attack and severely damaged the pirates. He followed a policy of keeping a significant patrolling presence on the Konkan and Kanara coasts after being appointed commodore and commander-in-chief of the Bombay Marine two years later.[11]

Following the death of Sambhaji, Tulaji's succession created a new dynamic, which altered the existing order. Tulaji refused to recognise the Mahratha Peshwa (prime minister) as his overlord. As a result, in 1755 Peshwa and Company soldiers jointly launched an attack on the Angrian strongholds of Gheria and Severndrug. These collaborative amphibious operations were successful, and Severndrug was captured in a matter of days. As for Gheria, in February 1756 the Commander-in-Chief, East Indies, Vice Admiral Charles Watson attacked the stronghold, and was aided by Colonel Robert Clive with his army contingent. The Third Rates HM Ships *Kent* (74) and *Cumberland* (66), together with the Fourth Rates *Tiger* (60), *Salisbury* (50), and the Company's Fifth Rate *Protector* (44) provided the heavy firepower. They provided support for 1,400 men, a company of artillery, two smaller Royal Navy ships and nine Company ships. The Angrian forces included bomb ketches, four Maratha grabs, and forty galivats. The pirate fleet was torched after two days of bombardment, and Gheria also fell with the unusually low casualties of 'nineteen men dead and injured'.[12] The Battle of Plassey in 1757 also saw Admiral Watson and fifty Royal Marines support Colonel Clive.

A view of the attack made on the Fort of Gheria by Admiral Watson, 13 February 1756.
An etching print by Pierre-Charles Canot (1710–1777), dated between 1756 and 1777.
(British Museum, London)

European wars on Indian soil
In the War of Austrian Succession (1740–48), the Bombay Marine fought alongside the Royal Navy. In 1745 French privateers active off the coast of Madras appeared before Bombay, but not much fighting happened. Commodore Thomas Griffin, Commander-in-Chief of the Eastern Station, arrived from England with a squadron of eleven ships to reinforce the Marine in 1747. On July 1748 Admiral Edward Boscawen arrived from England with six ships of the line and auxiliaries and conducted a naval expedition against the French at Pondicherry, which was a French colony in South India. However, they were unsuccessful against the sturdy defence put up by the French under the governor-general of French India, Joseph François Dupleix.

In the Seven Years War (1756–63), the English began their hostilities with France and were soon enough able to destroy the French trading outpost in Bengal at Chandannagore. Eventually, after the Battle of Plassey, the East India Company obtained a prominent foothold in the region. After Admiral Watson died in 1757, command of the Marine passed on to Admiral George Pocock. In March 1758 a squadron from England, led by Commodore Charles Stevens, joined Pocock's force. In April of that year, Stevens had defeated a stronger French fleet off St Davids, Wales, with a British force that included the Bombay Marine's Sixth Rate frigate *Protector* (44). In August 1759 *Protector* and the Bombay Marine Sixth Rate frigate *Revenge* (28) were on detached service off India's Coromandel coast under the direction of Admiral Pocock, when his forces defeated the stronger French fleet off Ceylon.[13] Under the command of Rear Admiral Samuel Cornish and Colonel Eyre Coote, East India Company warships were a component of the naval-military force that participated in an attack on Pondicherry. The French garrison surrendered in January 1761. Nonetheless, two Indiamen, *Advice* and *Mermaid*, and the Bombay Marine's *Protector* sank in a hurricane during these final missions.

Fighting against the local powers
From the 1760s onward, the East India Company fought a multitude of wars against local kings and rulers, among which the Marathas and Mysore stood out. A minor conflict broke out between the Sidis and the Mughals (a branch of the Timurid dynasty of Turco-Mongol origin from Central Asia) around Surat, where the local nawab (indigenous governor) of Surat asked for English help, and the Bombay Marine was sent. As a result, the Company was commissioned to carry out the duties of the Sidi with a Bombay Marine officer appointed as the 'Moghul Admiral' on an annual basis. The Marine's Surat squadron carried out this duty and it remained their responsibility until 1829.

Early in 1768 the Bombay government sent out an expedition consisting of a squadron of their ships and four hundred Europeans and a large body of sepoys (Indian soldiers serving under British orders) to attack the western seaports of Hyder Ali's domains on the Malabar coast. The forts were captured with little loss, and the squadron captured nine ships of considerable tonnage.

After 1772, the East India Company decided to take the islands of Salsette, Kanary, Elephanta, Caranja and Hog from the Marathas. Subsequently, the Company signed a treaty with the Marathas in 1775 that granted these lands, along with Bassein and its surroundings, to the Company, in return for providing support to the Maratha Hindu General Raghuji. However, when the treaty did not materialise (the treaty which the British Bombay council made, which is also known as the Surat treaty), the British Calcutta council declared it null and void and signed a new treaty known as the Treaty of Purander, resulting in wars with the Marathas. The East India Company fought the Maratha navy in the subsequent war.

The Maratha navy comprised six ships: one of forty-six guns, one of thirty-eight, one of thirty-two, and three of twenty-six guns, with five ketches of from twelve to fourteen guns and twelve galivats having from six to ten guns each. The British encountered this fleet off the coast of Gheria. Commodore John Moore, in the frigate *Revenge*, and Captain Sheriff, in the Bombay grab, pursued the fleeing Maratha force. The English ships pursued the largest ship, *Shum-sher Jung* (46). Eventually, Sheriff in his little grab skilfully managed to bring *Shum-sher Jung* into action. The commodore came to Sheriff's assistance, and after an engagement of twelve hours, *Shum-sher Jung* exploded. Her commander and a significant portion of the crew perished. The war ended on 31 May under orders of the British colonial administrator and governor-general of Bengal, Warren Hastings, and the British signed a treaty in Purander with Raghunath Rao, the Peshwa of the Maratha empire.

Mr Abraham Parsons, a European commercial consul and traveller who was looking for new commercial opportunities spoke of the Bombay Marine's order of battle at the time of his visit:

The Company's Marine, on the Bombay establishment, are more than twenty in number, the largest of which is the *Revenge*, mounting twenty-eight guns, twenty of which are 12pdrs; the second is the Bombay grab, the remainder are from sixteen to eight guns; and as there are several little piratical States, both on the north as well as on the south coast of Bombay, the coasting trade could not be carried on in safety without being convoyed by such vessels belonging to the Company. It is usual to see sixty or eighty coasting vessels sailing between Surat and Bombay, convoyed by one or two of these vessels.[14]

The Bombay Marine also took a proactive role in the Second Anglo-Mysore War (1780–84). At the same time, the naval power of Hyder Ali was on the rise. In December 1781 the small craft of a squadron led by Vice Admiral Sir Edward Hughes engaged the Nawab fleet comprising two ships, a large grab, three ketches, and many small vessels, which were at anchor at their naval base in Mangalore.[15] Despite being outnumbered, Hughes's force inflicted enormous casualties, and only the large grab was able to escape. Two Bombay Marine ships provided cover fire for these operations.

During the siege of Tellicherry, the Bombay Marine's ships, the Indiamen *Neptune* and *Royal Admiral*, participated in the siege until mid May 1782. During Sultan Tipu's departure, Bombay Marine units led by Commodore George Emptage captured Rajamundroog at the mouth of the Merjee (or Merjan) river before proceeding to Onore. The galivat *Wolfe*'s officers and men, both European and indigenous, were involved in the desperate defence of Onore. On 'home' territory, the Marine also helped to defend Bombay when the Marathas besieged it. This period also saw the loss of one of the famous ships of the Marine, when the frigate *Revenge* ran into a violent gale off the coast of Bombay en route for Anjengo (Anchuthenhgu, in modern-day Kerala).

The Marine also participated in the Third Anglo-Mysore War, which began in the 1790s, where the ships of the Marine took part in reducing many of Sultan Tipu's coastal fortifications. The Marine also gave the British logistics support to Royal Navy operations in Malabar. Soon enough, the war ended with the succession of one-third of the Sultan's Mysore territories to the British.

Surveying operations of the Marine

In 1772 officers of the Bombay Marine fitted out their first surveying expedition to better understand the Indian coastlines and their environments. The expedition consisted of the schooner *Fox*, of about 100 tons and carrying six guns; the ketch *Dolphin*, of a similar armament but somewhat smaller; and a patta mar, or native craft. With Lieutenant Thomas Robinson in command, they explored the coast of Mekran, Sindh and Kathiawar, part of Persia, and some parts of Arabia between the coasts of Muscat and Ras-ul-Hadd. The Marine conducted the expedition with great precision and accuracy despite having inferior equipment.[16]

Between 1777 and 1795 Lieutenant Archibald Blair conducted surveys of the Kathiwar coast, Salsette, and the Andaman Islands. The official report of the survey of the Andamans was laid before Lord Charles Cornwallis, governor-general of India, in June 1789. The report delineated the topographical and natural features of the coast and suggested the creation of a penal colony and three harbours in the Andamans. The spot chosen for the first British colony in Port Cornwallis, or Port Blair, was Mark Island, now called Chatham Island.

Lieutenant John McCluer, hydrographer and commander of the Bombay Marine, surveyed the coast of the Persian Gulf, as the previous versions of charts in that area contained numerous inaccuracies. His first survey included the southeastern part of the coast, from the entrance of the Gulf, for a distance of three hundred miles. The accuracy of the principal points rendered it superior to any others in existence. The second survey covered the remainder of the coast, with the principal channel of the Shatt-ul-Arabas as far up as Bussorah (Basra, Iraq), a distance of about thirty leagues from the sea. At that time, Bussorah was the centre of commerce and communication between India and the Turkish dominions. Bussorah was much frequented by the Company's ships.

In 1793 Lieutenant John Hayes commanded a surveying expedition consisting of the vessels *Duke of Clarence* and *Duchess*, which were despatched to explore the coast of Van Diemen's Land, now known as Tasmania. Between 1812 and 1820 Lieutenant Daniel Ross and draughtsman Philip Maugham conducted surveys on the Chinese coast to have a better understanding of the location of harbours and shoals. Additionally, a small detachment of the Marine led by Lieutenant John Wood, Scottish naval officer and surveyor, and British naval officer and hydrographer, Lieutenant Thomas Greer Carless, led a survey of the coast of Karachi at the mouth of the Indus River.[17]

Bombay Marine in the nineteenth century

While conducting research on the Bombay Marine 1802, historian Rathbone Low noted that:

> The following were the ships of the Bombay Marine: The frigates 'Cornwallis,' of fifty-six guns – built at Bombay, in 1800, and named after the Governor-General – and 'Bombay,' thirty-eight. The sloops-of-war 'Mornington,' twenty-two, launched at Bombay in 1800, and named after the then Governor-General; Teignmouth, sixteen, built in 1799, and named after Sir John Shore; and 'Ternate,' sixteen, built in 1801. The fourteen gun brigs, 'Antelope' and 'Fly,' were added to the Service in 1793. The snows 'Drake,' eighteen (1787); 'Panther,' fourteen (1778); 'Viper,' fourteen; 'Princess Augusta,' fourteen (1768); 'Princess Royal,' fourteen (1768); 'Comet,' ten (1798); and 'Intrepid,' ten (1780). The ketches 'Queen,' fourteen; and 'Rodney,' fourteen. Besides these vessels, there were prizes and others purchased into the Service, for special, or temporary, uses, such as the 'Swift,' 'Star,' 'Les Freres Unis, 'Alert,' 'Assay'e,' and others; and there were also some small craft and patta mars, armed with guns.[18]

The French islands of Mauritius provided a haven for French warships and privateers who would sortie into the Indian Ocean to capture East India Company shipping. In 1809 a force of ten thousand men led by General Sir John Abercromby, commander of the Bombay Army, and ships of the Company's Marine captured the islands from France.

The early 1800s saw the rise of piracy along the coasts of Kathiawar, Konkan and Kutch. In 1811 the British sent an expedition under the command of Colonel Lionel Smith with the help of Captain Sealy as the senior naval officer and a squadron from the Marine. Marathas also sometimes attacked Company ships, including *Aurora* in 1812. The problem would be solved only after the complete dissolution of the Maratha empire in 1818.

During this time, the Arab Joasmis tribe, based along the Persian Gulf coast at Ras Al-Khaimah (present day United Arab Emirates), increased their piratical activities under their leader Abdul Wahab. From 1815 the Joasmis began to appear off the coasts of Daman and Diu. The East India Company finally

Maratha pirates attacking the sloop *Aurora* of the Bombay Marine, 1812. Oil painting (c1816) by Thomas Butterworth (1768–1842).
(© National Maritime Museum, Greenwich, London, BHC1084)

decided to put an end to such piracy. In December 1819 an expedition departed from Bombay under the command of Major-General Sir William Grant Keir with the assistance of the Royal Navy's Fourth Rate *Liverpool* (50), together with the Sixth Rate *Eden* (26) and brig-sloop *Curlew* (18). They were joined by the Bombay Marine sloops *Teignmouth* (16), *Benares* (16), *Aurora* (16), brig-sloops *Nautilus* (14), *Ariel* (10) and brig *Vestal* (10) that escorted the convoy of eighteen transports (carrying 1,600 British and 1,400 Indian troops). Three Marine ships, the sloop *Ternate* (16), the brigs *Mercury* (14) and *Psyche* (10), had already been patrolling the Persian Gulf when they joined the main force.[19] When they arrived at the Gulf's head, the Imam of Muscat provided two frigates and six hundred soldiers (with another two thousand marching on Ras Al-Khaimah separately).

The town was taken following two days of bombardment, primarily from ships' artillery. Eighty pirate ships, each between 40 and 250 tonnes, were sunk in the harbour. The Joasmis had, however, already made a nocturnal retreat to the interior prior to the attack. Landed forces dealt with them while the naval forces exacted revenge up and down the coast, completely destroying forts and vessels. A treaty between the British government and all pertinent seagoing Arab tribes was established in January 1820. Sultan bin Sagar (Saqr), ruler of the towns of Sharjah and Ras Al-Khaimah, Jazirah Al Hamra and Rams, all Trucial States in their time and now part of the United Arab Emirates, was deposed in the year 1809/10 by another ruler, Hassan Bin Rahmah, during whose reign attacks on British shipping increased. So in 1820, in exchange for controlling the Arabs, Sultan bin Sagar, who was sympathetic to the British, was again placed on the throne and obtained all the former Joasmi ports. The British viewed this as a huge victory, both militarily and diplomatically.

The Marine participated extensively in the last campaign of the Anglo-Burmese War, which was primarily a coastal and riverine campaign. The Fourth Rate HMS *Liffey* (50), Sixth Rates *Slaney* (20), *Larne* (20), and the sloop *Sophie* (18) made up the majority of the invasion force, sailing out of Port Cornwallis for Rangoon, while the Marine's Fifth Rate *Hastings* (32), sloop *Teignmouth* (16), brig *Mercury* (14), sloop *Prince of Wales* (14) and *Jessy* set sail carrying nine thousand troops. The Burmese resisted the invasion by sending fire ships down the Rangoon river from Kemmendine. They proved difficult to handle. But, once they were neutralised, the combined force seized Rangoon with minimal resistance. Additional operations then took place at Martaban, Tavoy, Ramree, Dalla Creek, Cheduba and Mergui. Eventually, Ramree was taken after successive failures, and ultimately, Pegu, Bessein and Donabu on the Irrawaddy River were occupied. The Marine's sloop *Ternate* (16), brig *Vestal* (10), survey ship *Research*, as well as a variety of small gun brigs, schooners, and even smaller armed rowing boats, continued to make contact along the Arakan coastline.[20] The Bengal Marine, the Company's other naval defence force, participated as well, with their wooden-hulled, steam-powered paddle steamer *Diana* serving as a support vessel. Engagements took place, particularly at Chanballa, which were described as 'sharp', on the Mayu and Kaladan rivers. These soldiers' ultimate objective was Arakan, which they eventually captured by assault in March 1825.

The service's organisational structure underwent some positive adjustments between 1827 and 1830. By 1827, London had received complaints about the Bombay Marine's status, salary and benefits, and working conditions. The first action taken that year to improve the situation was to grant officers of the Bombay Marine a status similar to that of officers of the Royal Navy of corresponding rank, with the caveat that officers of the Royal Navy would have precedence over officers of the Marine. The introduction of command and control was another wise move. Unless both the British government and the East India Company agreed to it, neither service was given any authority to command the other. The Bombay Marine's only units up until this point had been 'Red Ensign' ships. But, on 12 June 1827 King William IV granted the Marine the right to have its ships fly the Union Flag and the St George's Cross flag. The King's decision was part of the greater reorganisation that replaced the civil servant position of superintendent of the Bombay Marine with a service officer, Captain Charles Malcolm RN being the first.

Another organisational development occurred in 1829, which focused on the discipline of the Bombay Marine. Despite the existence of a method for establishing a court of inquiry, the naval court could not pass judgement or impose punishments on Bombay Marine personnel, as these were the prerogatives of the East India Company. To standardise the judicial system, martial law, which was already in use by the British Army in India, was implemented on the Bombay Marine. To avoid legal ramifications, a strange formula was established in which naval officers were given army commissions in addition to their naval commissions and the Bombay Marine was renamed 'Marine Corps'. The curious name 'Marine Corps' lasted only a year, as the force was renamed the Indian Navy in 1830 in recognition of its great services at sea for nearly two centuries.

Conclusion

The Bombay Marine, from its humble beginnings, gradually grew into a disciplined service and reached the stature of a small navy. No doubt the presence of their 'big brother', the Royal Navy, overshadowed their activities and stole their glory to a great extent. As Admiral Sir H W Richmond observed:

The fact that no spectacular battles were fought at sea by that force must not blind our eyes to the importance of the work of this detached flotilla; for though in normal times, when no European naval forces were in the Eastern seas, it was a navy in itself, with its own capital ships and lesser classes ... [21]

It is the force that made the difference between the British and other colonial powers. The Bombay Marine made important contributions in almost all the coastal wars in which the East India Company participated whilst the Marine supported the Company's control over much of India. Additionally, by surveying important coastline locations and protecting the Indian waters from the wrath of pirates, this Marine force helped the East India Company in making India the most valuable colonial asset of the British Empire — the 'jewel in the crown'.

Portrait of the East Indiaman *Neptune* in two positions off the Downs, see colour plate 2

Russian Naval Power During the Eighteenth Century

Kenneth Flemming

Peter the Great (1672–1725) had spent a substantial portion of his youth in the German quarter of Moscow and was greatly impressed by the culture of the Western world. He fully realised the backwardness of his country and that it was essential that Russia break out from its landlocked position. He wanted a 'Window on Europe'.[1]

By the time of his death, Peter had transformed Russia into a European power; he had created a Western capital with access to Europe, launched a navy, mobilised a victorious army, brought women into society, demanded religious tolerance, and promoted the nation's industry and commerce. However, despite these substantial changes, he had not truly reformed Russia's contradictory legal structure; the government departments were disorganised and administration throughout the empire was inefficient and corrupt.

With Peter's death, successive rulers worsened the confusion in Russian law.[2] For the next half-century, chaos at the highest levels of government led the nation into stagnation. This article tells the tale of how Catherine the Great brought Russia back to a competitive footing with the nations of Europe, and revived the Russian Navy.

The Russian Navy prior to Catherine the Great

With Peter's death, his second wife, Catherine I, came to power. She died two years later, making the twelve-year-old grandson of Peter the Great, Tsar in 1728. The immediate effect on the Russian Navy was that the twelve-year-old Peter II ordered that only four frigates and two flutes could go to sea, while only five more frigates were ready for cruising. The remaining ships were to remain in port, 'saving the treasury'. Thus, only a fraction of the fleet was operational. To the argument of fleet commanders that it was necessary to keep the fleet at sea, the boy Tsar replied, 'When the need calls for the use of the ships, then I will go to sea; but I do not intend to walk on it like a grandfather'. The boy Tsar died two years later.

His decision to restrict the navy's operations, coupled with the poor state of the treasury and irregular salary payments led to an outflow of officers, causing a drop in discipline among those on the lower deck. Peter's actions caused the Russian fleet to deteriorate. However:

It is a high tribute to Peter the Great that much of the work he had done in establishing Russian sea power survived the reigns of the six mediocrities who followed him to the throne. When Catherine the Great came to power the fleet was, of course, weakened in both size and quality, but there had been no eclipse of Russian sea power nor had there been any disastrous defeats.[3]

The Russian Navy revitalised: Catherine the Great (1729–1796)

Katharina II after Stefano Torelli
(1712–1784) in Russian national costume.
(State Historical Museum of Russia)

Ekaterina II, known as Catherine the Great, was Empress of Russia from 1762 until her death in 1796. She came to power following the overthrow of her husband and second cousin, Peter III, who became Tsar upon the death of Empress Elizaveta (Elizabeth) I in 1762. Catherine became the country's last empress and longest-ruling female leader: 'Catherine's concern with naval matters proved her a worthy successor to Peter the Great, for she carried out many of his plans and followed many of his general policies'.[4]

During the first decade of her reign, Russia undertook a monumental naval building programme. By the time of her death in 1796, the Baltic and White Sea shipyards had built eighty-nine ships of the line and forty frigates, while the Black Sea shipyards had built fourteen ships of the line and fifty frigates for the sailing fleet.[5] These numbers exclude the hundreds of smaller craft, such as oared galleys, bomb ketches and floating batteries that were built to equip the Russian Army's fleet or flotilla.

This ambitious programme was secured in part by acquiring the talents of European naval architects, engineers and shipbuilders. Additionally, Catherine's talent hunt included acquiring the services of foreign naval officers. As a result, the Russian Navy of the eighteenth century had many officers of British origin, including several whose careers in the Royal Navy can be traced before and after their service in Russia.

One such officer was Lieutenant Samuel Greig RN, who joined the Russian

Navy in 1764 and was promoted to captain at twice his previous salary. He was to prove Russia's leading foreign commander. Samuel Greig, or Samuil Karlovich Greig as he became known in Russia, was born at Inverkeithing, Fife, Scotland, in 1735.[6] Greig quickly rose to the rank of admiral. His son, Alexey Greig, would go on to have his own spectacular career in the Russian Navy. Like his father, he became an admiral of the Russian Navy, privy councillor, and knight of all the Imperial Russian Orders.

Following Peter the Great's success against the Ottoman Empire, which expanded Russian control south to the northern shore of the Black Sea, the Tsarina successfully conducted two Russo-Turkish wars that gained control of all of what is modern Ukraine to include the Crimean peninsula. In her treaties with the Ottoman Empire, Catherine insisted on her right to intervene in Ottoman lands on behalf of fellow Orthodox Christians. The revitalised Russian Navy played a significant role in Catherine's wars.

Admiral Samuil Karlovich Greig (1736–1788), 1790 (Admiral Samuel Greig). Oil on canvas after Dmitry Levitzky (1735–1822). This portrait shows the Star of the Order of St Andrew and the Star of the Order of St George.
(Collection, Russian Museum)

In addition to the land campaign, she sent a portion of her Baltic Fleet into the Aegean to carry the war to Turkey from the sea. The idea of sending the Russian Navy to fight the Turks in their own waters first emerged in November 1768. By January 1769, preparations were underway to bring the Russian fleet into a seaworthy condition, fitting out first in Kronstadt, then the main base of the Baltic fleet. The navy had entirely gone out of repair since Peter the Great; Catherine saw in it 'only ships and men, not a fleet and sailors', and described it as 'scarcely fit to catch herring.'[7]

Catherine was said to be extremely enthusiastic at the thought of the noise she would make in Europe with the appearance of a Russian fleet in the North Sea, English Channel, Atlantic and the Mediterranean. Such a vision was to prove one of the most notable advertisements to Western Europe of Russian power on land and at sea.

Catherine's initiative gained recognition in the British publication, *The Annual Register: or, a View of the History, Politicks, and Literature for the Year 1769*:

> That great and enterprising woman has not however confined her views merely to the operations of a land war: that are much more extensive; and to the astonishment of Europe, from the bottom of the Baltic, a Russian fleet is issued to shake the remotest parts of the Mediterranean; to excite and support the insurrections of the Greek Christians, and to leave nothing in any part of the vast empire of enemies free from alarm and confusion. This naval expedition of Russia stands particularly distinguished amongst the events of this year, and is indeed a remarkable era in naval history.[8]

Seen as such a challenge to the traditional balance of maritime power, the growth of Russia's navy required extensive diplomatic preparation, causing much anxiety in France. In July 1769 Catherine instructed her London ambassador to negotiate and pay for the friendly reception of Russian ships in British harbours compatible with British neutrality in the Russo-Turkish conflict. She avoided the touchy issue of Russian sovereignty: being forced to dip her ensign first to ships of the Royal Navy. Instead, she gave her Russian admirals orders not to lower their flags before entering the Channel, in which case they would merely make a gunfire salute. This would be the first time in the history of the Russian Navy that it would operate in waters away from the homeland.

The Russian fleet manned its eleven ships of the line by taking peasants off the land and pushing them into service. However, these landsmen could not stand naval life. Only those crew who had come from the area of Archangel proved efficient. By the time the fleet put into Hull in October 1769, more than eight hundred were on the sick list. The fleet wintered at Spithead, Portsmouth. By the end of October, Samuel Greig joined Admiral Spirodov, commander of the Russian fleet.[9]

The year 1770 was to become the *annus mirabilis*. Russia's army routed a massive Turkish force of a hundred and fifty thousand with just twenty-five thousand men at Lake Kagul, one of the most significant land battles of the eighteenth century. Russian success opened the territory between the Danube and Dniester rivers, effectively giving Southern Ukraine and Moldova to the Russians. In February of that same year, the Russian squadron, having sailed from Portsmouth, arrived in the Eastern Mediterranean.

Battle of Chesme, 5–7 July 1770
The Battle of Chesme significantly enhanced Russian naval prestige. It was the battle in which Samuel Greig distinguished himself. The Turkish fleet of fifteen

ships of the line plus frigates and galleys met near Chesme Bay, western Turkey, and was much superior to the Russian force of nine ships of the line and three frigates. However, after a severe but indecisive battle, the Turkish line fell into disorder and withdrew to the harbour of Chesme during the night, where land batteries protected them.

At 1am Captain Greig bore down upon the enemy with his fire-ships and destroyed the Turkish fleet. Greig and his subordinate, another British officer, Lieutenant Drysdale, both set the match to the fire-ships. With this perilous duty performed, Greig and Drysdale leapt overboard and swam to their boats, under tremendous fire from the Turks and at the imminent hazard of being killed by the explosion of their fire-ships. The entire Turkish fleet was destroyed with the loss of eleven thousand men.[10]

Destruction of the Turkish Fleet in the Bay of Chesme, 1771, by Jacob Philipp Hackert (1737–1807).
(Hermitage Museum, St Petersburg, Russia, public domain)

Following this success, the Russian fleet attacked the town and batteries on shore, and by 9am, scarcely a vestige remained of the town, fortifications, or Turkish fleet. The victory was greeted with indescribable joy in St Petersburg where the euphoric empress showered rewards on every man in the fleet. For this critical service, Captain Greig, who had been appointed commodore in command of the fire ships, was immediately promoted by Count Alexei Grigoryevich Orlov, commander-in-chief of the fleet, to the rank of admiral. The Tsarina immediately confirmed the promotion and named him Admiral of the Russian Empire. Later she would select him as the governor of the port city of Kronstadt.

With the Ottoman fleet out of the way, the Russians were in complete command of the Aegean and Eastern Mediterranean. Their ships were active from Egypt to the shores of Thrace, destroying Ottoman trading vessels and bombarding shore establishments. These operations did little to hamper Ottoman commerce, but they did great harm to the Greek struggle for independence.

Admiral Orloff had aroused the Greeks to revolt at the city of Morea. His squadron occupied Navarino and his landing force occupied other Aegean coastal towns: 'The intervention of Russia proved disastrous to the Greeks ... The available landing force was too small to obtain any permanent success, and on the arrival of Turkish and Albanian troops the revolt was crushed with great bloodshed.'[11]

While Russian naval operations in the Aegean continued, the Russian Army had re-established an outlet on the Black Sea:

Russian fleet in the Bosphorus Strait, by Mikhail Ivanov (1748–1823), St Petersburg. (Wikimedia Commons, public domain)

The war ended with the Peace of Kainardji, signed on July
21st, 1784, which gave to Russia Kilburn, Kertch, Yenikale,
and the district between the Dnieper and the Bug, confirmed
her possession of Azof and Taganrog, opened the Bosphorus
and Dardanelles to her mercantile marine, and prepared the
way for the formal annexation of the Crimea nine years
later.[12]

During the intervening years between the peace and the second Russo-Turkish
war, shipbuilding got firmly underway at Kherson and later at Sevastopol.
Enormous traffic developed in timber rafting down the Dnieper each spring. At
the same time, the production of sailcloth and rope increased to about 16 tons
per week, together with oakum and miscellaneous items of rigging. By 1784
production exceeded the demands of the Russian Black Sea Fleet and left a
large surplus for export to Britain.[13] However, the loss of Kherson and Crimea
brought the Ottoman Empire to declare war against Russia.

Between 1787 and 1792 Russian was engaged in two wars, the Russo-
Turkish War (1787–92) and the Russo-Swedish War (1788–90).

The Russo-Turkish War (1787–92)
But for the battle of Kerch Strait in 1790, 'the naval operations in the South
[Black Sea] were of small importance' to the outcome of this second Russo-
Turkish war. For the most part, the Black Sea Fleet conducted inshore
operations in support of the Russian army, which at the conclusion of the war
had 'retained Oczakoff and the country between the Bug and Dnieper'.[14] But
one successful action by the Russian Navy had major strategic
import.

Kerch Strait, 1790
The Russian Black Sea Fleet, under the command of
Admiral Fyodor F Ushakov, received reports that an
Ottoman fleet had been observed south of Crimea,
heading eastward toward the Kerch Strait, the narrow
entrance which leads into the Sea of Azov. With the
understanding that the Ottoman fleet would land an
army to retake Crimea, Ushakov sailed from Sevastopol
to intercept the Ottomans on 13 July, anchoring at the

Admiral Fyodor Fyodorovich Ushakov, 1912, by Peter Bajanov (1851–
1913). (Central Naval Museum, Russia – Wikipedia, public domain)

mouth of the straits on the morning of 19 July. Receiving word the Ottoman fleet was in sight, Ushakov weighed anchor, and headed toward 'the Turks, who were probably about twenty per cent superior to the Russians'.[15]

During the afternoon, both fleets manoeuvred against one another as the wind shifted from east-northeast to north-northeast. With the changing wind conditions, Ushakov manoeuvred to 'put the Russians into line on the Turk's weather quarter'. Seeing this, the Ottoman fleet withdrew and firing ceased just before sunset.[16] Ushakov had prevented the Ottomans from retaking Crimea.

The Russo-Swedish War (1788–90)

The third war between both countries in the eighteenth century was started by King Gustav III of Sweden. It was his attempt to regain Finnish territory lost to Russia during the Great Northern War (1700–21).[17] The Swedish plan of attack was a three-pronged offensive, which had part of the Swedish army advancing across the Finnish interior, with another part of the army advancing eastward along the Finnish coast supported by the Swedish Navy's coastal flotilla into the Gulf of Finland. The third prong had another element of the army sailing with the Swedish battle fleet in order to land on the Gulf of Finland's south coast and nearby St Petersburg, forcing Catherine to capitulate.

Northern Theatre of War. Sea battle on 17 July, between the Russian fleet under Commander-in-Chief Admiral Greig and the Swedish fleet under Commander-in-Chief Duke of Südermannland, on the Baltic Sea, 7½ miles west of Hogland (Gogland), 1788, by Johann Caspar Weinrauch (1765–846). (Wikimedia Creative Commons, public domain)

All three offensives failed. The third culminated in the Battle of Hogland on 17 July. Admiral Samuel Greig, 'with seventeen ships of the line, engaged the Duke of Sudermaina, with fifteen ships of the line and four 40-gun frigates, off the island of Hogland'.[18] Although Greig's fleet suffered more casualties and damage to his ships, the Swedes abandoned the offensive and withdrew westward to Sveaborg.[19] Greig quickly repaired his damaged ships and pursed the Swedish fleet, blockading them at Sveaborg.

Unfortunately for Greig, shortly after his success against the Swedish Navy, he succumbed to a fever:

His death occasioned national mourning on an unprecedented scale, certainly for a foreigner … a state funeral held at the Lutheran cathedral in Revel … Catherine had a gold medal struck in his memory and ordered her architect Giacomo Quarenghi to design his mausoleum … Count Zavadovskii [Catherine's secretary] called him 'the first admiral the Russian navy had ever had' and looked with an apprehension … at the people who were to succeed him.[20]

In 1789 Gustav renewed his offensive against Russia. In July the Russian fleet, commanded by Admiral Vasiliy Chichagov, engaged the Swedish fleet

Greig's tomb, Indian ink and watercolour, c1790s, by Giacomo Quarenghi (1744–1817). Original in State Hermitage Museum, Russia. (Wikimedia, public domain)

Battle of Vyborg Bay, June 25, 1790, by Ivan Aivazovsky (1817–1900), 1846.
(Wikimedia Commons, public domain)

off Öland and forced the Swedes back to their base at Karlskrun, Sweden. In August the Russian galley fleet defeated the Swedish galley fleet at the First Battle of Rochensalm (Svensksund).[21]

The war on the Baltic continued and reached its crescendo the following year. On 13 May the Swedish fleet attacked the Russian fleet anchored in Reval Harbour. The attack was repulsed with the loss of two Swedish ships of the line. Two days later, the Swedish galley fleet, commanded by King Gustav, attacked the Russians at Frederickshamn (now Hamina) in Finland, destroying several small craft and large quantities of naval stores. Then on 4 July the Swedish Navy suffered heavy losses at the Battle of Vyborg Bay. One week later, the Swedes defeated the Russians at the Battle of Svenska Sound. These battles left the 'resources of Sweden … nearly exhausted; on August 14th peace was signed, and Catherine was able to bring her undivided energies to bear against Turkey'.[22]

Catherine the Great's legacy
Captain Robert A Theobald USN wrote in 1954 that:

> If Peter the Great had been the father of the Russian Navy, then certainly Catherine must have been its greatest benefactor. When she died in 1796, she left Russia still the dominant naval power in the Baltic; she had re-established the Black Sea Fleet and extended her country's coastline on

that sea from Azov to the mouth of the Dniester. Based solely on numerical strength, Russia was the world's second naval power, second only to England.[23]

Catherine's legacy would carry the Russian Navy through the rest of the eighteenth century and into the nineteenth.

Russian naval operations in the Mediterranean, 1798–1800

The Anglo-French Wars of 1793–1815 saw 'the Russians … allied first with one side and then the other, shifting their allegiance a total of four times'.[24] An unintended consequence of Nelson's victory at the Nile was that it brought the Russian Navy back into the Mediterranean.

Under Catherine's son, Tsar Paul I, Russia allied with Britain, Austria and the Ottoman Empire against Revolutionary France. After Napoleon seized Malta, a Russo-Turkish squadron, under the command of Admiral Fedor Ushakov, entered the Mediterranean in September 1798. In one of its first operations, the combined squadron obtained the surrender of the Ionian Islands (minus Corfu) from the French who had occupied the islands a year earlier.[25]

Anticipating the arrival of the Russians and Turks, the Admiralty sent orders to Lord St Vincent to co-operate with them. That task fell upon Nelson, who had much to deal with. In addition to his responsibilities to co-operate with the Russian and Turkish squadrons, the Admiralty had placed him in Naples to protect 'the coasts of Sicily, Naples and the Adriatic; [promote] active co-operation with the Austrian and Neapolitan armies; cutting off France from Egypt; blockading Malta'.[26]

Although Ushakov never subordinated his forces to Nelson, he did assist Nelson in the Adriatic by interdicting the French and their Neapolitan republican allies' shipping, whilst Nelson did the same on the Italian west coast. Ushakov provided his marines in recapturing the Neapolitan republican ports of Bari and Foggia on the Adriatic. Russian and Ottoman forces supported Neapolitan royalists under Cardinal Ruffo in retaking Naples during the summer of 1799, thus restoring the Kingdom of the Two Sicilies after the French had overrun it six months earlier.

However, the British, Russian and Ottoman alliance was a fragile one. Shortly after the restoration of the Neapolitan crown, Tsar Paul pulled out of the alliance. Russia had several reasons for ending what was the greater War of the Second Coalition against Revolutionary France. Two of the reasons involved the Russian Navy's Mediterranean Fleet.

The first was the affront Paul I felt when Nelson broke the terms of surrender that Admiral Ushakov obtained with the pro-French forces defending Naples:

A [Russian] naval bombardment of Naples on May 18 was followed by a lengthy siege. The city was taken, and Russian landing parties assisted in the elimination of pro-French holdouts. Ushakov and his subordinates granted generous terms to the prisoners – terms which were later violated by Lord Nelson when he seized the prisoners and turned them over to the king of Naples, who publicly tortured and executed the vast majority.[27]

The second reason involved Malta. The Tsar wanted Russian forces to capture Malta from the French, since the Knights of St John, the order that he headed as their protector, had previously ruled the island. Nelson would have none of it, as it was his ships that were blockading the island: 'Paul resentfully issued an order to Ushakov on December 22, 1799 directing his return to the Black Sea'.[28] However, the Ionian isles, which Ushakov liberated from the French, remained under Russian control.

Russian Navy in the Baltic: lack of action
Relations between Russia and Britain deteriorated further when on 16 December 1800 Paul I and Sweden formed the Second League of Armed Neutrality: 'Denmark and Prussia immediately acceded'.[29] The revival of the league was a form of protest against Britain's 'right of search' for French contraband aboard neutral shipping. Paul ordered the seizure of all British shipping in Russian ports.

The British answer was to embargo all Russian, Swedish and Danish shipping. This included the issuing of letters of marque for the capture of their shipping. Shortly after the onset of 1801, Britain dispatched a fleet under Sir Hyde Parker, with Nelson in second command, to the Baltic:

This move caught the Baltic nations napping. Had the navies of the three powers been prepared and united, the British would surely have been decisively outnumbered; Russia alone had 47 of her 82 battleships in the Baltic. However, inasmuch as only 15 Russian battleships were in fighting condition and no move was made to unite the three navies, the British were able to deal with each in turn.[30]

Nelson urged Hyde Parker to attack a squadron of the Russian Baltic Fleet that was laid up for the winter at Reval (now Tallinn). But Hyde Parker overruled him and instead, the British fleet entered the Sound on 31 March and approached Copenhagen. Subsequently, 'The Battle of Copenhagen was both the climax and the end of the Danish-Norwegian fleet as a European naval power'.[31]

With the Danes out of the way, Hyde Parker and Nelson entered the Baltic and made for Reval. Prior to the British fleet's arrival, news reached both commanders that Tsar Paul I was assassinated on 24 March, and the new Tsar, the young Alexander I, ordered the Baltic Fleet not to engage the British. In May the British force, now under Nelson's command, reverted from a combat role to a diplomatic one.

Nelson set out for Reval with twelve ships of the line. Prior to reaching his destination on 12 May, he stopped his force briefly at Karlskrona to inform the Swedes their fleet would be attacked if they put to sea. Once at Reval, Nelson informed the Russians his mission was a peaceful one. On 18 May Nelson learned that Alexander had removed the embargo on British shipping and released the dozens of British merchantmen held in Russian ports. Conversely, Britain released the Russian ships it had seized.

The Russian Navy under Alexander fared differently from that of Catherine and Paul: 'He was not interested in developing naval administration. He concentrated on cutting costs while at the same time demanding an efficient and modern service and sponsoring maritime exploration'.[32]

In May 1803 the Treaty of Amiens fell apart. At first, Russia held off entering the war, even though Alexander's admiration for Napoleon had dwindled, especially after French victories threatened Germany and the Ottoman Empire. However, Napoleon's control over northern Italy (proclaiming himself King of Italy in 1805) and the threat he posed to Russian control of the Ionian isles, forced Alexander to join Britain, Austria and Prussia in the short-lived Third Coalition against Napoleon. A provision of the treaty Russia and Britain signed was an agreement to provide security to the Kingdom of the Two Sicilies against Napoleon.[33]

From a naval perspective, the years of the coalition were punctuated by the Royal Navy's victory at Trafalgar. But the years 1805/6 saw another major land war across central and southern Europe. The Russian Navy was active again in the Mediterranean, responding to Napoleon's seizing most of northern Italy and taking the Dalmatian providences from Austria.

The Mediterranean/Dalmatian Campaign (1805–1807)

Early in 1805 Alexander directed the Russian forces based at Corfu to proceed to Naples to support the King of Naples, who had joined anti-Napoleon forces. This force, comprising a Russian squadron under the command of Commodore A Sorokin, conveying approximately fourteen thousand Russian soldiers under General Lacy, was joined by a British squadron conveying another 7,500 soldiers from Malta: 'The two, proceeding together, reached the Bay of Naples on the 19th of November'.[34]

Through the first half of December the operations of the Allies in Naples, though purely defensive, proceeded smoothly. The Neapolitan battalions gradually grew larger, and a Russian reinforcement of some 6,000 men was landed in Puglia and helped to swell Lacy's army to respectable proportions. But any hope of an eventual advance [against Napoleon's Army in Italy] was crushed before Christmas by the news of the defeat of the Austrian and Russian Emperors at Austerlitz.[35]

With the defeat at Austerlitz, Tsar Alexander instructed Lacy's army to return to Corfu, while the British force would retire to the Sicilian side of the Straits of Messina. The evacuation was effected by their respective navy squadrons and transports.

The Russian army's repositioning back to Corfu relied on additional naval reinforcements sent out from the Baltic. Sorokin's squadron was augmented by Admiral Dmitry N Seniavin with five ships of the line and various lesser vessels in February 1806. This brought the Russian Mediterranean Fleet to nine ships of the line, eight frigates, six corvettes, seven brigs, a schooner and twelve gunboats. Two transports and a hospital ship made for a respectable number of forty-six sail.[36]

For most of 1806 the Russian Mediterranean Fleet concentrated their operations in the Adriatic. Despite the French occupying much of the Dalmatian coast, Seniavin successfully occupied many of the ungarrisoned port towns along the coast and conducted amphibious operations against French garrisoned port towns with mixed success. His frigates and corvettes were successful in interdicting French coastal shipping on both sides of the Adriatic. However, his efforts were undercut by his Tsar, who again, becoming annoyed with the British, ordered Seniavin on 4 September to hand over his conquests to the French and withdraw his fleet to the Black Sea. Adding insult to injury, the terms of the Treaty of Tilsit, concluded between the Tsar and Napoleon in July 1807, saw that the 'liquidation of Russian interests in the Mediterranean was completed with the surrender of the Ionian islands to the French and the withdrawal of 4,740 men in six battleships and three brigs to Trieste. These ships were turned over to the French; the crews went home through Austria'.[37]

The Russian Navy and the Turkish War (1806–12)

However, Admiral Seniavan's plan to take his fleet to the Black Sea was thwarted when the Ottoman Empire, at the urging of Napoleon, declared war on Russia on 30 September 1806. Seniavan, still in control of Corfu, was ordered to take his fleet, consisting of eight ships of the line and lesser craft, to enter the Aegean Sea, seize the island of Tenedos, and attack Constantinople.

His force was part of a greater Anglo-Russian naval force that planned to sweep the Ottoman Navy from the Aegean Sea, blockade the southern mouth of the Dardanelles and, with the Russian Black Sea Fleet, attack Constantinople.

Reaching the Dardanelles on 7 March 1807, Seniavan found the British fleet under the command of Admiral Sir John Duckworth. Duckworth had already attempted to blast his way past the Ottoman defences, only to be beaten back. Duckworth declined Seniavan's request to join in a combined attack. Duckworth sailed away one week later, leaving Seniavan to his own devices, especially as the Black Sea Fleet had been totally unsuccessful in sweeping the Ottoman fleet before Constantinople.

Seniavan then sailed and 'took possession of the islands of Lemnos and Tenedos, garrisoned the latter, and then proceeded to blockade the Dardanelles'. Between May and early July, Seniavan successfully defeated the Ottomans' attempt to recover Tenedos, with the Ottomans losing three ships of the line and two frigates in addition to the loss of about a thousand men.[38]

Seniavan's success was undermined by the Treaty of Tilsit, which now had Russia changing sides, becoming Napoleon's ally. Seniavan had been ordered

After the Battle of Athos, 19 June 1807, Aleksey Bogolyubov (1824–1896).
Wikimedia Commons, public domain)

to return his fleet to the Baltic, which was now impossible. Attempting to return to the Baltic, Seniavan's fleet pulled into Tagus, Portugal, in November. Shortly after arrival, his fleet immediately met with a British blockade. Almost a year passed before Seniavan agreed to surrender his ships to the British under a condition that his ships and their crews would be returned to Russia. With Seniavan's surrender, the Russian Mediterranean Fleet ceased to exist. When war with the Ottoman Empire renewed in 1809, it was prosecuted indecisively by the Russian Black Sea Fleet.[39]

Baltic operations renewed (1807–1809)

Tsar Alexander's agreement with Napoleon at Tilsit renewed the long war against Sweden. The Russian army invaded Swedish Finland and quickly defeated the Swedes. The Russian Baltic Fleet was not as strong as the combined Swedish and British fleet which exercised naval superiority on the Baltic. Despite this inferiority, the Russian Baltic Fleet successfully supported the Russian army as it advanced through Finland, and in doing so, inflicted considerable losses on the craft and crews of the Swedish Navy. However, when the Royal Navy supported the Swedes, the Russian main battle fleet withdrew to Port Baltic (Baltischport, Russia, now Estonia) to be blockaded.[40]

With the main Russian sailing fleet blockaded, the Russian and Swedish inshore flotillas, consisting of small sail and rowing craft, fought several sharp actions along the Finnish coast in support of their respective armies. Neither side dominated and the campaign ended with the arrival of winter in 1808.

Little happened the following year, although the Royal Navy engaged the Russians in a few small-scale actions during the summer months. Despite success on the Baltic, the Swedes lost the land war and with the Treaty of Fredrikshamn signed in September 1809, Sweden lost all of Finland, the Åland Islands, and all Swedish territory east of the Gulf of Bothnia to Russia. The treaty also required the Swedes to join Napoleon's Continental System and close its ports to British trade.

However, the following year saw Alexander becoming increasingly alarmed over Napoleon's expansionism, especially as it concerned the lands that had been Poland. Conversely, Napoleon was greatly displeased with his Russian ally not aggressively enforcing the Continental System, the economic weapon Napoleon hoped would bring Britain to its knees. By 1811 both were preparing for war, a war that would lead to the invasion of Russia by Napoleon's Grand Army in 1812. One factor that led to Napoleon's subsequent defeat was Anglo-Russian naval operations on the Baltic, which interdicted Napoleon's seaborne logistics supply lines through amphibious and blockade operations.[41]

Russian Navy status post French Revolutionary/Napoleonic Wars
With the end of the French Revolutionary/Napoleonic Wars, the Russian Navy was unchallenged in the Baltic and the Ottoman Empire on the Black Sea had been significantly weakened. The Russian Navy would be employed against the Ottomans during the immediate decade after the French wars.

The Russian Navy's first naval actions were against the Ottomans' attempt to suppress the Greeks in their efforts to become independent. In 1827 Russia joined Britain and France in sending a strong naval force to the Eastern Mediterranean to blockade the Ottoman Navy. The blockade turned to an actual battle in October with the destruction of the Ottomans' Mediterranean Fleet at Navarino. This action kept the nascent Greek Republic from disintegrating. But it would take the Russo-Ottoman War of 1828, as well as France sending an expeditionary force, to ensure Greek independence. This war also gave Russia additional territorial gains along the northeastern shores of the Black Sea and autonomy to Romania and Bulgaria. The Russian Black Sea Fleet was instrumental in ensuring these gains.

At the end of Alexander's reign, the Russian Navy was second only to the Royal Navy in the number of ships of the line and lesser vessels. But there was a massive gap in the quality of the Russian fleet in ships and their crews.

With Alexander's successor, Nicholas I (1825–55), the Russian Navy saw a sharp increase in expenditures that facilitated the introduction of steam, the screw propeller, shell-firing guns, mines and torpedoes. There was even an attempt to develop a submarine. The first ironclad in the Russian Navy was built on the Black Sea in 1838. Additionally, both Alexander and Nicholas facilitated scientific exploration and territorial expansion of the Russian empire. They used the navy for the former, which greatly increased geographic and scientific knowledge in the nineteenth century. However, Nicholas's interest in the navy waned, and by the first decade of Queen Victoria's reign, the French Navy became the world's second largest navy.[42]

Diplomacy, Restraint and Protection: The Actions of Saumarez's Baltic Fleet 1808–1812

Andrew Venn

Vice Admiral James Saumarez was appointed commander-in-chief of the Royal Navy's Baltic Fleet in early 1808, with orders to blockade the Russian fleet, maintain diplomacy in the region and support the continuation of Britain's merchant shipping interests. The campaign that followed, which spanned several years, would test Saumarez's restraint and diplomatic prowess. Taking the indomitable First Rate *Victory* (104) as his flagship, the admiral was given virtual autonomy over how to conduct business, leading to many shrewd decisions that would shape the course of the war in the Baltic.

Vice Admiral James Saumarez (1757–1836), oil on canvas by Edwin Williams, 1862. Saumarez is shown here in his vice admiral's full dress uniform. (© National Maritime Museum, Greenwich, London)

This article will focus on three key aspects of Saumarez's campaign: maintaining diplomatic ties with a neutral yet volatile Sweden, keeping the threat of the Russian fleet at bay, and defending against the fiery Danish gunboat threat to merchant shipping. Each of these three sections will draw upon key examples to illustrate the importance of Saumarez's actions to the wider context of the changing face of the Napoleonic Wars.

Following the climactic battles of Austerlitz and Trafalgar in 1805, on land and sea respectively, the war between Britain and France had reached somewhat of a stalemate. While the Royal Navy boasted dominance of the seas, Napoleon commanded similar authority over much of mainland Europe. However, despite this impasse in direct conflict, the Napoleonic Wars raged on through other means, namely intrigue and economic manoeuvring. If Napoleon could exploit Britain's reliance on foreign trade by denying them such trade, he would have a clear advantage in the war. In particular, northern Europe was a key source for Britain's imports and exports, and cutting off this trade could lead to a crippling recession for the country.[1] Such action would also greatly diminish Britain's supply of stores critical for the Royal Navy. As François Crouzet suggested, cutting off the entire Continent to Britain's trade would prove too difficult for Napoleon to achieve, particularly with the strength of the Royal Navy hindering his plans, but cutting off the right parts could still have severe consequences for Britain.[2] In particular, a lack of revenue from import duties and taxes could seriously hurt the Royal Navy, potentially opening the door for the French navy to assert its dominance.

Trade with northern Europe was a particularly large part of Britain's economy at the start of the nineteenth century. In 1805 it was estimated that Britain exported almost double the amount of goods to the region, more than it did to the rest of Europe combined. On the other hand, the Royal Navy relied on vital shipbuilding materials such as fir, hemp, pitch and tallow from the Baltic region to keep its ships afloat and in good condition.[3] The November 1806 Berlin Decree marked the start of Napoleon's Continental System, which prohibited European states under French influence from trading with Britain, while also claiming British shipping as 'fair prize'.[4] Britain responded with its own measures, including blockades on French ports, the seizure of French-affiliated merchants and the issuing of licences to circumvent the Continental System. This was becoming not a war of direct action, but rather one of attrition through economic warfare.

Sweden

A major aspect of Saumarez's early Baltic responsibilities was maintaining good relations with Sweden, ensuring Britain still had an ally in the region. Sweden was ruled by the unstable, Napoleon-hating, King Gustav IV, who Saumarez would have to manage wisely to avoid any unnecessary flare-ups.[5] The country was surrounded by enemies in the Baltic, namely Denmark (and Danish-controlled Norway), Russia and Prussia. Sweden had to be particularly wary of a Russian invasion of Finland, its territory for over seven hundred years. The Treaty of Tilsit of July 1807 complicated matters, with Russia putting further pressure on Sweden to close its ports to Britain and declare war, and threatening to invade Finland if they did not comply. This threat would become reality, as

Russian troops crossed into Finland in March 1808, a few days after the Tsar had declared war on Sweden. Additionally, Gustav was watchful that a French army could cross the Øresund Strait from Denmark.[6] Despite these threats, Gustav also had his own designs on Norway. Instead of using the brunt of his forces to repel the Russians, Gustav decided to turn his attentions to an invasion of Norway.

Saumarez's diplomacy was immediately tested in 1808 as he stepped in to maintain relations with the Swedish crown following a failed expedition by Lieutenant General Sir John Moore.[7] Britain provided Moore's army of ten thousand to Sweden to assist with Sweden's war effort. However, it was not the intention of the British force to submit themselves to the full control of Gustav, but rather to provide general support where needed to keep Sweden from capitulating, which would result in Britain losing a key ally in the overall war against Napoleon. Upon their arrival in Sweden, the King prevented Moore's troops from disembarking from their transports until their use was agreed upon. Gustav objected to Moore having independent control of his own men, instead preferring to absorb the British force into the pool of Swedish soldiers. Gustav also planned for the British soldiers to either attack Danish Zealand, which was heavily defended by a Danish force superior in number, or assist in the assault on Norway, which had suffered from poor planning.[8] Moore personally negotiated with the King, but after these negotiations turned sour, the general was forced to flee Stockholm, seeking refuge aboard Saumarez's flagship *Victory*. Saumarez's actions and calm manner helped preserve relations between Sweden and Britain, laying the groundwork for a rapport that would assist him greatly later in the conflict.[9]

Anglo-Swedish relations would become more complicated in the following years, testing the limits of Saumarez's abilities. In 1809 Gustav was removed in a coup that would turn Sweden towards French influence, and what started as Sweden closing its ports to Britain evolved to their joining

Gustav IV Adolf, oil on canvas by Johann Baptist von Lampi the Elder, c1830. King Gustav IV was deposed in an 1809 coup. (Nationalmuseum, Sweden)

Napoleon's Continental System; however, the country wished to remain amicable towards Britain.[10] In the spring of 1810 France began to apply more pressure on Sweden to fully turn its back on Britain, and in October of the same year French Marshal Jean-Baptiste Bernadotte was elected crown prince and next in line to the Swedish throne.[11] Sweden declared war on Britain in November 1810, which appeared to end friendly relations between the two countries; however, Saumarez managed to maintain an air of diplomacy which still enabled trade to flow despite the changing conditions.[12] Sweden managed to discreetly keep its ports open to British shipping and still supplied Saumarez's fleet. Bernadotte's ambition perhaps also helped, as he longed to forge his own path away from the control of his former rival Napoleon.[13]

On occasion, Saumarez would even disregard instructions coming from Britain, thinking them to be detrimental to what he was hoping to achieve.[14] Although Saumarez had been given the authority to fire the first shot if necessary, he used his discretion to prevent an escalation of conflict.[15] Throughout his tenure in the Baltic, Saumarez kept his cool and maintained cordial relations when dealing with the difficult Swedes, ensuring that vital stores and trade continued to flow.

Russia

Another example of Saumarez's restraint and control came in his dealings with the Russian fleet. Once again, the admiral managed to avoid conflict and keep the political situation in the region under control. On 7 August 1808 Saumarez dispatched the Third Rates HM Ships *Centaur* (74) and *Implacable* (74) to reinforce the Swedish fleet in the Gulf of Finland, which was under threat from a Russian fleet that had sailed from Kronstadt.[16] Poorly maintained and with low morale, the eleven Swedish ships under the command of Admiral Henrik Johan Nauckhoff desperately needed the assistance of their British allies. The two British ships joined their Swedish counterparts on 20 August, and a few days later, on the 25th, weighed anchor and began a pursuit of the Russian fleet. Overnight, *Centaur* and *Implacable* raced ahead of the Swedes and caught up with the Russian ship of the line *Sevolod.* A short firefight followed, ending as soon as it had begun after the Russian vessel struck her colours. With the remainder of the Russian fleet bearing down, *Sevolod* was abandoned until the danger was over. The ship eventually became lodged on shoals and had to be burned; the British ships took her crew as prisoners.[17]

With the Russian fleet blockaded once more in Rogervik (modern Paldsiki, Estonia), Saumarez arrived on 30 August with further reinforcements to assist the Swedish fleet. He wanted to attack the Russians at anchor, but he showed restraint. There was good reason for this: such an attack would have been hard

The Russian ship *Sevolod*, after the action with *Implacable*, destroyed in the presence of the Russian fleet in Rogerwick Bay in September 1808, Spottiswoode & Co lithograph, London. *Sevolod* was burned by the British after striking her colours in a short-lived action.
(Navy Records Society, public domain)

enough to accomplish with a full complement of British ships, let alone with a force of Swedish ships in poor material condition. After further reconnaissance, Saumarez eventually decided on a fire-ship attack, but after several attempts being frustrated by previously unseen Russian fortifications, he called off this form of attack in September.[18]

The short-lived affair ended with the Russian fleet being allowed to retreat to Kronstadt. Saumarez was criticised for allowing the Russians to escape, his action regarded as overly cautious.[19] However, Saumarez's decision to allow the Russian fleet to return to Kronstadt prevented a war with Russia, which would have destabilised the entire Baltic region.[20] Another result of Saumarez's decision was that it made the Russians cautious of any fleet action in which they could lose additional ships. After all, the British had captured the Russian Mediterranean Squadron in Lisbon in 1807 with the ships being held at Portsmouth. They were released later in 1809.

The Russian conflict in the Baltic grew quiet from 1809 onwards, although several gunboat actions preceded the signing of a peace treaty between Sweden and Russia, ending the war between the two nations. After this point, Russia would officially attempt to hinder British shipping, but their enforcement of the

Continental System was not strictly applied. Russia would eventually turn out to be an ally to Britain after the souring of relations between Napoleon and the Tsar led to the former choosing to invade Russia in 1812. Napoleon had grown tired of Russia's indifference towards the Continental System and their previous commitment at Tilsit to become allies. Saumarez's fleet supported its new Russian allies in 1812 by hindering French coastal troop movements during the war, aiding Russia's resistance from the sea.[21]

As in his dealings with Sweden, Saumarez used diplomacy and restraint to prevent a conflict between Britain and Russia in 1808, which would eventually pay off after the latter switched sides in the war. Had the Baltic conflict between Britain and Russia developed, perhaps the Tsar would have enforced France's Continental System more vigorously, dissuading Napoleon from making an enemy of Russia.

Denmark

Perhaps the biggest nuisance to the British fleet in the Baltic were the Danes, who actively sought to harass British trade. Richard Woodman argued that, 'in the Danish gunboats, the Royal Navy met its toughest opponents', suggesting that, apart from American privateers and the frigates of the fledgling United States Navy, the navy of the kingdom of Denmark–Norway posed the biggest challenge to British naval power at the time.[22]

In May 1803 Britain broke the uneasy truce between itself and Napoleon's France that had been created by the Treaty of Amiens: 'Denmark–Norway kept out of the war, but in the following years the kingdom's situation became more and more difficult.'[23] The Danes found themselves under immense pressure from both Britain and France: 'An alliance with France's Napoleon would do a lot of harm to shipping which was one of the country's most important sources of income. An alliance with England might almost certainly mean that French troops entrenched south of the border would move up into Jutland'.[24] To the Danes, Napoleon's army posed the bigger threat.

Seeing that French coercion would force the Danes to turn against Britain, the British made their move. A British force led by Admiral James Gambier arrived off Copenhagen in July 1807 under the pretence of negotiation, but with the secondary motivation of a pre-emptive strike against the Danish Navy.[25] The Danes were given an ultimatum to surrender their fleet, which they refused. Their time ran out and bombardment of the city started. On 2 September the British fleet commenced bombarding the city, continuing for three consecutive nights.[26] At least two hundred Danes were killed in the bombardment, and approximately a third of the city was destroyed by fire.[27]

As a result of the bombardment, the Royal Navy confiscated eighteen Danish ships of the line, fifty-two smaller vessels, and 20,000 tons of naval stores worth £305,655.[28] Only four of the ships of the line were actually commissioned to the Royal Navy, and the most valuable prize for Britain was undoubtedly the stores.[29] Nevertheless, the Royal Navy had managed to take a sizeable number of ships out of the hands of Napoleon, which would prove vital to the overall war effort and maintaining British superiority at sea. However, the bombardment all but confirmed to Denmark that it should enter into an alliance with France, with Brian Lavery suggesting the Danes held lasting bitterness towards Britain as a result.[30] Denmark formally declared war on Britain on 4 November 1807.

Upon his appointment to the post of Commander-in-Chief of the Baltic Fleet, Saumarez received orders from the Admiralty concerning the Danish problem. These orders included preventing the movement of French troops into Zealand, or worse, onto the Scandinavian peninsula via Norway. He was also ordered to assist in the safe passage of trade through the Danish Straits and was advised to secure the strategic island of Anholt to help in this endeavour,[31] which Saumarez's forces did in 1809. He used the island as a base to protect shipping and also as a vital water resource, removing the British fleet's reliance on volatile Sweden for supply.

Denmark positioned 173 gunboats in the Danish Straits, supported by around nine hundred privateers, posing a constant threat towards the Baltic Fleet and the shipping it was protecting.[32] However, these vessels would prove to have little real effect on a large scale. For example, in the second half of 1809, 2,210 merchant vessels successfully made the trip through the straits, without a single loss.[33] In the same year, Britain managed to export £13.6 million worth of goods to northern Europe, the highest amount since 1802.[34] James Davey disagreed with Woodman's sentiments, stating that although the Danes did pose a real threat to British shipping; they lacked the power to challenge the Royal Navy, meaning the threat had declined by 1811.[35] Ole Feldback added that there was realistically little that Denmark could do against the professionalism of Saumarez's force and the organisation of British convoys.[36]

Although the Danes posed a nuisance to the Royal Navy, they were not a threat to Britain's foothold in the region. In terms of Britain's fight against the Danes, the Royal Navy captured around 1,400 Danish merchant vessels during the course of the war, proving Britain's superiority in offensive actions as well as defensive.[37] Denmark also suffered as a result of being forced to adopt the Continental System, virtually bankrupting the country by 1813; the only thing stopping them from signing peace terms with Britain was a threat of occupation by France.[38]

Conclusion

Saumarez's overall campaign in the Baltic was vital work, ensuring that the Continental System did not trouble Britain too much. By maintaining diplomatic relations and preventing the escalation of conflicts, he was able to hold out for long enough until the other nations capitulated, either due to internal pressure or financial difficulties. Whereas other commanders might have led their fleets down a path of escalation, Saumarez managed to keep his cool, bide his time and wait for the situation to fall in his favour. With Sweden, Saumarez's good relations with the Swedish court helped keep the country's ports open to British shipping, even after war was declared. With Russia, Saumarez's restraint prevented any unnecessary losses to his fleet in daring raids or battles, and also prevented Russia from becoming a direct enemy to Britain, something which would prove useful later on in the Napoleonic Wars. Finally with Denmark, the professionalism and organisation of Saumarez's fleet helped ensure that the Danish gunboat problem was managed and that the only entrance to the Baltic Sea remained open to British shipping.

Lavery stated that it has never been established whether Saumarez's appointment to the Baltic Fleet, with his excellent diplomatic skills, was intentional or just a stroke of luck.[39] In a 2017 biography of Saumarez's life, Anthony Sullivan stated that Saumarez shaped his own foreign policy in the Baltic in response to the vagueness of instructions coming out of Britain.[40] Saumarez was able to thrive under the relatively free rein that he was given, keeping his cool in situations where other commanders might have led their fleets into battle. Iain Ballantyne and Jonathan Eastland argued that the Baltic campaigns of 1808–1812 were just as vital to the overall war effort as Trafalgar, albeit without the notability or violence.[41] Woodman added that the presence of the Baltic Fleet enabled British trade to flow, in turn funding the war effort elsewhere.[42] Although the actions of the Royal Navy in the Baltic may not be regarded in the same esteem as major battles such as Trafalgar, the work carried out was no less vital in the grand scheme of the war, ultimately hindering Napoleon's ambitions.

Karl XIV Johan in general uniform on a white horse, see colour plate 3

Introduction to Three Chapters from
The Baltic Cauldron

Peter Hore

The Baltic Cauldron – originally published in Swedish as *I Fred och Örlog* (*In Peace and War*) – was conceived as a celebration of the quincentenary of the Royal Swedish Navy in 2022. A navy which was created when, during the Swedish War of Liberation, the future King Gustav Vasa bought a fleet of ten ships which arrived in Sweden on 7 June 1522. In researching the story it soon became clear that there was another story to be told, of several centuries of Anglo-Swedish naval relations. Then at the beginning of 2022 the book acquired a new resonance, the unending fight for the principle of the freedom of navigation, for the freedom of the seas and thereby the freedom of trade, and for independence from aggressive neighbours bordering the Baltic Sea.

Was the Baltic to be a lake, a preserve of its littoral states, or was it a gateway from which much of Europe's raw materials were to be exported? Was the Baltic to be *mare liberum*, open to all, or *mare clausum*, a closed sea, as Russia always wanted?

So, *The Baltic Cauldron* became a history of the Baltic Sea and its approaches, from the Skagerrak to the gulfs of Bothnia and Finland. Throughout history, navies have naturally supported civil society and the prosperity that international trade brings. Historically international trade has been seaborne, and still today some 90 per cent of trade is borne in merchant ships which are global by nature, traversing oceans and transcending terrestrial jurisdictions.

It is navies – warships – which can either facilitate or prevent this trade. Warships visit many countries and can be used to project foreign policy, helping to develop relationships during port visits or while on joint exercises and operations. Naval officers are not only sailors but often diplomats too.

Two navies in a particular have played a significant role in the Baltic, and *The Baltic Cauldron* portrays the relationship between the Swedish Navy and the Royal Navy over the centuries. Starting in the 1700s, Britain became a global naval power and developed doctrine, ships and culture which were copied by others, but the relationship with Sweden became special and helped to shape the Swedish Navy, its self-image, tactics, materials and traditions.

Much of the interaction between the two navies centred around thrilling, colourful, strong individuals, whose stories tell of their good sense and sound judgement which created friendship and trust, rather than discord and conflict. Remarkably, only once during the centuries have the two countries been at war with each other, and then not a shot was fired by either side. In chapters by outstanding American and British scholars like John Hattendorf and Andrew Lambert, and first-class Swedish authors, *The Baltic Cauldron* shows how British naval officers influenced not only the development of the Swedish Navy but of Sweden itself.

The three chapters reproduced here in the *Trafalgar Chronicle* focus on the late eighteenth and early nineteenth century, but the whole book is highly recommended.

Editors' note: The Baltic Cauldron (English version) was edited by Michael Ellis, Gustaf von Hofsten, and Derek Law and published in 2022 by Whittles Publishing, Dunbeath, Scotland. The translation from Swedish was paid for, in part, by donations from members of The 1805 Club. With permission, we selected these representative chapters by Peter Hore and Christer Hägg, who are both 1805 Club members.

The Baltic Fleet 1715–1727 and Sir John Norris

Peter Hore

To be properly told and understood, the history of the Great Northern War, and within that of Anglo-Swedish naval relations, cannot be written except in its context of centuries-long trade, regime change in Europe, Jacobite rebellion in Britain, Russian expansion, privateering and personalities.

The Baltic trade

The Eastland Company, founded in London in 1579 to foster trade between England and the countries bordering the Baltic Sea, was an attempt to challenge the Hanseatic League's commercial dominance in northern Europe. At first, the principal exchange was English wool for grain from the ports of Livonia, Poland, Pomerania and Prussia.

In the early 1600s government and commercial interests in England and Holland combined to found two East India companies, the Honourable East India Company (HEIC) and the Vereenigde Oostindische Compagnie (VOC), whose trade was in silk, tea, spices, furniture, porcelain, precious stones and other luxury items from India and China and ports and islands in between. The HEIC and VOC competed for a monopoly of the trade with the East, and it was not until over 100 years later that the Svenska Ostindiska Compani (SOIC) was founded in Gothenburg in 1731 in an attempt to break into this lucrative market. The SOIC made a mere 132 trading voyages to the East using thirty-seven different ships, typically like *Götheborg*, a sailing replica of an East Indiaman launched in 2003. The SOIC grew to be the largest trading

Admiral Sir John Norris, by George Knapton, 1735.
(Royal Museum of Greenwich, BHC2922)

company in Sweden during the eighteenth century and turned Gothenburg into a centre of trade for northern Europe. Think of the effort and organisation and resources needed to build just one ship like *Götheborg*: by comparison, the English and Dutch commercial effort was many hundred times greater, and already by 1700 both nations had built or hired scores of East Indiamen like *Götheborg* in addition to their warship building efforts – and hundreds more warships and merchant ships would be built in the eighteenth century.

The enormous demand for raw materials to build these ships far outstripped any domestic supply and the Eastland trade increasingly supplied the essential raw materials to build the large fleets of merchant ships and warships of England and Holland. Timber was needed for masts and planks from Russia, hemp and flax for ropes and sails from the southern Baltic lands, and iron, copper, tar, pitch, and more timber from Sweden and Finland. In England, the Navy Board particularly appreciated the tar, for treating ropes, and pitch, for caulking hulls and decks, which was available through the Swedish Tar Company, a monopoly whose product was better, cheaper, and more abundant than from elsewhere. England and Holland depended upon raw materials from the Baltic and when Russia invaded Finland, this supply was threatened.

Regime change

For most of the seventeenth century the Baltic had been a Swedish lake, but the deaths within a short number of years of Jan Sobieski of Poland (1696), Ivan V of Russia (1696), Karl XI of Sweden (1697), and Christian V of Denmark (1699) led to this settled period in northern affairs being disrupted by the Great Northern War (1700–1721) in which the newly crowned Tsar Peter I led a series of shifting coalitions which challenged the Swedish empire. In Spain in 1700, Carlos II's death led to the War of the Spanish Succession (1701–1714), in which Felipe V struggled to hold the Spanish empire together.

In England, the death of Mary II (1662–1694) and of her husband, William III, William of Orange (1662–1702), who was also stadtholder and de facto ruler of the Dutch Republic, brought Queen Anne to the throne. Anne's husband was Prince George [Jørgen] of Denmark and Norway (1653–1708), brother and uncle to the Kings of Denmark, a marriage which had been arranged with a view to improving Anglo-Danish relations, but though Anne gave birth seventeen times, sadly, none of her children survived. George was easy-going and unambitious, and his appointment as Lord High Admiral in 1702 was honorific. However, Britain was wracked by Jacobitism, support for the House of Stuart and the person of James Stuart (1688–1766), also known as James III or the Old Pretender, which found shape in a series of armed rebellions and attempted invasions which occurred intermittently between 1689 and 1746.

The SOIC East Indiaman *Götheborg*. (Painting by Christer Hägg and printed here with permission.)

Sound Dues

The King of Denmark levied a toll on ships passing through the Sound, known as Sound Dues, which was the King's personal income for several centuries until the 1800s. All foreign ships passing through the Sound paid these dues at the rate of 1 to 2 per cent of the value of the cargo, cargo which by 1700 included many luxury goods. To deter captains of ships from understating the value of their cargo, the Danish king reserved the right to purchase the cargo at its stated value.

It was an easy toll to collect, cargoes in and out of the Sound were mostly carried in small ships, much smaller than the East Indiamen which made oceanic voyages to India and to China, with small crews, and they were often obliged to wait off Elsinore, on the Danish side of the Sound, for the right wind to carry them through or out of the Sound. Though the actual number of ships varied with the intensity of war, most years hundreds of Dutch, English, Scottish and Swedish merchant ships were involved: Sound Dues made up two-thirds of the Danish king's income, making him independent of his nobles and his commoners.

Kaparkriget

The King of Sweden had his own method of taxing shipping; taxes that he needed to pursue the war. As the cost of war and Swedish casualties increased, Karl XII raised taxes and debased the coinage. He also licensed privateers, issuing letters of marque to individual private ship owners, licences to attack enemy merchant ships in return for a share of the value of the captured cargo and ship. These Swedish privateers were supposed to cut trade out of Reval (modern Tallinn), Riga, Narva and other Baltic ports, so that Peter I could not take advantage of his conquests along the southern Baltic coast. Karl XII also sought by licensing privateers to cut communications between Denmark and Norway, to stop the trade in Norwegian timber, prevent Norwegian seamen reaching Copenhagen to man the Danish fleet, and halt reinforcements and supplies to the Danish army in Norway. In turn, Danish and Russian privateers were licensed to try to cut off Sweden's foreign trade, and Karl XII levied a convoy tax on Swedish shipping waiting at Gothenburg to be escorted out into the North Sea.

In theory the Swedish privateers were only licensed to prey on the ships of the King's enemies, and ships of neutral countries were exempt, but if part of the cargo or the crew were suspected of belonging to the enemy, they too could be captured and carried into a Swedish port. Ironically, Swedish merchants who shipped their goods on neutral keels risked having their cargoes seized by Swedish privateers. To prevent privateering blurring into outright piracy, it was carefully regulated by Admiralty Courts, which ruled on what happened to the privateers' prizes. In the 1710s at least 156 Swedish privateers, most with Gothenburg as their home port, were licensed. Karl XII also authorised the privateers to fly the three-tongued Swedish war flag and, apparently, he hired out his own ships to these new Vikings, who were otherwise respectable merchants and rich landowners. This so-called *kaparkrig* sparked protests from both the British and the Dutch.

Lasse i Gatan

The Gothenburger, Lasse i Gatan, otherwise Lars Gathe (1689–1718), was the pirate king who owned or held a financial interest in some one-third of the Swedish privateers, and many of his sea captains were English Jacobites. Not least due to their ruthlessness, Lasse grew rich on privateering, and as a measure of royal approval of his achievements, he was ennobled in 1715 as Lars

Gathenhielm. On his death he was succeeded by his young wife Ingela, who as pirate queen continued the *kaparkrig* until the end of the Great Northern War. Though it barely mattered to the victim, there was a distinction between privateering (*kapari*), licensed by the state, and piracy (*sjöroveri*), outlawed by all nations. Though in theory they were two different acts of violence, Lasse's captains became increasingly pirate-like, individual members of the crew and passengers were robbed during acts of privateering, and if, at the end of a long and otherwise unsuccessful cruise, there had been no legitimate privateer targets, well, what witnesses would there be to an act of piracy?

During the 1710s at least 136 British ships were taken by privateers operating out of Gothenburg and several smaller ports on the Swedish west coast, and in 1710–14, 110 prizes were brought into Gothenburg to be adjudged by the Admiralty Court, thirty-five Danish and Norwegian ships, and sixty-one ships from the Netherlands and Lübeck. Lasse's privateering operations stretched further and further into the North Sea and the English Channel, where they claimed many more victims, and these were taken into Dunkirk in northern France, long a hub of privateering and piracy, and where there was something of a black market in stolen goods.

It was only British and Dutch concern that Russia might become too strong in the Baltic which deterred the two maritime powers from tougher punitive measures against Sweden, but Swedish diplomats had a difficult task trying to ameliorate the effects of the *kaparkrig*. When Karl XII lost control of lands to the south, he declared a blockade of the Russians' newly acquired southern Baltic ports, but the British and the Dutch needed those naval stores from the Baltic and could not and would not suspend their trade, thus setting the scene for a conflict with Sweden.

Lars Gathenheim, alias Lasse i Gatan (1689–1718) cropped, by unknown artist. (Gothenburg Museum, public domain)

Sir John Norris

In early 1709, the year of the Battle of Poltava when Karl XII was defeated and exiled in Turkey, Admiral John Norris (1671–1749) was sent to the Baltic, to intercept a grain convoy bound for France, but his expedition, like other English expeditions before him, reached no further than the Sound and returned without having fired a shot.

John Norris was a naval officer of unusually wide experience and long service. Norris came from the Anglo-Irish establishment settled around Dublin; politically he was a Whig, he was strongly Protestant, and he supported the Hanoverian succession in Britain. He went to sea at the age of nine or ten and for the next ten years he served mostly in the Mediterranean under Admiral Cloudesley Shovell, and he met many of the senior English naval officers who would ensure that during the Glorious Revolution of November 1688, the English navy deserted James II in favour of William and Mary. Shovell took a shine to Norris and steadily prompted him, so that at the age of just twenty-three he was Shovell's flag captain in the battleship *Britannia* (90). In the following years Norris took part in every major campaign of the English navy. In 1710/11 Norris commanded the Mediterranean Fleet when operations brought him into close contact with the future Holy Roman Emperor Charles VI, and he won the friendship of Prince Eugene of Savoy, an imperial councillor known to share in Vienna's distrust of the Elector of Hannover's territorial aspirations. The experience turned Norris into an effective diplomat.

However, when in 1714 the Elector of Hannover became George I of Great Britain, Britain was drawn into the Great Northern War. Although Britain had been at peace with Sweden, Hannover was not. As Elector, George had bought from Denmark the territories of Bremen and Verden which Denmark had conquered from Sweden. Karl XII wanted these territories back and it did not help when he accused George I of prostituting the honour of the British flag in order to serve the interests of Hannover. When Swedish privateers began to seize British ships which were alleged to be carrying arms, ammunition and stores to Russia, who was at war with Sweden, protests by the British minister at Stockholm were ignored. The Dutch had similar causes of complaint against Karl XII and found it equally difficult to obtain either redress or apology.

Norris's first expedition, 1715

So, in 1715, for the first time, a British naval expedition penetrated further than before through the Sound, with orders to intimidate the Swedes and to prevent further interference with shipping. Norris, commanding twenty ships, reached the Sound on 10 June 1715 where he joined forces with twelve sail under Dutch Rear Admiral Lucas de Veth, and a large convoy of merchant ships was escorted southward into the Baltic proper. While Swedish, Danish and Russian forces fought out another year of the Great Northern War, Norris's ships broke the Swedish blockade. However, the chart of the Baltic was a blank to Norris and his officers, and he had been unable to find any pilots in London, so although he carried some troops, any other operations such as an amphibious landing, were impossible.

Letters were sent to Karl XII insisting that the privateers should desist and demanding compensation for earlier captures, but the King declined to answer. Nevertheless, at the end of the season, the assembly of merchant ships which Norris and his Dutch allies escorted westward out of the Baltic was the largest ever convoy of merchant shipping – 340 – to leave the Baltic in any one month during the Great Northern War.

Significantly, during a three week stay in Reval in July/August 1715, Norris had met and won the liking and respect of Tsar Peter.

Norris's second expedition, 1716

Over the winter the British learned that Karl XII had given indirect support to the Jacobite rising of 1715, and so Norris's orders for a second expedition to the Baltic in 1716 were more directly anti-Swedish. Norris reached the Sound on 17 May with twenty-one warships and ninety-eight merchant ships. He was still unwilling to adopt strong measures against Sweden unless he had the gravest reasons for doing so and sent an officer to Stockholm to inquire if British merchant ships would continue to be seized. Norris spent several weeks in Copenhagen, hoping for a positive reply from Karl XII, but preparing to assist in a Dano-Russian invasion of south Sweden. When Karl XII sent a vague and ambiguous reply, Norris consulted with Tsar Peter himself, who was at Copenhagen where he commanded a squadron of Russian warships. It was decided that while a British, Danish and Russian fleet would stay off Bornholm in a demonstration of force intended to dissuade the Swedes from any further meddling with trade, an Anglo-Dutch fleet would convoy merchantmen into the Gulfs of Riga and Finland.

The Swedish fleet retired into Karlskrona, and while the British and Dutch covered their merchant ship convoys, Tsar Peter used the opportunity to pass the troop convoy westwards towards his army in Mecklenburg. A crisis erupted among the allies when Peter abandoned the invasion of Sweden and revealed the full extent of his threat to Hanoverian interests. However, Norris collected a large homeward-bound convoy and sailed on 9 November 1716, passing Copenhagen the next day and without waiting to pay any Sound Dues, set out in bad weather, losing one ship, *August* (60), when she ran aground on Anholt. Norris's nickname in the fleet was 'Foul Weather Jack'. However, he preserved the convoy, which dispersed off the Nore on 29 November 1716.

George Byng's expedition, 1717

Over the winter of 1716/17 Swedish diplomats in London were suspected of being involved in Jacobite plots and Parliament passed a bill which banned commerce with Sweden and voted funds for a third naval expedition to the Baltic. It was decided to send a more senior officer, George Byng, under whom Norris refused to serve. Peter I was visiting Holland and instead Norris was sent on a mission to improve George I's relations with the Tsar and to promote a commercial treaty between Britain with Russia. The Tsar's prevarication rendered the mission abortive, and Norris's better acquaintance with the Tsar turned him into a Russophobe.

Admiral George Byng (1663–1733), who later became Viscount Torrington, had first to oversee the defences of Sheerness where it was feared that Karl XII might launch an attack, but on 30 March Byng sailed for Copenhagen with twenty-one ships of the line, with frigates and fire-ships. Byng was authorised to co-ordinate his actions with Denmark, but saw little of the Swedish fleet, though he did see one of the few occasions on which the British and the Swedes came to blows. Between Gotland and Öland on 28 June the one-month-old Swedish *Jilderim*, built to a design by Karl XII himself, under command of Commodore Charles Gustaf Ullrick, met two British frigates, *Dartmouth*, commanded by Edward Falkingham and *Dragon*, commanded by Byng's brother-in-law, Streynsham Master. Few details of the engagement are known, but both Falkingham and Master were injured while *Jilderim* was captured. Her crew were put ashore at Helsingborg, and their ship was sold to the Danes, who renamed her *Pommern*. The incident did not

Admiral George Byng, 1st Viscount Torrington (1683–1733), by Jeremiah Davidson. (Licensed for *Trafalgar Chronicle* from National Portrait Gallery, London, NPG 14)

82

harm Ulrich's career, as he was soon promoted and given command of *Jilderim*'s sistership *Jarramas.*

However, Ulrich's orders from the Swedish Admiralty, which were captured in *Jilderim,* revealed Swedish policy for pursuing the war at sea. Ulrick, commanding a squadron of five ships, was ordered to bring all ships laden with hemp or masts 'of whatever nation they are' into Karlskrona, while sixteen named Dutch merchant ships and one English ship, *Angel of London*, were to be allowed to pass, Swedish ships laden with foodstuffs and tar were to be escorted to safety, and the enemy, described as 'the Muscovites', was to be engaged only if he was found to be weaker. Otherwise, Byng joined the Danes in blockades of Gothenburg and Karlskrona, but, apart from an aggressive reconnaissance of the latter, he left any fighting to the Danes.

Byng's force was steadily withdrawn during the year by the need to reinforce the British fleet in the Mediterranean, and by mid November the last of the merchantmen had cleared the Sound and, apart from three warships which overwintered at Flekkerø in Norway, all were home.

The madness of Madagascar

At the beginning of the 1700s, the two centres of English privateering – and piracy – were Bristol, in the West Country, and New York, then still an English colony. The main areas of operation were the waters around Europe, the North Atlantic, the Caribbean, and the Indian Ocean, where the island of St Mary's, five miles off the northeast coast of Madagascar, was home to some hundreds of pirates and slave traders. The majority of these were English (or American) and Scottish, who were unable to return to Britain without a pardon for their crimes. They had attempted to negotiate an amnesty with William III and with Queen Anne, and when their proposals were rejected, the Madagascar pirates offered money and ships to Holland and then France in return for pardons.

When they were again rebuffed, the pirates turned to Sweden, realising that in Karl XII's costly war with Russia he needed both money and ships. In May 1714 an English pirate, Simon St Leger, offered 500,000 pounds sterling, a fleet of twenty-five ships, and the services of 1,400 pirates in return for a Swedish pardon. After Simon St Leger left to return to Madagascar, he was never heard from again, but his son, Samuel St Leger, obtained a letter of marque from the King permitting him to capture Danish vessels in the North Sea, and by 1716 he had entered the service of Lars Gatenhielm.

In 1717 Karl XII's factotum Baron Georg Heinrich von Görtz began negotiating with William Walton of New York who styled himself leader of the Madagascar pirates, though he appears to have been a shipowner, merchant and slave-trader who had never left the city. In 1718 captured letters revealed that the pirates were also negotiating with the Danes, and when this was rejected, the pirates renewed their offer to Karl XII. Their proposal was to help Sweden to colonise Madagascar, to establish an East India trading company in Gothenburg, and to establish trading posts in Madagascar and along the East African coast. The King invited representatives of the Madagascar pirates to meet with him, and in 1718 Jasper Guillaume Morgane and Jean Monnery arrived in Gothenburg from France and joined up with Englishman John Norcross, whom they previously met in the French port of St Malo, Normandy, to buy a 40-gun frigate on behalf of Lars Gatenhielm.

John Norcross (or Northcross) was English and also a Jacobite. Born in 1688, Norcross had served in the Royal Navy from his youth, but after the failed rebellion of 1715, he had fled to Gothenburg where he met Lars Gatenhielm and became another of his feared captains. The Madagascar agent with the French-sounding name, Jasper Guillaume Morgane, was also a former English naval officer, whose real name was Casper William Morgan. Based in St Malo, Normandy, Morgan was a Jacobite agent who had recruited troops and bought ships and weapons for the 1715 rebellion. Only Jean Monnery may have been the genuine article, a Madagascar pirate.

Karl XII took the time to meet Morgan, Monnery and Norcross at Strömstad in late June 1718. The pirates expressed their wish to put an end to their present lifestyle and were successful in convincing the King to offer them an amnesty and Swedish nationality. On 24 June 1718 Karl XII issued a letter of protection for the Madagascar pirates, granting them permission to move themselves, their ships and all their belongings to settle in Sweden. He also gave Morgan an order to claim St Mary's for Sweden, to colonise Madagascar itself, and to begin trading and signing treaties with neighbouring countries. Morgan was made governor of St Mary's with the right to issue letters of marque to privateers to attack Sweden's enemies trading in the Indian Ocean – which could only mean the ships of the HEIC and the VOC.

In the midst of planning an invasion of Norway, the King is supposed to have promised twelve thousand troops for an expedition to the Indian Ocean. Otto von Klinckowström, who had shared the King's exile in Turkey, was appointed to lead the Madagascar expedition, accompanied by four other Swedes who were to assess the alleged, rich mines of Madagascar and the possibilities for trade, left overland for France while Morgan travelled ahead to St Malo to wait there with two frigates to escort the expedition to Madagascar. However, British spies in St Malo suspected that this was a cover for Swedish participation in another Jacobite rebellion, and that Morgan's two ships and the troops waiting in Gothenburg were actually about to participate in an invasion of Great Britain. By October 1718, Klinckowström had reached Amsterdam where he learned from Morgan that, although he had two fully equipped frigates, the voyage could not depart until the next spring because the harbour was infested with British spies. Instead, Klinckowström went to Paris where he delivered a personal letter from Görtz to Cardinal Giulio Alberoni, another ardent supporter of the Jacobite claim to the British thrones.

Although it was suspected that Karl XII's twelve thousand men were intended for an invasion of England, when a Jacobite fleet did sail from Spain for England later in 1719, it sailed without Morgan, and the fleet was disbanded by storms.

Norris's third expedition, 1718

Meanwhile, overtures of peace between Russia and Sweden in 1718 were accompanied by a growing suspicion by Britain of Russian intentions. Norris sidestepped a proposal that he should turn full-time diplomat and negotiate with the Tsar, and instead sailed from the mouth of the Thames on 28 April with a squadron of ten sail of the line, a bomb ketch, and a fire-ship and a number of merchantmen in convoy. Arriving off Copenhagen, he was joined by a Danish squadron, but no naval action ensued. Karl XII skilfully made peace with Peter I, and having freed himself of anxiety in one direction, turned with renewed energy to prosecute his land war with Denmark.

Pirate graveyard on St Mary's Island Madagascar. Photo by Jailiang Gao.
(Wikipedia Creative Commons)

Norris's orders were to prevent the formation of a Russo-Swedish fleet, and he heard rumours that he was to be ordered to go to St Petersburg, where it was thought that he might help to head off growing hostility between Britain and Russia. Norris avoided this commission by sailing early from the Baltic and not opening these new orders from London until he was clear of the Kattegat in late October.

On 11 December, Sweden suffered the loss of the brave but quixotic Karl XII, who was killed by stray grapeshot from the fortress of Frederiksten in Norway. It was not until February 1719 that the members of the Madagascar expedition in St Malo learnt of Karl XII's death, and that Görtz had been arrested by Karl's sister Ulrika Eleonora, who was now regent. Görtz was tried, sentenced to death for embezzlement and treason, and executed by hanging on 19 February. Queen Ulrika Eleonora decided upon a more conciliatory policy towards England, while in England there was a growing realisation that the threat to trade came not from Sweden but from Russia.

Norris's later expeditions

The Danes were surprised when in the summer of 1719 Norris anchored with a fleet off Copenhagen. They were more surprised to learn that he had not come to join them in their war against Sweden, but to aid the new Queen Ulrika Eleonora in her war with the Tsar, who had adopted terror tactics and who had sent Cossacks on raids inland against the Swedish population, known as the 'Russian Ravages', aiming to force concessions over the Åland islands.

Norris with sixteen ships, two frigates, two sloops and two fire-ships, did not enter the Baltic until late in the season, but on 26 August he rendezvoused off Karlskrona with Admiral Claes Sparre (1673–1733). Sparre's father was an admiral and two of his uncles were field-marshals in Karl XII's army. Sparre himself had gained much of his experience in the Dutch navy and subsequently enjoyed quick promotion to *schoutbynacht*, the Dutch title for a flag officer or admiral, at the age of twenty-seven, and he became a privy councillor and president of the Swedish Board of Admiralty. Norris and his officers, it will be remembered, knew little about Swedish waters, and sailing in company with Sparre they learned a good deal about navigating the intricate channels of the *skärgård*. Norris confided in his log 'the coast is full of small islands and rocks at the water's edge and blind ones under water'.

Sparre, with eight battleships, escorted Norris to an anchorage off Dalarö and there Norris met the Queen. She wanted the combined Anglo-Swedish fleet to attack the Russians, but they, at the mere rumour that Norris was on his way, had given up their depredations and had long since retired. Nor did Norris know the Gulf of Finland, where he suspected that the Russian galley fleet would have the advantage, and it was already late in the season. Besides, it was one thing to support Sweden but another matter to start a war with Russia. Norris rejected the idea of overwintering in the ice but undertook to return the following season and to consider a joint Anglo-Swedish attack on Reval if the government in London agreed.

Norris – remember he was called 'Foul Weather Jack' – was windbound for several weeks off Dalarö and could not sail until the end of October. On his passage through the Sound the Danes were surly and resentful of his support to the Swedes, and in the North Sea his fleet was scattered, the last ships not staggering into port until the New Year. Nevertheless, he had set the scene for that winter's peace talks in which Sweden regained some of her lost possessions.

Norris did return in mid May 1720 with fourteen ships over 60 guns, six 50s, and eight smaller ships, to reunite with a Swedish fleet of eight ships over 60 guns and three 50s. This was an overwhelming force to confront the Russian main fleet, but could not stop the Russian galley fleet from razing Umeå. There was criticism of Norris for allegedly blundering about the Baltic without fighting the Russians, but his manoeuvres deterred Peter I from major action.

One more expedition was needed, and on 27 April 1721 Norris was at Copenhagen again, this time with twenty-one ships, and, with new confidence in new knowledge of the waters, sailed on to Kapellskär where the British fleet anchored for most of that summer. The Russian main fleet dared not venture to sea, though some hit-and-run raids were carried out by the galley fleet. Norris exercised his diplomacy by writing to all the Russians he knew, including the Tsar, and on 30 August peace was agreed. Russia would give back Finland but keep Viborg, and compensate Sweden for the loss of Livonia, Estonia and Ingria with a payment of two million riksdaler.

On a cliff on the island of Marö i Rådmansö Sparre and Norris left a memorial (in Latin): *'Here lay a fleet of warships of Sweden and Great Britain, united under the command of Admiral of the Fleet his Excellency Count Sparre and the English Admiral John Norris; they lay at anchor together with lesser vessels in the year 1721.'* Norris also spent some time in Stockholm but was able to sail a month earlier than normal and by 19 October was back in the Thames. During these several expeditions to the north, Norris seldom had occasion to fire a gun in anger, and his proceedings were throughout uneventful and unexciting, yet, thanks to his tact, patience, and diplomatic ability, and to the recognised strength and efficiency of the forces under him, he was able to exercise a very weighty influence upon the leaders of the northern powers, and peacefully bring about results which a less capable officer might have failed to secure even by fighting for them.

To prove that his achievements were not just happenstance, in 1727 Norris, now Admiral of the Fleet Sir John Norris, sailed again for the Baltic, arriving in Copenhagen on 12 May. Russia was again in a threatening mood; Tsarina Catherine I menaced Sweden and was casting envious eyes on the Danish province of Schleswig-Holstein. However, she died five days later, and the appearance of Norris's fleet put a halt to events. The Russians laid up Catherine's fleet and abandoned her designs. Once more Norris returned without having had occasion to fire a shot in anger, thus setting a standard for himself and for others, like Nelson and Saumarez, to follow.

Further reading

David Denis Aldridge, 'Admiral Sir John Norris 1670 (or 1671)–1749: His Birth and Early Service, His Marriage, and His Death', *Mariner's Mirror*, vol 51 (1965), pp73–183.

David Denis Aldridge, *Admiral Sir John Norris* (Lund: Nordic Academic Press, 2009)

R C Anderson, *Naval Wars in the Baltic During the Sailing Ship Epoch 1522–1850* (London: Gilbert-Wood, 1910)

Cyprian Bridge, *History of the Russian Fleet during the Reign of Peter the Great by a Contemporary Englishman 1724* (London: Navy Records Society, 1899)

Sir William Clowes, *The Royal Navy: A History from the Earliest Times to the Present*, vols 2–3 (London: Sampson Low, Marston, 1898)

Lars Ericson Wolke, *Kapare och pirater I Nordeuropa under 800 ar* (Lund: Historiska Media, 2014)

John D Grainger, *The British Navy in the Baltic* (Woodbridge: Boydell Press, 2014)

David Kirby, 'The Royal Navy's Quest for Pitch and Tar During the Reign of Queen Anne', *Scandinavian Economic History Review*, no 22/2011, pp97–116

Brian Tunstall (ed), *The Byng Papers*, vol III (London: Navy Records Society, 1932)

Vice Admiral Lord Nelson Threatens the Swedish Fleet in Karlskrona 1801

Christer Hägg

Background

Towards the end of the eighteenth century, the British gradually became increasingly aggressive towards the seagoing trade of Sweden, Denmark, Russia and Prussia. Many British merchant ships had also been captured and the vital Baltic trade had been severely disrupted, but the Baltic trade was an absolute necessity, mainly for the import of naval stores. In 1800 the four Baltic Sea countries formed the League of Armed Neutrality, an alliance created to protect and facilitate their merchant shipping and to impose restrictions on the British. This challenged the core interests of Great Britain and could not be accepted and so the League had to be fought by force and broken. As the biggest threat, Denmark was first in line.

At the beginning of 1801 Great Britain organised a Baltic Fleet under the command of Admiral Sir Hyde Parker with Vice Admiral Sir Horatio Nelson as his second in command. Parker was a cautious admiral and not a man with a feverish desire to be active, but who now had a subordinate admiral who was his antithesis. In addition, Nelson had patrons in high places and had become a national hero after his crushing victory over Napoleon's fleet at the Battle of the Nile on 1 August 1798. Parker's friends pitied him for having been landed with this livewire as his deputy, while Nelson was unhappy too, as he had thought he would be appointed fleet commander. Nelson's own plan to break the League of Armed Neutrality was to first focus on Russia, which was the leading power in the League, and force it out of the League with a victory over its fleet in Reval.

Once the trunk had been felled, he saw no difficulty in cutting off the branches. But the cautious Parker excluded Nelson from his strategic conferences, which proceeded at a slow pace. Parker had nothing against this as he was newly wed to an eighteen-year-old girl and appreciated his marital happiness. The First Sea Lord, Admiral St Vincent, described the girl as a 'whipped pudding'.

The British fleet consisted of twenty-two ships of the line and forty-six other ships of different kinds – frigates, bomb vessels, fireships and gun-brigs. On 12 March 1801 the fleet set sail and passed The Skaw on 19 March. Severe weather drove part of the fleet towards Vinga outside Gothenburg, where it was sighted. King Gustav IV Adolf was only twenty-two years old and was in Gothenburg, where in January he had already ordered the reinforcement of the city's defences. The British fleet appeared earlier than expected but, to the general relief of everyone, it continued heading south towards The Sound. The King followed along the coast and stopped at Landskrona to observe developments. He ordered that the fleet in Karlskrona be armed swiftly and go to sea to take positions between Flintrännan and Drogden (the site of the present day Öresund Bridge), in order to support the Danes in their fight against the British and prevent the British from penetrating the Baltic. The Swedish squadron consisted of seven ships of the line and three frigates. The King was assured that the fleet would be ready to sail on 1 April and he expected to 'get to see my fleet become a participant, in an honourable way worthy of the kingdom, in the battle that may perhaps soon occur.'

The sortie was delayed by stormy weather and then by southerly winds that prevented the squadron from leaving Karlskrona roadstead. The King sent

Nelson in HMS *Elephant* leading his squadron past Helsingborg and out of reach of the guns of Kronborg Castle. The Swede chose not to fire on the passing ships. (Painting by Christer Hägg. Reprinted with permission from the artist)

several orders for the fleet to go to sea, but each time the commanding admiral in Karlskrona cited obstacles. The squadron commander had many concerns; the crews were almost completely untrained and had been partly reinforced with infantry from the Närke-Värmland regiment. The squadron consisted of seven ships of the line, all faithful old servants from Gustav III's War of 1788–1790 – namely *Gustaf III*, *Vladislaff*, *Wasa*, *Dristigheten*, *Tapperheten*, *Försiktigheten* and *Manligheten*, and three frigates: *Bellona*, *Camilla* and *Fröja*. Going into battle against a stronger, well-trained and superior British fleet three times their size in the narrow and shallow waters of the southern Sound could only lead to disaster.

In the meantime, the British fleet had anchored at Lappegrund, just north of Elsinore. Parker wanted to wait, but Nelson wanted immediately to continue on towards Copenhagen. Eventually, Nelson was ordered to attack the Danish fleet of twelve ships of the line and seven frigates, anchored in defence in the King's Canal outside Copenhagen. Parker intended to move towards Copenhagen via the Great Belt, but due to headwinds had to turn and go through The Sound. The time factor was critical because it was expected that the Swedish and Russian fleets would come to the aid of the Danes in accordance with the terms of the League of Armed Neutrality.

Lord Nelson delivers a toast to a successful victory with his 'Band of Brothers' the night before the Battle of Copenhagen on 1 April 1801. Painting by Thomas Davidson, 1898.
(Wikimedia, public domain)

On 1 April Nelson's division anchored just south of Middelgrund at the entrance to the Kungenskanal channel. During the night, a reconnaissance of the channel and locations of the Danish fleet was conducted. Buoys to mark the shoals were laid out, and in the evening all the ships' captains were summoned to join Nelson for dinner and orders.

That evening, at a late hour for the date, Nelson sat down to dine in Foley's well-appointed ship, with a large but choice party of comrades in arms. The signal to prepare for battle had been given. Darkness had hidden the sullen line of enemy hulks and substantial fortress guarding a northern capital of fantastic towers and steeples. Candle and lantern light illuminated the faces and figures of Nelson's second-in-command, Admiral Graves, an old and valued acquaintance; Colonel Stewart, whom he had met for the first time at Portsmouth; Riou, whom he had met for the first time yesterday; Hardy, Fremantle and many others whose names would be for ever remembered together with his own. He was in the highest of spirits and drank to a leading wind and to the success of the following day.
(From Carola Oman's book, *Nelson*).

The Battle of Copenhagen

The battle took place on 2 April and was very violent. The Danes suffered heavy losses, with over a thousand dead and wounded, while the British also suffered badly, with almost as many casualties. Six ships ran aground, and several ships sustained such damage that it would probably not have been possible for them to manoeuvre out of the channel. Nelson decided on a stratagem. Under a flag of truce, he sent a letter to the Danish Crown Prince Regent proposing that unless Denmark ceased fire unconditionally and accepted negotiations for a permanent ceasefire, Nelson's squadron, which was 'now winning the battle' (which was in reality highly uncertain), would be forced to set fire to the captured Danish ships without any possibility of taking off wounded Danes first. Nelson called it an act of humanity to cease fire. That same afternoon, the battle was ended by both sides and negotiations between Nelson and the Prince Regent began the next day. The ceasefire was ratified on 9 April and so Denmark had been forced out of the League of Armed Neutrality. As Prussia had no navy, now only Sweden and Russia remained.

The Swedish king was frustrated by the inaction of his fleet and the commander-in-chief, Admiral Claes Adam Wachtmeister, was replaced by Admiral Carl Olof Cronstedt. Squadron commander Palmquist was also removed and replaced by Rear Admiral Rudolf Cederström. In Karlskrona, everyone who could carry a weapon was mobilised. Retired admirals were appointed as battery commanders.

After the fourth order from the King to sail, the Swedish squadron finally left Karlskrona on 9 April and was outside Ystad on 15 April, where it was sighted by the British frigate *Amazon* (38). With the exception of Nelson's flagship, HMS *Saint George* (98), which was aground on a sand bar off Copenhagen, the British fleet had sailed eastward. Nelson had a six-oared gig made ready and set off after the fleet which, according to the report from *Amazon*, was pursuing the Swedish squadron on its way back to Karlskrona in conditions of light winds. After many hours of rowing, Nelson reached HMS *Elephant* (74). When Hyde Parker received a report that the Swedish squadron had arrived in Karlskrona, the British fleet returned to Köge Bay, near Copenhagen. The Swedish squadron had escaped by a margin of a few hours, and this tipped the strategic balance as the Swedes were now free to sail and unite with the Russian fleet in Reval.

On 27 April Parker was recalled. The Admiralty had been particularly dissatisfied with the signal (number 39, 'Discontinue the action') hoisted by Parker when the battle at Copenhagen was at its peak. Nelson had chosen to ignore the signal and is said to have put the telescope to his blind eye, announcing to his flag captain: 'You know, Foley, I only have one eye – I have the right to be blind sometimes – I really do not see the signal.'

Lord Nelson threatens the Swedish fleet in Karlskrona

Nelson was now appointed commander-in-chief of the British fleet and at the same time made Viscount Nelson of the Nile. On 7 May the fleet set sail for the Gulf of Finland in order to force Russia out of the League of Armed Neutrality. As the fleet passed Karlskrona next day, Nelson sent a letter in English to 'His Excellency, the Swedish Admiral'. It read:

> Sir, The former commander of the British fleet in the Baltic has, at the request of the Russian Tsar, permitted the Swedish trade in the Baltic to sail by sea. I would be saddened by any event that even for a moment, would disrupt the renewed friendship (I hope) between Sweden and Great Britain. I would like to inform Your Excellency that I have no orders to refrain from hostilities if I were to face the Swedish fleet at sea, which it is in your power to prevent. I am sure you will receive this communication as being the most peaceful act on my part and convey it to your Sovereign. I request that Your Excellency believe me, with all due respect.

The letter was written in English and not in the customary diplomatic language – French. The King perceived this as an insult and responded very evasively in Swedish, which caused Nelson a problem. On 1 June he wrote to the Admiralty and attached a translation of the response from the Swedes and apologised for not having sent it earlier because it could not be translated until the day before. Nelson also wrote that the Sea Lords would hardly be surprised, as the letter had been published in the *Hamburg Gazette* a few days after he himself had received it.

If the Swedish squadron were to leave Karlskrona and attempt to join the Russians, the consequences were crystal clear – it would be annihilated by the superior British fleet. The commanding admiral in Karlskrona had no intention of allowing the fleet to leave Karlskrona and so it was time to adapt for defence. It is interesting that Nelson wrote that he would fight the Swedish squadron if it went to sea, not that he would go into Karlskrona to fight it and bombard the shipyard and the city. In a letter to the British ambassador to Prussia on 8 May, Nelson wrote that: 'It is my intention to send a letter to the Swedish admiral because in the current circumstances it would be disagreeable to seek battle with the Swedes inside Karlskrona; if anything happens after they have received my letter, the blame will lie with them.'

Nelson's primary goal was now to force Russia out of the League and conclude peace. Sweden and Prussia would then quickly follow and the League would thus become history.

A strongly fortified Karlskrona
The Swedish squadron of seven ships of the line and three frigates anchored with springs inside Aspö Sound between the Drottningskär bastion and Kungsholms fort, with the ships formed with broadsides facing the inlet. A boom made from spare masts was laid to seaward of the ships and beyond that, a sea palisade with metal-tipped pointed poles was fixed 3m below the surface of the water. These poles were intended to rip open the bottoms of ships that attempted to break into the roadstead. There were gun launches between the outer islands and inside Karlskrona, batteries had been set up in several places, and blockships placed. The bastions were Kungshall on Stumholmen, Söderstjerna, Neptunus (now the figurehead gallery on Lindholm) and Drottninghall (the location of the shipbuilding hall in the current shipyard). Special batteries were also set up on Lindholmen and at the Femfinger docks.

The city of Karlskrona, the shipyard, the roadstead and the inlet were thus strongly fortified. Added to this was the fact that with southerly winds the British might break into the roadstead but would find it impossible to get out again – it would then become a matter of victory or death. With northerly winds,

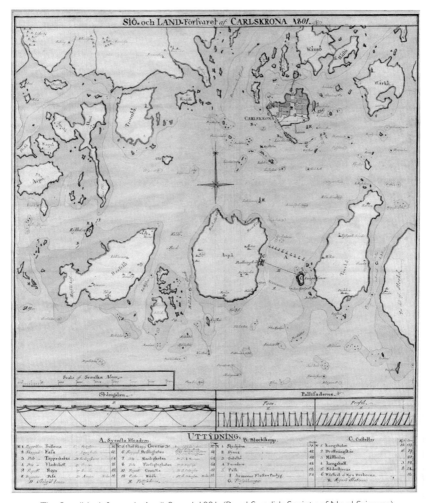

The Swedish defences in Aspö Sound, 1801. (Royal Swedish Society of Naval Sciences)

it was simply not possible to get into the roadstead. Parker's great hesitation to attack Karlskrona and Nelson's later ambivalence is easily understood given the rule of thumb that wooden warships should avoid getting into battle with fortifications of stone.

Nelson had now received information that Tsar Paul had been assassinated on 23 March and replaced by Tsar Alexander I, who was more inclined to be friendly to the British. In addition, Nelson discovered that the Russian squadron in Reval had left harbour nine days earlier and sailed to Kronstadt. The Russian fleet, which included forty-three ships of the line, was now blockaded inside the Gulf of Finland. Thus the danger of the Swedish fleet uniting with the Russian fleet had practically disappeared. When Nelson became persuaded of the new Tsar's desire for peace and that Russia would leave the League of Armed Neutrality, he departed from Reval on 17 May, leaving Captain Murray with six ships of the line outside Karlskrona to watch that the Swedish fleet remained in port, which it did.

On 26 May the frigate HMS *Jamaica* (26) sailed into Karlskrona with a new letter from Nelson:

> Sir, I am most honoured by the letter from Your Excellency of 24 May, with the attached proclamation from His Swedish Majesty respecting the right of British merchant ships to free shipping, for which I am very grateful. I hope that in a few days, we can restore the old friendship between our countries, so important to both our interests and hope that I will have the opportunity to meet Your Excellency in order to assure you with respect I am your most obedient servant.

On 19 June Nelson, who had requested a return to Great Britain for health reasons, handed over command of the Baltic Fleet to Vice Admiral Charles Pole and set sail aboard the brig HMS *Kite* (18), arriving in Yarmouth on 1 July. On 21 July the Baltic Fleet weighed anchor and sailed through the Great Belt to Great Britain.

In Karlskrona, the defence arrangements were dismantled. The old ships of the line were laid up and rotted alongside their dolphins. In the next great crisis of 1808–1812, it was again to be Sweden's foreign trade that was brought into focus through the Continental System imposed by Napoleon. That and the fate of Finland represented the biggest threats to Sweden, but this time the British Baltic Fleet would be on Sweden's side.

And so, in a little under three months, the Baltic Fleet had broken up the League of Armed Neutrality by force, by threats of force, and by diplomacy. British sea power had demonstrated who ruled the Baltic.

Further reading
Nicholas Harris Nicolas (ed), *Horatio Nelson – The Dispatches and Letters of Vice-Admiral Lord Viscount Nelson*, vol 5 (London: Henry Colburn, 1846)
Carola Oman, *Nelson* (London: Hodder & Stoughton, 1947)
Tom Pocock, *Horatio Nelson* (London: Brockhampton Press, 1987)

The Battle of Copenhagen on 2 April 1801, see colour plate 4

Plate 1. George Anson's victory off Cape Finisterre, 3 May 1747; a painting by Samuel Scott, c1749.
(© National Maritime Museum, Greenwich, London, 1861)

Plate 2. Portrait of the East Indiaman *Neptune* in two positions off the Downs. Oil on canvas, 1817, by Thomas Lucy (1759–1837). (Wikimedia Commons/Bonhams)

Plate 3 (left). *Intåget i Leipzig 1813 med Karl XIV Johan i generalsuniform på en vit häst i spetsen för sin stab* (The entry into Leipzig in 1813 with Karl XIV Johan in general uniform on a white horse at the head of his staff), oil on canvas by Fredric Westin, circa 1818–1844. Marshal Bernadotte would later be crowned King Charles XIV John. (Skoklosters Slott)

Plate 4 (above). The Battle of Copenhagen on 2 April 1801. Painting by Nicholas Pocock, early nineteenth century. (Wikipedia, public domain)

Plate 5 (following page). HMS *Clyde* arriving at Sheerness after the Nore Mutiny, 30 May 1797 (1830), by William Joy (1803–1865). One of a pair of oil paintings commissioned by Charles Cunningham. (Royal Museums, Greenwich)

Plate 6 (right). Rear Admiral Kempenfelt, 1781; oil painting by Tilly Kettle (1735–1786). (© National Maritime Museum, Greenwich, London, BHV 2818).

Plate 7 (below). French xebec *L'Espérance* and cutter *Swift*, in the Mediterranean Sea, 1804. Watercolour by Nicolas Cammillieri, 1809. (Licensed for the *Trafalgar Chronicle* by Mariners' Museum, Hampton Roads, Virginia, accession number 1934.1737.000001).

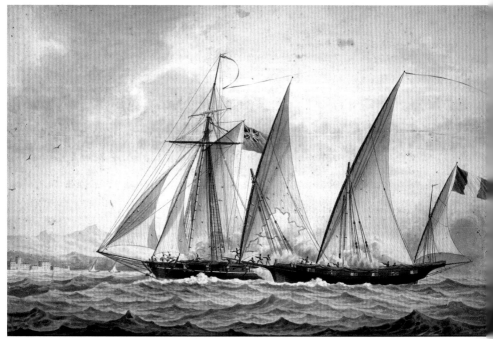

Swedes at Trafalgar

Peter Hore

Some eighty-five Swedes fought at the Battle of Trafalgar on 21 October 1805, where three Swedes were killed. There were four Swedes in the flagship, HMS *Victory*, and there even was a Swedish Nelson, 23-year-old Ordinary Seaman John Nelson in HMS *Dreadnought*.

Fair enough, John Nelson's mother probably knew him as Johan Nilsson, but that we know any of this is because the muster books of all the British ships which took part in the battle have survived. The names of a further twenty-five Swedes who had recently left the fleet are also recorded. The muster books (or registers) show that in total there were 18,282 officers, seamen and marines in the British fleet off Trafalgar, and a further 3,099 names of men who – like the twenty-five Swedes – were absent for whatever reason, making a total of 21,381. This would have been one-sixth of the Royal Navy's authorised manpower of 120,000 seamen and marines. Trafalgar is a large sample, and we can say that if the proportion of Swedes were the same throughout the Royal Navy as it was at Trafalgar, then in 1805 there were some 520 Swedes serving under the White Ensign.

There were men of many nationalities in the fleet off Trafalgar in 1805. About half (11,248) of these came from England, principally the four counties of Devon (1,341), Lancashire (720), Gloucestershire (618) and Cornwall (587). About one quarter (4,642) came from Ireland, which was part of the Union with the rest of the United Kingdom, 1,557 from Scotland and 727 from Wales. The remaining quarter of the men in Nelson's fleet off Trafalgar came from other nations, including some 526 North Americans, fifty-seven Danes, forty-one Norwegians, eight Finns (Finland was still united to Sweden), and, of course, the 110 Swedes. Where the place of origin is specified, the Swedes were from Stockholm (25), Göteborg (15) and Karlskrona (5), Ekenäs (1) and Västervik (1), and two places that have not been identified, Alinsforth and Calsand.

Mustering before the ship's clerk

Before analysing these numbers more closely, it is important to understand how the muster books were written up. A man newly arrived in a British warship stood before the ship's clerk and verbally gave his name, his age, and his place of birth. Close your eyes to listen to this conversation and it is easy to imagine

On the deck in battle, the crew had to show what they were made of. The Hero of Trafalgar. Painting by William Heysham Overend. (Royal Museums of Greenwich, PA16141)

how the clerk wrote Lillyagreen for Liljegren or Beorg for Bjorg, but some of the other transliterations are difficult to imagine. Even placenames were not safe from the clerk's ignorance, and while Stockholm was always correctly spelled in the muster books, Karlskrona is spelled differently on each of the five occasions it occurs, there were four ways of spelling Göteborg, and several

different ways of spelling Sweden (including three versions of Swedeland).

While the newcomer was talking to the clerk, one of the ship's officers would be assessing his ability and giving him a rating. There were three basic ratings: a landsman was an unskilled labourer who had little or no seagoing experience, an ordinary seaman would have one or two years' experience at sea, whereas an able seaman was a prime sailor with an intimate knowledge and understanding of the way of the sea and of ships, and who could 'hand, reef, and steer'. Looking at the nominal list of the Swedes, one is struck that few of them were in the lowest rating, landsman (12); the rest were ordinary seamen (40), able seamen (46) and the others were higher ratings, including two petty officers. Also, the average age of the Swedes was twenty-nine, at least five years older than the average of all the other men. Swedish seamen were always highly prized (fifty years later one British admiral advised another that there were plenty of good seamen in the Baltic, but don't let the Norwegians and Swedes serve together!). It is clear that the Royal Navy wanted skilled seamen and was recruiting, or pressing, the best of them in 1805.

The Swedes included both pressed men and volunteers
For the record, the oldest Swedes at the battle were volunteers: Able Seaman Jan Jansson, aged forty-nine in 1805, in the frigate *Phoebe*, born in 1745 in Göteborg, and Ordinary Seaman Peter Fosslines, aged fifty-one, in HMS *Agamemnon*, born somewhere in Sweden in 1744. It appears that Jansson was

taken in a French merchant ship, *Poulette*, when she was captured in 1804 in the Mediterranean, and that he was happy to transfer his loyalty to the White Ensign. Peter Fosslines was discharged to Deal hospital in November 1806 where he died, whether of wounds or of old age is not known. There was also 63-year-old Michael Luxan from Finland, one of the oldest men in the fleet, who must have been an experienced hand with previous service under the White Ensign, because, when he volunteered in HMS *Belleisle* in 1802, he was immediately rated as a quarter-gunner; that is, a petty officer who would have been in command of a battery of six guns.

Popular histories are filled with lurid stories of men being shanghaied or snatched by the press gang to serve at sea. It is true that between the years 1803 to 1805, the authorised manpower of the Royal Navy increased rapidly from 50,000 to 120,000, and that consequently there was a 'hot press' for seamen. The press gang was only supposed to take British men of seafaring habits between the ages of eighteen and fifty-five years and in theory no foreigner could be impressed, although they were able to volunteer. If, however, the foreigner was married to a British woman, or had worked on a British merchant ship for two years, his protection from the press gang was lost and he could be impressed.

We know that at least four Swedish volunteers had wives in England. Ordinary Seaman Andrew Synburg, in *Agamemnon*, made a will to Catherine Bos of Shadwell, while the prize money and Parliamentary Award which were due to Able Seaman Nicholas Rundquist of *Neptune*, one of three Swedes who were killed at the Battle of Trafalgar, was paid to a Lisa Jones. Andrew Sanderson and Martin Leaf, of whom more below, were also married.

There were other exemptions from the press gang, exemptions which were often ignored, and in the years of rapid expansion of the fleet, especially in the years 1803 to 1805, it can be assumed that the press gang was pretty indiscriminate. However, analysis of the muster books shows that 10 per cent of sailors were noted as pressed men while 49 per cent were volunteers. Amongst the Swedes, the percentages were slightly different: 51 or 46 per cent were volunteers, and 24 or 22 per cent were pressed. However, these numbers should be treated with caution, since there was a bounty, up to £5, which was the equivalent of several months' wages, paid to volunteers. So, some men, once taken by the press gang, would decide to make the best of their circumstances and, by taking the bounty, become volunteers. Whatever their source, whether pressed men or volunteers, their conditions of service, including pay, were the same.

Why should anyone volunteer for a harsh life at sea in the Royal Navy and its discipline? Well, this navy was one of the largest, most efficient, and effective in the world. Onboard, the officers were dedicated to keeping their men well-fed and healthy, and while the pay might seem low (the pay of an able seaman was £1 13s 6d per lunar month), there were few overheads, there was medical care and access to hospitals (unheard-of elsewhere in eighteenth-century society), and always the chance of a share in the prize money which was paid when an enemy ship was captured. To many, life in the Royal Navy must have seemed preferable to farming and fishing for subsistence on a barren island in the Stockholm archipelago.

There was one condition of service which was rather special: under a standing Admiralty Order a foreigner was entitled to claim his discharge from the navy, and the muster books show that no less than twenty-five Swedes were successful in claiming their discharge 'by Admiralty Order', some after only a few days or weeks.

The earliest Swedish volunteer to be found in the muster books is Marine Alexander Janson Pike, who was recruited at Chatham in 1796, but was killed at Trafalgar in HMS *Colossus*. The majority (60) of Swedes served between one to four years in the Royal Navy, but a small corps of men (7), like Pike, served longer. The longest serving seems to be Able Seaman Andrew Stallett, who joined *Victory* on 14 June 1803, but was drowned in an accident in Bermuda in 1814. The second-longest serving Swede was Marine William Johnson (Vilhelm Jansson?) from Karlskrona, who served ten years without promotion, and, curiously, was discharged in 1814 with the annotation 'bad character'. Ordinary Seaman John Godfrey joined *Leviathan* on 30 July 1797, but six years were enough. He did not want to take part in the blockade of Brest, so he claimed his rights as a foreigner and was discharged by Admiralty Order on 1 December 1803.

The percentage of pressed Swedes appears to be almost twice as large as the average in the fleet. Nine men were pressed in 1803 and 1804, but nearly three times that number were pressed in 1805, when the press gang was hottest. These latter pressed men included eight Swedes, mostly experienced seamen, who were press-ganged in late July 1805 and placed onboard HMS *Orion*, but by the end of the month each of them had been discharged 'being a Swede'. The record for having served the least time under the White Ensign falls to Frederick Kyerman who was pressed on 24 July 1805 and discharged by Admiralty Order 'being a Swede' on 27 July, having spent just three nights under the White Ensign. When four other pressed Swedes, who deserted or were discharged by Admiralty Order, are counted, the percentage of pressed men falls to 12 per cent, much in line with the overall figure.

In the days before personnel directors and human resources departments, there was little management of the common sailor's career. The best a man could do, if he did not like his ship, his officers or his shipmates, was to desert,

Martin Leaf from Stockholm was the only Swede who lived long enough to be retroactively awarded the Naval General Service Medal with the Trafalgar Clasp in 1847.

shown in the ship's muster book by the annotation 'R', meaning 'run'. Ships were usually short of men, and it was easy enough to change one's name and to join another ship. In the days before birth certificates and identity cards, three Swedes are known to have used aliases. So, desertion was commonplace and, not surprisingly, the books show that fifteen Swedes ran. A case in question is Stockholmer John Brown who had been in *Victory* for over two years, including Nelson's blockade of Toulon and the chase of the Combined Fleet to the West Indies and back, but who ran in Portsmouth on 13 September 1805 – two days before *Victory* sailed to join the blockade off Cadiz. Brown was arrested ashore, spent a night in prison, and on the next morning remustered in HMS *Africa*, using the name William Brown, and on the same day that a draft of five pressed

Swedes arrived in Portsmouth from the Nore. Did he recognise one of the pressed men and prefer to sail with him?

A far more serious case of desertion occurred in *Neptune* after the Battle of Trafalgar. *Neptune* was a hard-worked ship, which spent years on the blockade of French Atlantic ports, including two winters off Brest. For whatever reason, her ship's company were due over two years' wages when she returned to Plymouth in May 1805. There was little opportunity to spend their cash ashore, the money burned a hole in men's pockets, and disciplinary problems arose in the ship, with thieving and gambling. The muster book tells us that on 24 March 1806 a dozen men deserted 'to the enemy in Gibraltar with the cutter in the night'. The majority were Irishmen, there was one American, and two Swedes, Able Seamen Hans Englebuckt and Jacob Salmon, and a Finn, Ordinary Seaman Matthew Hekell, who had all joined *Neptune* in December 1803. What makes this incident curious is that these dozen deserters were mostly volunteers, who had each served between one and three years in *Neptune*, and they were all experienced and skilled seamen. By deserting they gave up their share of the prize money and, eventually, of the Parliamentary Award which were equivalent to another half a year's wages. Were they escaping their gambling debts or making off with their winnings?

What the muster books can tell us

Because the men are listed in the muster books with their ships' book numbers, it is sometimes possible to follow an individual though several musters. Peter Andersson, for example, saw service in the both the French and the English navies. On 19 July 1805 off Puerto Rico, four French ships, the 40-gun French frigate *Topaze*, the 22-gun corvette *Départment des Landes*, the 18-gun corvette *Torche* and the 16-gun brig *Faune*, captured and burned the British 36-gun frigate *Blanche*. However, the fortunes of war changed on 15 and 16 August 1805 when the 74-gun English *Goliath* and the 20-gun frigate *Camilla* met this French squadron at the entrance to the English Channel. After a long chase, *Faune* and *Torche* were captured: both ships were carrying English prisoners-of-war from *Blanche*. The French crews now became prisoners-of-war and among them was 30-year-old Peter Andersson (written Andrisson) from Stockholm and John Negroot from Finland.

Andersson and Negroot were carried into Plymouth, where two weeks later on 30 August they were entered into the muster book of HMS *Ajax* as prisoners-of-war, and next day as seamen. There they found a fellow Swede, Landsman Andrew Linque, who had been in *Ajax* since 29 July 1804: Linque had been wounded at the Battle of Cape Finisterre on 22 July 1805 and awarded £5 from Lloyd's Patriotic Fund. *Ajax* would be destroyed by an accidental fire which broke out on the evening of 14 February 1807 while she was anchored off the Aegean island of Tenedos. Many men who had been at Trafalgar lost their lives that night, but 380 people were rescued, including Andersson. Whatever loyalty Andersson felt – to the British or the French – he was evidently an experienced seaman with few ties in Sweden, and he appears to have been content in the Royal Navy. After *Ajax*, he was happy to serve in the 98-gun HMS *Windsor Castle* until at least 8 April 1807, when we lose trace of him. Negroot's fate is not known.

Two other Swedes found under the French flag were Stockholmers, both prime seamen, Isaac Hickland, and Martin Leaf. The richly laden East Indiaman *Lord Nelson* was on her return voyage to London when on 14 August 1803 she was captured by the three-masted French privateer *Bellone* off Cape Clear, Ireland. After several attempts at recapture by English privateers and by the sloop HMS *Seagull*, on 26 August a squadron led by HMS *Tonnant* came into sight and *Lord Nelson* surrendered. When the English boarded *Lord Nelson*, they found five of her original crew, who were accused of serving the guns during the fight against *Seagull*. These protested that they were Americans and not renegade Englishmen, but the prize crew put them in chains. Also, in the original crew of *Lord Nelson* were Hickland and Leaf, who promptly volunteered and joined *Tonnant*'s crew. Hickland was discharged to the depot ship in Plymouth in February 1805, but Leaf went on to serve several years in the Royal Navy. In a subsequent battle in the Channel, Leaf received wounds to the head and body, and in 1837, now a widower, he was awarded an annual pension of £16 from Greenwich Hospital. Leaf was also the only Swede to live long enough to be awarded the Naval General Service Medal with the Trafalgar clasp when it was awarded retroactively in 1847.

In HMS *Achilles* were two men who must have had several years' experience under the White Ensign: Hendrick Roughtrough, aged thirty-one, who joined from the sloop HMS *Kite* was placed in the sailmaker's crew; while Henric Miller, aged thirty, who had previously served in HMS *Windsor Castle*, was made a petty officer and yeoman of the sheets – as such he would have had charge of the sail locker. Both men would claim their discharge under the Admiralty Order in early 1806. There was one other petty officer in the fleet, 43-year-old George Teel, again a man who must also have had long experience in the Royal Navy, because, when he transferred from the frigate *Andromache* to *Temeraire*, he was immediately rated as yeoman of the powder room, a position which he would not have been given unless he was well-trusted and well-known.

In the summer of 1805, when there was a dearth of seamen in southern England, HMS *Africa* was hurriedly brought out of reserve and rapidly manned,

Crippled but unconquered, HMS *Belleisle* at Trafalgar 1805, by William Lionel Willie (1851–1931). *Belleisle* had to fight against seven enemy ships and lost her rigging early on. She fought for forty-five minutes before other British ships came to her assistance. Original in Army and Navy Club, London. (BritishBattles.com)

and her captain was presumably grateful for the nine Swedes who joined his ship in September. Three were Landsman Michael Mollynew from Karlskrona, Lawrence Rickman (alias Beckman and Buckman) from 'Sweedland', and Landsman William Brown, who has already been mentioned. The others were men who had been pressed from a single Swedish merchant ship in the Thames, including Nils Magnus Hoffström from Västervik (written Westerwich) on the Baltic coast; Johan F Nordland, whose place of birth is given as 'Ekenaas', which we may presume to be the Swedish-speaking harbour of Ekenäs in southwestern Finland; and Stockholmers Carl Johan Wolffe, John Boddell, John Nestrow and Lawrence Norman. Mollynew died at sea in 1806, the fate of Rickman is unknown, but between December 1805 and February 1806, all of the other seven Swedes in *Africa* were discharged by Admiralty Order.

In HMS *Defence* were two pressed men, John Jacobs and Andrew Spackman, and a volunteer, Nicholas Lice. There they were joined by two prime seamen, Jan Janfors and Peter Bjorg, who were both captured in a Dutch ship on 4 April 1804 and promptly volunteered. Jacobs and Spackman deserted on 10 and 12 June 1805, the dates suggesting that they colluded in their escape, but Lice, Janfors and Bjorg fought at the Battle of Trafalgar. Janfors and Bjorg were sufficiently reliable men to serve for seven days after the battle as part of the prize crew of the Spanish *San Ildefonso* which, though dismasted in battle and despite a storm, was successfully sailed to Gibraltar, where they rejoined *Defence* on 6 November 1805.

There were three Swedes in HMS *Defiance*. Able Seaman Nicholas Coleman volunteered on 6 July 1803, but on 11 February 1805 he was sent to the naval hospital at Paignton suffering from venereal disease; he was not cured until 30 May. The other two were Alexander Walin – surely Alexander Wallén – and the curiously named Juiro Flackness, who both volunteered at Cawsand Bay on 6 August 1803.

Even the smallest English ship off Trafalgar, *Entreprenante*, carried two Swedes in her crew of thirty-two. *Entreprenante* was just over 20m in length, certainly the wettest ship off Cadiz, and one wonders where the crew all slung their hammocks. Able Seaman Andrew Sanderson appears to have been thoroughly anglicised. He was a volunteer, and a skilled man serving – though he could not write – as carpenter's mate in the little *Entreprenante*. He was also a family man who remitted a large portion of his wages to his wife Charlotte, who lived near Plymouth. His service was long enough for him to receive both a share of the prize money and £4 12s 6d from the Parliamentary Award. Able Seaman Angus Pillstream, or more likely Adolphus Pilström, aged twenty-four, was another Swedish volunteer in *Entreprenante*: though he was awarded a share of the prize money and of the Parliamentary Award, he disappeared from the ship and the historical record before he could collect either and the proceeds went to Greenwich Hospital.

Ordinary Seaman Oliver Westerland in HMS *Mars* (more probably Olaf Västerland or Westerlund) was wounded at the Battle of Trafalgar. Injured in the back, he spent five days in the naval hospital at Gibraltar, before returning to England in *Mars* and being 'DS' or 'discharged sick' to Haslar Hospital. In 1806 he was awarded a pension of £5 for one year from the Chatham Chest at Greenwich, and £20 from Lloyd's Patriotic Fund. These grants bring us a little more information about Westerlund: he was tall and of light complexion, and his parents were called John and Hannah Westerlund. Two others joined *Mars* on the same day as Westerland, 27 April 1805: Peter Martin, who was discharged 'being a foreigner' on 11 December 1805, and Peter Vikström (written Wickstram) who did not wait for the paperwork to come through and deserted in Portsmouth on 23 January 1806.

Able Seaman Jonas Augustine, one of four Swedes in HMS *Spartiate*, was also wounded in the battle, and was awarded £10 from Lloyd's Patriotic Fund when he was discharged by Admiralty Order 'being a Swede' on 11 December 1805, but he ran before he could collect any prize money or his share of the Parliamentary Award, or even the £10 which he was awarded for his wounds.

Little more is known of the three Swedes who died at the Battle of Trafalgar. Marine Pike and Able Seaman Nicholas Rundquist have already been mentioned. The third was 28-year-old Able Seaman Caleb Goldberry who was killed in *Temeraire*.

In 1805 Finland was part of Sweden, and the Finlanders John Negroot, Johan F Nordland, Matthew Hekell and Michael Luxan have already been mentioned. There were four other Finns on the ships' books: Able Seaman Andrew Anderson, a pressed man; Marine Andrew Easterman who served 1805–10; and two men who deserted, Able Seaman Alexander Rossenberry before the battle, and Ordinary Seaman John Johnstone after the battle and without collecting the prize money and the £10 he was awarded from Lloyd's Patriotic Fund for the wounds he received.

As for John Nelson, he was pressed into service in *Dreadnought* on 9 May 1803, but he was discharged by Admiralty Order on 15 May 1805 'being a Swede', and so, unlike his namesake, he missed being part of Nelson's victory.

Of all these men, it has been possible, so far, to trace only two. Nils Magnus Hoffström was a professional sailor, who married on Gotland in 1803, had six children, and he died there in 1834; and Johan F Nordland (or Nordlund), who enjoyed a career in the Finnish Coastguard, or Suomen Meriekipaasi, became a *kaptenleutnant* in 1844, and died in 1848 in the Ålands. If any reader has more information about these men, please contact this author.

Further reading

P Ayshford & D Ayshford, *The Ayshford Complete Trafalgar Roll* (Brussels: SEFF, 2004) (CD-ROM)

Peter Hore, *News of Nelson, John Lapenotiere's Race from Trafalgar to London* (Brussels: Seff Publications, 2005)

Patrick Marione, with a foreword by N A M Rodger, *The Complete Navy List of the Napoleonic War 1793–1815*, Ageofnelson.org/NavyList/ (2007), also available on CD-ROM

Nicholas Slope, *Nelson's Navy: Recruitment, Promotion, Discipline, and Death* (Tring: Incitatus Books, 2019)

'An Officer of Great Merit': Captain Charles Cunningham and the Nore Mutiny

Andrew Field

Rear Admiral Sir Charles Cunningham (1755–1834) was born in Oak Lawn House, Eye, in 1755. Now largely forgotten, his prominent memorial in St Peter's and St Paul's Church in Eye suggests a distinguished naval service. When researching the service of naval officers between 1793 and 1815, it is easy to be swept up by the spectacular exploits of such officers as Nelson, Pellew, Cochrane and others. Perhaps it's time to assess another, less renowned 'officer of great merit'. This article presents a summary of his daring actions and decisions at the Nore in 1797 when he sailed his ship out of the mutinous fleet.

Charles's early naval service

At age fifteen, inspired by Defoe's *Robinson Crusoe*, Charles Cunningham began a life at sea. By 1775, at the age of twenty, he was rated master's mate, judged fully capable of standing a watch. On the outbreak of the American war, he entered the Royal Navy. Initially rated able seaman, but soon re-rated master's mate, he joined the Fifth Rate *Aeolus* (32) on 6 November 1776, and sailed to the West Indies.[1] Here he served on the flagship, the Fourth Rate *Bristol* (50), the brigs *Ostrich* (14) and *Port Royal* (18), and served briefly as Nelson's acting first lieutenant on the Sixth Rate *Hinchinbroke* (28).[2] As master and commander of *Admiral Barrington* (14), he distinguished himself during the failed attempt to recapture the Turks and Caicos Islands, closing inshore to give supporting fire.[3] Confirmed lieutenant, in November 1782 Charles served on the Fifth Rate *Pallas* (36), and the Third Rates *Ajax* and *Tremendous*.

With war's end, Charles returned home, marrying Mary Boycatt of Burgh St Peter in 1783. After five years on half pay, he was offered the position of third lieutenant in the Third Rate HMS *Crown* (64), by William Cornwallis, MP for Eye, who had just been appointed as commodore of the East Indies Squadron. Cornwallis had the pick of the many unemployed officers desperate for a seagoing appointment, and Charles was fortunate to be chosen.

Returning home in 1793, Charles was given command of the newly built brig *Speedy* (14), and joined Lord Hood's Mediterranean Fleet. Here, he further

Portrait of Rear Admiral Cunningham in the undress uniform of a rear admiral, painted between 1834 and 1845 by Henry Wyatt (1794–1840). (Royal Museums, Greenwich)

distinguished himself, and in October 1793 *Speedy* formed a part of Rear Admiral Gell's squadron in the attack on Genoa, where two French frigates, *Modeste* and *Imperieuse*, had been violating Genoa's neutrality, attacking British trade. During the action, boats from *Speedy* cut out two privateers and in recognition of this, Lord Hood gave Charles command of the prize, *Imperieuse*, confirming this with a commission dated 12 October 1793.[4]

Charles commanded until March 1794, when he exchanged with Captain Wolseley of the Fifth Rate *Lowestoffe* (32), and further distinguished himself supporting operations on Corsica. In another clear sign of approval, Hood gave Charles the honour of carrying his despatches back to London, praising his actions and recommending him to the Admiralty as 'an officer of great merit, and highly deserving any favour that can be shown him.'[5]

Following another spell at home, Charles was appointed to the Fifth Rate frigate *Trent* (36), to supervise her fitting-out, before being appointed to another new, fir-built Fifth Rate frigate *Clyde* (38). A powerful ship, she was to be Charles's for the next six years.[6]

The Nore Mutiny

In 1797 Charles and his men found themselves playing a significant role in the Nore Mutiny, one that Charles felt important enough for him to recount in *A Narrative Of Occurrences That Took Place During The Mutiny At The Nore In The Months Of April, May, June 1797*, published in 1829. Looking back at events of thirty-two years earlier, Charles acknowledged that he would be biased, that his narrative was an officer's account, and that he neither intended to be, nor could he be, objective about the mutineers, or their motives.[7]

Unlike at Spithead, the ships at the Nore were, in historian James Dugan's words, a 'catch-all', with some ships, including *Clyde*, only temporarily at anchor, and the port admiral, Admiral Buckner, who flew his flag in the Second Rate *Sandwich* (90), guardship and receiving ship, 'an admiral of everything and nothing'.[8]

As a receiving ship, *Sandwich* was overcrowded, with volunteers, pressed men and experienced seamen all waiting to be posted to other ships.[9] Their inactivity, overcrowding, shipboard diseases and boredom made *Sandwich*, in particular, a powder keg, needing just a spark to set it off.

That spark was provided by growing dissatisfaction in the fleet as a whole, and brought to a head by the Spithead mutiny. The sudden influx of pressed men into the navy and many officers who had not been to sea for years created ill-feeling, exacerbated by poor conditions, low wages and monotonous blockades. Wider conditions may also have played a part, as there was a great mood of unrest throughout the country. After four years, war-weariness, inflation and failed harvests all combined to create opposition to the war and to the government.[10] Yet with the mutiny at Spithead seemingly resolved with concessions which applied to the whole navy, Charles, along with many other naval officers, struggled to understand why the men at the Nore mutinied, and primarily blamed outside agitation and the influx of 'quota men', unwilling recruits into the navy, with little or no seagoing experience.

According to Edward Brenton, a friend and former shipmate of Charles, a later author of a five-volume history of the Royal Navy between 1783 and 1822 and a biography of the Earl of St Vincent, the blame lay with quota men. At the time a lieutenant on the Third Rate *Agamemnon* (64), of Admiral Duncan's North Sea Squadron, Brenton believed that the bounties of up to £70 paid to them were a major cause for discontent amongst serving seamen, many of whom had joined the navy in 1793 and had only received a bounty of £5. He described quota men as 'the very refuse and outcasts of society, flying from justice and the vengeance of the law'.[11]

Cuthbert Collingwood, then a captain, held similar opinions, and in a letter to his sister described them as 'debtors, drunkards, unemployed and radicals, who had taken the bounty and brought dangerous, political ideas on board the navy's warships'. More recent historians, including Professor Christopher Lloyd in *The British Seaman*, have agreed. Lloyd wrote that 'the original outbreak was promoted by a small body of such sea lawyers, appalled by the prospects of a life at sea and not yet inured to its hardships.'[12]

Whilst some of the mutineers were undoubtedly politically radicalised, far from being disgruntled pressed seamen, in reality many of the leaders of the Nore Mutiny were experienced senior ratings or petty officers; many others, often experienced sailors themselves, were resentful of being ignored and left on *Sandwich*, rather than being posted to seagoing ships.[13] Skilled leading hands, it would have been easy for them to cajole and organise confused raw recruits into refusing duty. Other mutineers, including experienced sailors, often went along with the extremists, either through intimidation, or just passively, welcoming the temporary change of routine and feelings of power. These were men happy to just to 'sit on the fence', content to bide their time and await developments. Ships whose crews opposed the mutiny seemed in a minority.

Certainly, the mutiny was not spontaneous. On 12 May, with most captains ashore attending a court martial, the men of *Sandwich* refused to shift her berth, instead climbing the shrouds, and cheering. This was the agreed signal for other ships to join in. Taking control proved a straightforward task. In all of the confusion, it proved easy to disobey officers, defying their attempts to restore order. Red flags were quickly hoisted on the mutinous ships.

In all of this, *Clyde*'s men were what historian James Dugan calls, 'reluctant fellow travellers in the cause', a fact that reflects well on their respect for Charles.[14] So, whilst *Clyde*'s log recorded the discontent and insubordination on other ships, there is no mention of any violent outbursts on *Clyde*. In fact, the log noted that a boatswain from the Third Rate *Inflexible* (64), one of the most radical ships in the Nore, attempting to board to speak to the crew, was refused permission by the officer of the watch, and that 'after some conversation the ship's company said they had no cause of complaint and were determined to remain quiet.'[15]

Such outright defiance toward the mutineers placed *Clyde*'s crew in a difficult position. Complete opposition would be dangerous, so the crew complied with demands to elect two of their number as delegates, who duly set off for *Inflexible* and *Sandwich*. On their return they demanded the keys to the ship's magazine from Lieutenant Kerr, the senior officer aboard. After remonstrating, rather than force a confrontation, Kerr reluctantly complied.[16]

Nevertheless, *Clyde*'s crew remained concerned about their situation and when *Inflexible* shifted her berth and sailed past: 'Many of our ship's company came aft and said to the First Lieutenant that they had received intimation from the crew of the *Inflexible* that if the *Clyde*'s company did not cheer them as they passed they would certainly sink the *Clyde*.'[17] *Clyde*'s crew was allowed to cheer, but it was clear that they feared a confrontation.

Although over the coming days *Clyde*'s log routinely recorded her crew as in a state of mutiny, and not under normal discipline, they remained reluctant mutineers, despite daily haranguing from their own and other delegates. Pushed into making some sort of mutinous gesture, they eventually expressed dissatisfaction with Mr Gardiner, their surgeon, describing him as an excellent man, but not a satisfactory surgeon.[18] These were hardly the words of ardent mutineers. Nevertheless, Gardiner was told to leave the ship and on 16 May was rowed ashore in the boat sent to pick up Charles, who was ashore at a meeting with Buckner.

Quickly summing up the situation, and the challenge to his position, Charles ordered Gardiner back into the boat, and they both returned to the ship. Once back on board, Charles took the decision out of the crew's hands and gave his own order to send Gardiner ashore.[19] In doing so, not only was Charles exerting his authority as captain, but also saving his men from the charge of mutinous behaviour. Yet it must have been equally obvious to him that he, and they, were in a difficult position. It would need all of his skill and his authority to retain the loyalty and respect of his men. Just one misjudgement on his part could lose him his ship. For their part, Charles's crew had to be seen to be active, not reluctant, mutineers, not least for their own safety.

Charles also made his own stance clear in an incident he recounted in his narrative. A group of officers was present when Admiral Buckner met with Parker and a body of delegates, attempting to negotiate a settlement. According to Charles, Parker openly challenged Buckner, using 'mutinous language'. Charles described being enraged and infuriated by this disrespect to an admiral, losing his temper and drawing his sword, fortunately being restrained by Captain Blackwood of *Brilliant* (28). James Dugan puts it more colourfully, describing one of the captains yelling, 'I'll kill the insolent bugger.'[20] Given Charles's well-known quick temper, had he not been restrained, events could quickly have taken a much more serious turn.[21]

Still, the mutineers attempted to gain some control over the unreliable ships, by sending orders on 23 May to *Clyde*, *San Fiorenzo*, *Brilliant* and *Iris* to shift their berths nearer the mutinous ships. The outcome further shows both Charles's attitude toward the mutineers, and the support he had from his men.

One of the mutineers' leaders, James Hockliss, was sent over from *Sandwich* to pilot *Clyde* to a new anchorage. Charles was having none of this and he argued and delayed as long as he could, only agreeing once the mutineers issued the further threat, that unless *Clyde* shifted her berth immediately, *Inflexible* would be brought alongside to make her do so.[22] Unwilling to force a confrontation that would have led to bloodshed and the loss of his ship, Charles reluctantly agreed. But only in part. The ship would move, but he would retain command.

Charles had allowed Hockliss onboard, but he was not going to allow him to issue orders. With his men looking on, Charles browbeat the hapless Hockliss, who, unsupported and overawed, gave way and Charles slowly shifted *Clyde* to her new anchorage.[23] At one point *Clyde* swung towards the sloop *Swan* (14) anchored nearby. Seeing Charles, *Swan*'s crew panicked, expecting to be boarded, and although Hockliss tried to reassure them that they were safe, they remained unconvinced, and soon shifted *Swan*'s berth away from the frigate. Later, the sloop *Pylades* (16), whose crew were obviously made of sterner stuff, anchored between *Clyde* and *San Fiorenzo,* with her guns laid on both ships.[24]

This whole incident was both another snub to the delegates, a clear indication that Charles and his crew were opposed to the mutiny. By obeying Charles, not Hockliss, *Clyde*'s men had placed themselves in a more precarious position, though. This clearly could not continue indefinitely, and Charles began thinking about escape.

Charles retained his crew's loyalty, and five days later, another incident occurred, which was the point of no return for *Clyde*'s crew. Whilst Charles was attending a midnight meeting with Admiral Buckner and the other captains, they were interrupted by the arrival of *Clyde*'s Lieutenant Hughes, with the disturbing news that, in Charles's absence, Richard Parker, erstwhile leader of the mutiny, had boarded *Clyde* and was urging the crew to join in a bombardment of Tilbury Fort the next day. The aim was to distract the defenders, and allow four ships, the Second Rate *Neptune* (98), the Third Rates

Agincourt (64) and *Lancaster* (64), together with the newly commissioned Fifth Rate frigate *Naiad* (28), to sail into the Nore from the Thames and join the mutineers.

These ships would have made a useful addition to the mutinous fleet. In fact, they had been ordered by the Admiralty to sail into the Nore to intimidate the mutineers, but Parker was hopeful that their men, many of them pressed men of dubious loyalty, or, in the case of *Lancaster*, men from the recently wrecked *Albion*, turned over without any opportunity for leave, would prove willing mutineers.

Aboard *Clyde*, however, the crew refused to go along with Parker, the log recording that 'this diabolical proposal was received by the people with indignation and instantly rejected.'[25] Parker's plan was unravelling. The ultimate humiliation for Parker came when he urged all who were in favour of the bombardment to join him on the forecastle. Only *Clyde*'s two delegates and one other seaman did so, the rest – officers and men, remaining in the waist. Parker, along with his three companions, was left isolated, angry, frustrated and humiliated. Leaving the ship, Parker singled out Lieutenant Kerr and threatened, 'you and your damned Captain have too much the confidence of the Ship's Company; and I will take you both and hang you, or the *Inflexible* people shall do it.'[26]

On Parker's departure, Lieutenant Hughes was sent to fetch Charles back.[27] Once Charles returned, the men begged him not to leave the ship again and to take the ship out of the Nore as soon as possible.[28] If it had not been suspected before, their rejection of Parker's proposal now made it clear there were no supporters of mutiny and Charles's crew anticipated that consequences would not be long in coming. Remaining at anchor was just too dangerous. Meanwhile, aboard *Sandwich*, thwarted in his plans, Parker cancelled the Tilbury bombardment, and turned his attention to *Clyde*, a focus for the disruption and dissension that Parker could not ignore.

Ashore, events were also developing. Two members of the Board of Admiralty, the First Lord, Earl Spencer, and Admiral Young had arrived, not to negotiate, but to issue the King's Pardon and see the ships returned to duty. As Spencer refused to meet with Parker in person, he selected the two captains most guaranteed to be unsympathetic to the mutineers, Sir Harry Neale of *San Fiorenzo* and Charles Cunningham to speak in his stead.

They met with Parker and the delegates at The Chequers, the Sheerness inn favoured as his headquarters, but the meeting failed before it had scarcely begun. When Neale began explaining the purpose of their visit, according to Charles, 'a person (a Stranger) not sitting at the table, rose up and observed that if there were only two Lords of the Admiralty, they did not form a Board.'[29]

Whoever this mysterious stranger was, he seemed well-known and well respected, because as soon as he spoke, the delegates left.

Charles and Neale reported back on their failure. Spencer and Young next decided to attempt to speak directly to the mutinous ships, sway their crews' loyalty and return them to duty. Rowing out to the anchored fleet, they first read the King's Pardon to the crews of the most loyal ships, *San Fiorenzo*, *Clyde*, *Brilliant*, *Isis*, *Grampus*, *L'Espion* and *Niger*.

Even so, they met with mixed success. Fights broke out among the various factions. On *Grampus* and *Isis*, men who wished to accept the pardon unsuccessfully fought mutineers, before being driven off the ships. Aboard *Brilliant*, Blackwood briefly managed to hoist the White Ensign, before being compelled to strike it again.[30] Complicating matters, the crew of the Third Rate *Director* (64) hoisted a Blue Ensign, an indication of their willingness to reach a negotiated settlement, and also sent a message. They were prepared to follow *Clyde* and *San Fiorenzo* out of the Nore. Soon, though, *Director*'s Blue Ensign disappeared, replaced once again by the Red.[31] As for the men on the other ships in the Nore, they refused to receive copies of the pardon on board, or listen to it.[32]

Tension in the anchorage continued to mount, as *Inflexible* manoeuvred to bring her broadside to bear on *Clyde*, still flying a White Ensign, compelling Charles to reluctantly strike the flag, and replace it with a Red. He was not yet ready to act or be pushed into premature action.[33] Well aware of his situation, he knew decisive action was called for, and soon, but it had to be planned. Events were drawing inexorably to a climax, and he did not want to lose control.

An opportunity seemingly presented itself when Spencer ordered the two captains to sail for Harwich, and embark the King's newly married daughter, Charlotte, and her husband, Frederick, Duke of Württemberg, for passage to Cuxhaven. Although this clearly provocative attempt to exert the Admiralty's authority could have risked loss of life, both Charles and Sir Harry felt compelled to act. Passively remaining at the Nore, awaiting events to unfold, was not an option either man would contemplate. So shortly before midnight on 29 May, after conferring, they both agreed to sail, whatever the risks, and sent word to Spencer. In reply, he sent them a change of orders. They were to sail for Sheerness, to support the defences there.

Making it more imperative to take action, Charles now received information from Thomas Yates, one of *Clyde*'s 'Committee of Internal Regulation', that *Inflexible*'s crew had volunteered to board *Clyde*, overwhelm opposition, and take Charles, his officers and every tenth man of the crew away to be punished for their defiance.[34]

The mood was tense, and Charles's men prepared to defend their ship when, out of the darkness, a boat approached. It was Neale, with news that he had secured a river pilot who was willing to sail the ships out. Both captains now finalised their plan to quit the Nore. They would cut their cables at two bells in the middle watch (1.00am), on the flood tide, a time when lookouts on the mutinous ships would, they hoped, be half-asleep and less alert. As *San Fiorenzo* lay nearest to *Sandwich* and was at the greater risk of being fired on, it was agreed that Neale should initiate the escape and send a boat across to Charles when he was ready to move.

Charles and his men prepared the ship for escape. Yet when two bells sounded across the anchorage, nothing happened. No movement, no signals from *San Fiorenzo* and no word from Neale. Shortly afterwards, yet another boat approached *Clyde*, with a dispiriting message from Neale. His pilot, struck by nerves, was now refusing to attempt the passage at night, claiming it was too dangerous with no lights or buoys to guide him. The plan seemed to have failed before it had even started. For Charles, though, the die was cast. He and his crew were committed, alert and ready for action. Fail to act and inevitably, lives would be lost, and Charles would lose his ship.

He acted decisively. Fortunately, William Bardo, the mate of the Sheerness Dockyard commissioner's yacht, had agreed to pilot *Clyde* into Sheerness.[35] Now Charles decided that Bardo would pilot *San Fiorenzo*, whilst Charles piloted *Clyde* himself.[36] Bardo was rowed across to Neale, whilst Charles ordered his anchor cables cut, and *Clyde*'s sails loosened. Luck was with Charles. *Clyde*'s delegates were meeting onboard *Sandwich* and planning to spend the night on her, leaving no one aboard *Clyde* to raise the alarm. Things could still go awry, though, and Charles wanted as much time as possible before their eventual discovery.

Slowly, the ship began to make her way downstream. Her escape could not go unnoticed indefinitely. Someone was bound to notice *Clyde* moving. As she moved downstream, everyone stood silently at their quarters, casting anxious looks towards the mutinous ships, waiting for the flash and roar of gunfire that would signal discovery.

Inevitably, the alarm was raised but, fortunately, few of the mutinous ships' guns could bear on *Clyde*. Those few guns that could bear were poorly served and no damage was inflicted, whilst the rest of the mutinous ships could only fire warning guns and rockets to raise the alarm and alert the patrolling guard boats. In the resultant confusion, the men manning the guard boats, unsure why there was gunfire and rockets, and possibly thinking it to be some sort of celebration, added to the noise and uncertainty by firing in reply.[37]

Onboard *Clyde*, Charles held his course towards Sheerness, where the

HMS *Clyde* escapes from the Nore Mutiny, 30 May 1797 (1830), by William Joy (1803–1865).
One of a pair of oil paintings commissioned by Charles Cunningham.
(Royal Museums, Greenwich)

garrison, alerted by the disturbance from the anchorage, had manned gun batteries and lit furnaces to heat red-hot shot, whilst anxious citizens crowded any vantage points, scanning the anchorage, fearful of an assault. Instead, dawn revealed *Clyde*, White Ensign proudly at her gaff, the flag of mutiny draped contemptuously over her quarter. Soldiers and civilians cheered her into the anchorage, Admiral Buckner came on board to offer Charles his congratulations and, later that day, hoisted his flag on *Clyde*, the first ship to escape the mutiny.[38]

Neale also managed his escape, although delayed until daylight and coming under fire. Damage to *San Fiorenzo* was also superficial, limited to the rigging, and no shots hit her hull, almost as if the mutineers hesitated to fire at fellow British seamen. There was one moment of danger, when some of Duncan's mutinous ships were spotted sailing into the Nore. But in all of the confusion, Neale had forgotten to strike the red flag, and as *San Fiorenzo* lay to, repairing her rigging, Duncan's mutinous ships sailed by her, cheering her as a fellow mutineer. Once repaired, and unable to make Sheerness, Neale sailed on to Portsmouth.[39]

The escape ended Charles's direct involvement in the Nore Mutiny, although, reinforced by Duncan's squadron, it continued, taking a more radical turn. However, things had peaked.

Government stood firm and denied supplies or medical help to the mutineers. Lacking leadership and organisation, short of food and drink, and with an attempt to blockade London failing, desertions increased, and the mutiny began imploding. Whatever authority Parker ever possessed finally ended when he ordered the fleet to sail for Holland or France. The crews refused, and one by one, ships began rehoisting their colours and surrendering.

Most of the ringleaders were eventually apprehended, although some escaped to France. Eventually, a total of over four hundred men were court-martialled for mutiny, although only twenty-nine men were eventually hanged. Others were transported or suffered flogging, but many were reprieved, so desperate was the navy's need for seamen. There was, of course, no mercy for Richard Parker, who, despite his protestations of being an unwilling, manipulated dupe, was court-martialled, found guilty and hanged from *Sandwich*'s yardarm.

After the Nore Mutiny
What of Charles? Both he and Sir Harry Neale were hailed as the heroes of the hour, lauded by the public and press. Charles's actions, in particular, were credited with weakening the mutineers' resolve, and giving hope to the undecided and unwilling participants.

Charles remained in command of *Clyde* until 1802, serving with the Channel

Fleet and becoming a senior captain of the Inshore Squadron, undertaking a diverse range of duties, including looking into Brest, disrupting coastal traffic, capturing privateers and the 28-gun frigate *Vestale*. He carried the artist Thomas Serres down the French and Spanish coasts, surveying and making detailed sketches of the coast for the Admiralty and ended the war as commodore, commanding a squadron cruising off the Channel Islands.

With the Peace of Amiens in March 1802, Charles paid off *Clyde* and returned to Suffolk. When war resumed in 1803, he was appointed to the Third Rate *Princess of Orange* (64), as a commodore in Admiral Dickson's North Sea Squadron, before his career took an unexpected turn. His former commander and now First Lord, Earl St Vincent, asked him to come ashore and join the Victualling Board. St Vincent intended to rid the Navy Board of corruption by appointing naval officers, sympathetic to the needs of the navy, to replace the existing commissioners when he could.[40]

This was an unsuccessful move, and Charles and his seven fellow commissioners found themselves overworked, overwhelmed by paperwork and the demands of war. Accounts remained unaudited, and contractors paid late, if at all. Crucially, though, the fleet was kept supplied. By 1804, with St Vincent ousted, the members of the Victualling Board were retired or replaced, having, according to one of their replacements, John Clerk, lost all oversight on their accounting and payments.[41]

Charles managed to survive to be appointed Commissioner of Deptford Dockyard, the navy's principal victualling yard, where he continued playing a crucial, if unglamorous, role in Britain's war at sea, that of keeping the King's fleet supplied. He stayed at Deptford until 1823, before moving to Chatham as Resident Commissioner until 1829, when he retired as a rear admiral. Returning to Suffolk, he passed away at his home, Oak Lawn House, in 1834.

HMS *Clyde* arriving at Sheerness after the Nore Mutiny, 30th May, 1797 (1830), see colour plate 5

Rodney and Kempenfelt:
How They Were Related

Hilary L Rubinstein

George Brydges Rodney (*c*1718–92) and Richard Kempenfelt (1715–82) were two of the most capable and cerebral British admirals of George III's reign. Rodney was the luckier of the two, his time at the top lengthy, and his record luminous since, aided by aristocratic sources of patronage that Kempenfelt lacked, he enjoyed quick promotion, had many opportunities to shine, and was well rewarded (Baronet, 1764; Knight of the Bath, 1780; Baron, 1782). Both men can be considered 'Precursors of Nelson', to borrow the title of a book of essays, one of which is devoted to Rodney.[1]

As midshipmen or lieutenants, Trafalgar captains Edward Berry (*Agamemnon*), John Cooke (*Bellerophon*), George Duff (*Mars*), Philip Durham (*Defiance*), William Hargood (*Belleisle*), and Robert Moorsom (*Revenge*) had all served, during 1781/2, in fleet actions under one or the other of these two admirals, and in some cases both. The fact that, through their respective mothers, Rodney and Kempenfelt were second cousins once removed is not generally known, having apparently escaped all previous historians. This essay, after briefly describing their careers for context, explains how they were related.

Backgrounds and naval service of Rodney and Kempenfelt

Rodney – whose father Henry (1681–1737), a well-connected captain in the marines left financially embarrassed by ill-fated investing, was a scion of an old Somerset gentry family – was baptised at London's St Giles in the Fields on 13 February 1718 (the baptismal record spells his middle name 'Bridges'); his precise birth date is elusive. Said to have attended Harrow School, he entered the Royal Navy in 1732, was commissioned in 1741 and posted in 1742. He commanded the Fourth Rate HMS *Eagle* (60) at Admiral Hawke's victory at Quiberon Bay in 1747 and a stellar future unfolded. Promoted rear admiral in 1759, vice admiral in 1762 and full admiral in 1778, he twice, when a flag officer, served as Commander-in-Chief, Leeward Islands.

Kempenfelt was born on 23 November 1715 (not October 1718 as some accounts state) and baptised at St Margaret's, Westminster, on 10 December. His father Magnus (*b*1665), a lieutenant colonel in the Coldstream Guards whose name was often spelled 'Campenfeld' in British military records, had left his native Sweden as a mercenary soldier. On Magnus's death in 1727 when lieutenant governor of Jersey in the Channel Islands, Richard Kempenfelt left Westminster School and entered the navy to help supplement his mother's income. Passing for lieutenant in 1737, he remained uncommissioned owing to a lack of vacancies. In 1739 he was a midshipman in Vice Admiral Vernon's squadron that achieved the Spanish surrender of Porto Bello. Vernon, who had known and admired Kempenfelt's father, was instrumental in the deserving, despairing young man becoming a lieutenant in 1741. But the demise of Vernon's career amid rancour in 1746 deprived Kempenfelt of his patronage. Posted in 1757 owing to constantly demonstrated merit, he served gallantly during the Seven Years War in three fierce engagements against the French off India's Coromandel coast. In the Philippines he participated in the capture of Manila in 1763, and was briefly governor of Cavite.[2]

Admiral Rodney at the Battle of the Saintes, 1783; oil painting by Thomas Gainsborough (1727–1788). Behind is the French fleur-de-lys naval ensign from the captured *Ville de Paris*. (Unidentified location, Wikimedia, public domain).

During the ensuing peace Kempenfelt wintered in France, familiarising himself with coastal fortifications and maritime developments; he also began his intense study of works on naval strategy and tactics by such eminent French thinkers as Mahé de Bourdonnais, Paul Hoste and Bigot de Morogues, knowing that the recommendations of those authors were studied in French naval academies and practised in French fleets. During 1779/80, when factional infighting rent the Royal Navy, and flag officers of the calibre of Howe declined to serve, Kempenfelt proved his worth aboard the First Rate *Victory* (104) as an outstanding 'captain of the fleet' (effectively chief of staff) to three successive Channel Fleet commanders-in-chief, Sir Charles Hardy, Sir Francis Geary and Sir George Darby, two of whom, Hardy and Geary, had left their glory days behind them. His wise counsel, not always heeded by those two, was sorely needed from the start, given the danger posed by a combined Franco-Spanish force aiming to land troops on the Isle of Wight.

He insisted on frequent gunnery practice and on regular fleet manoeuvres. He also trialled the numerary signal code that he was painstakingly developing, designed to free fleet commanders from the fetters of the old *Fighting Instructions* by giving them a fluent and flexible means of communication that would be readily comprehended. In private letters to his friend Captain Charles Middleton, Comptroller of the Navy (destined, when Lord Barham, to be First Lord of the Admiralty during the Trafalgar campaign) he shared his many and varied ideas for improvements in the Royal Navy; he did so not to aggrandise himself but to counter what he saw as deplorable past negligence.[3]

In January 1780 Rodney defeated, on a lee shore in stormy conditions, the Spanish admiral Don Juan de Lángara at the so-called 'moonlight battle' of Cape St Vincent, and proceeded to the relief of Gibraltar and Menorca. That April he won an incomplete victory over France's Comte de Guichen off Martinique, the outcome marred by the behaviour of certain British captains who, owing to an apparent misunderstanding of his signals and intent, failed to engage the enemy more closely. Interpreting this as symptomatic of a widespread indifference to his authority within his fleet's officer corps, he complained bitterly to the Admiralty, naming names, but only two lieutenants and one captain were court-martialled: the latter was the tough old veteran Nathaniel Bateman, who suffered the cruel penalty of dismissal from the service. Captain Walter Young's letter to Middleton from St Kitts that July, regarding Rodney's probable indifference to Kempenfelt's latest signal book just received, suggests that Rodney may have been either too impatient or too disdainful, or perhaps both, to believe Kempenfelt had anything to teach him. Rodney's defeat of Comte de Grasse off Dominica in April 1782, known as the Battle of the Saintes, was a spectacular triumph that raised Britain's morale during the American War of Independence. It famously featured the tactic of breaking the enemy's line, anticipating Trafalgar.[4]

Meanwhile, in September 1780 Kempenfelt had been promoted rear admiral. On 12/13 December 1781, off Ushant, with *Victory* as his flagship, he cunningly and cleverly intercepted and captured many French supply and troop transports bound for the West Indies that were under convoy by Comte de Guichen's fleet. It was a significant blow to France's plans and did Kempenfelt much credit. But to his chagrin, and much of Britain's, he was unable to engage with the enemy fleet itself, owing to the vastly inferior force with which the Admiralty had equipped him. He was still flying his flag in *Victory* when she was claimed by Lord Howe as *his* flagship prior to the Channel Fleet sailing to the relief of Gibraltar in September 1782. Obliged to shift into the First Rate *Royal George*

(100), which when heeled for a routine repair sank suddenly at Spithead on 29 August, he drowned, much mourned, with most of her crew, and was immortalised by poet William Cowper as 'brave Kempenfelt'.[5]

Kempenfelt's ancestry

Kempenfelt's Swedish ancestry was set out over fifty years ago by Åke Lindwall. But what of the admiral's English ancestry? When researching the loss of *Royal George* I discovered that Kempenfelt's great-uncle Nathaniel Hunt (1642–1709), a London lawyer, left £100 and his law books to his former clerk John Cowper. Could this man have been a relative of the poet? I also discovered that Nathaniel left £400 to his niece Anne ('Ann Kempenfeild' [*sic*]) and £200 to Anne's short-lived infant Magnus, his godson. That child, and Admiral Kempenfelt's brothers Jonas and Gustavus Adolphus, owed their names to their Swedish heritage, while brother Marmaduke was named in honour of an army colleague of their father.

In investigating Anne's ancestry I ignored the (very real possibility) that her sailor son was named after her husband's friend Richard Steele, the dramatist who wrote fondly of 'Colonel Campenfeld' in the pages of *The Spectator*, and followed my hypothesis that he was named after her father. And deducing that Kempenfelt's sister Anna was named after their paternal grandmother, Anna Kullberg, I surmised that their other sister, Mary, was named after Anne's mother. So, beginning my quest by looking at online probate registers for a credible Richard Hunt who was probably married to a Mary, I discovered that my quarry had indeed been named that. And so had his father.[6]

Born in 1595, the latter was a prosperous City of London mercer (a dealer in fine cloth) whose own father, George Hunt, Anne's great-grandfather, had been born in Shrewsbury, Shropshire. George was a London woollens merchant who in 1589 at the Church of St Benet Fink, in Threadneedle Street, married Derby-born Mary Sleigh, whose family was also in the wool trade. Edmund Sleigh MP was probably related to her. George and Mary Hunt's oldest surviving son, George, lived his adult life back in Shrewsbury, where during the mid-seventeenth century his descendants filled prominent roles. One of them, Queen's College, Cambridge graduate Thomas Hunt (1599–1669), a colonel in the Parliamentary army, was a Member of Parliament for Shrewsbury, 1645–53, and from 1657/8 mayor. After the Restoration he purchased Boreatton Hall, not far away, thereby founding the Shropshire gentry line known as the Hunts of Boreatton, whose members have included Vice Admiral Sir Nicholas Hunt (1930–2013).[7]

Like his cousin Thomas Hunt MP, Richard Hunt the mercer was a Puritan with Parliamentarian sympathies, who in the 1640s subscribed £100 to 'Ye Sea

Forces' necessary to establishing a Protestant plantation in Ireland. Often styled 'gentleman' following his acquisition of bishops' lands in Essex (which unfortunately for his progeny were forfeited after the Restoration), he had married, in 1625 in the hamlet of Ickenham (nowadays part of the London borough of Uxbridge), Mary Gascoigne. Her father William was said to be from Cleveland in north Yorkshire: if so, he was presumably from the well-known gentry family of that name.[8] Indeed, he was probably the William Gascoigne (c1568–1645) who 'matriculated' (that is, formally enrolled) at Exeter College, Oxford, in or about 1581, son and heir of Richard Gascoigne of Sedbury in the north Yorkshire district referred to in old records as 'Richmondshire'. From Oxford, this William proceeded to Middle Temple, qualifying as a lawyer. Knighted in 1599, he seems to have been a collateral descendant of the famous medieval Chief Justice of England Sir William Gascoigne.[9]

The mercer was ambitious for his sons (three of whom became lawyers) and sent Richard to Eton. From there, in 1645 Richard entered King's College, Cambridge (BA 1649, MA 1653.) Admitted in 1650 to Gray's Inn, the widely erudite young man was elected in 1654 professor of rhetoric at Gresham College, the proto-university established in 1590 by the Mercers' Company in conjunction with the City of London as the result of a bequest by Thomas Gresham, founder of the Royal Exchange. In accordance with the college's stipulation that only unmarried men could hold the professorship, Richard resigned it in 1659 upon his marriage to Mary (b1639; dead by 1692), daughter of William Hampton, rector of Bletchingley, Surrey. They lived in Romford, Essex before moving to Austin Friars where, during the Great Fire of London in 1666, Hunt's 'very choice and valuable' library was destroyed.

For some years thereafter, the Hunts resided at Bletchingley. In 1676 they moved to Reigate, Surrey, where Anne (1679–1766), Kempenfelt's mother, was born. Her sister Mary (b1663) married, in London in 1692, John Grainger, and in 1697 her sister Judith (1668–1742), married John Troughton, from 1708–28 librarian of the Middle Temple. Hunt was once described as 'Richard Hunt LLD of the Admiralty Division', implying that he sat on the Court of Admiralty, which adjudicated cases relating to prizes; however, his name is not included in a supposedly definitive list of such judges.[10] Hunt's final home was Hutton Hall in Essex. He was interred in the chancel of All Saints' Church at Hutton, the burial register describing him as 'one of the mirrors of learning of the age'. A noted Hebraist, he had studied under a learned Jew in Holland, and afterwards was often in the company of a rabbi (probably the Sephardic scholar and spiritual leader Isaac Abendana, who certainly knew him). Kempenfelt inherited Hunt's deeply entrenched instincts as a polymath. Compare these passages. Hunt's wife's nephew, a Sussex clergyman, on her husband: 'He was the best natured person I ever knew, and the freest to communicate his knowledge to others, so that very few had his company, but went away the better for him.' A lifelong friend of Kempenfelt: 'Admiral Kempenfelt was in all things original; I never left his company without hearing things I had never heard before.'[11]

Rodney's ancestry

And so to Rodney. His great-grandmother Mary Hunt married, in 1644, mercer Henry Newton; her lawyer brother Nathaniel (mentioned above) left her £400, as he did to Anne Kempenfelt and other nieces. Mary's son, (Sir) Henry Newton, baptised at Romford in 1650, attended St Mary Hall (an Oxford college incorporated into Oriel College in 1902), where he gained his Bachelor of Arts and Civil Law degrees. In 1678 he graduated from Oxford's Merton College with a doctorate in civil law. He became an eminent jurist and diplomat who served towards the end of his life as a judge of the Admiralty Court. Knighted in 1715, he died that same year and was buried in the chapel of the Mercers' Company. In 1687, at London's St Sepulchre's Church, Sir Henry married, as his second wife, Mary, daughter of Thomas Manning of St Dunstan in the West parish: the elder of their two daughters, Mary (b1689) married Henry Rodney and became Admiral Rodney's mother. Her sister Catherine, who died in 1655, married naval captain Lord Aubrey Beauclerk (killed in action in 1641), son of the first Duke of St Albans.[12]

Comparing Kempenfelt and Rodney

Apart from their obvious high intelligence and their aptitude and zeal for their profession, Rodney and Kempenfelt had little in common. Married (twice, first to a sister of the 8th Earl of Northampton) with children, Rodney was voluble, vain, foppish, extravagant and avaricious. He could also be arrogant, quarrelsome, ruthless and inclement. A bachelor, Kempenfelt was reserved and overly modest like his father; he wasted few words except among his intimates. Compassionate and fair-minded, he was rather endearingly eccentric, absentmindedly taking snuff repeatedly while in silent meditation on matters nautical and spilling most of it over himself. Drawn to Wesleyism, he composed impressive sacred verse. Rodney was an ardent Tory, Kempenfelt probably a Whig. Did they know they were related? It seems improbable that they did not.

Rodney certainly appears to have been conscious of the ancestral Hunt and Gascoigne connections. These ran deep: Richard Hunt, the mercer's cousin Rowland Hunt, of Shrewsbury, married Susan, daughter of a John Gascoigne of Manchester (as the mercer himself mentioned in a brief genealogy he prepared for Charles I's official heralds in 1634 when asserting his right to a coat of arms). And in 1661 at St Peter, Paul's Wharf, London, a George Hunt,

Kempenfelt - Rodney Family Tree

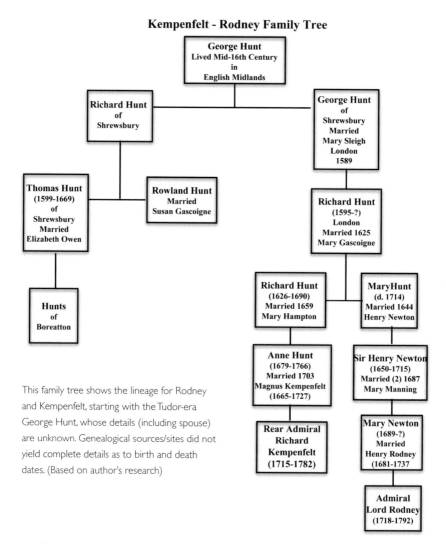

George Hunt
Lived Mid-16th Century
in
English Midlands

Richard Hunt
of
Shrewsbury

George Hunt
of
Shrewsbury
Married
Mary Sleigh
London
1589

Thomas Hunt
(1599-1669)
of
Shrewsbury
Married
Elizabeth Owen

Rowland Hunt
Married
Susan Gascoigne

Richard Hunt
(1595-?)
London
Married 1625
Mary Gascoigne

Hunts
of
Boreatton

Richard Hunt
(1626-1690)
Married 1659
Mary Hampton

MaryHunt
(d. 1714)
Married 1644
Henry Newton

Anne Hunt
(1679-1766)
Married 1703
Magnus Kempenfelt
(1665-1727)

Sir Henry Newton
(1650-1715)
Married (2) 1687
Mary Manning

This family tree shows the lineage for Rodney and Kempenfelt, starting with the Tudor-era George Hunt, whose details (including spouse) are unknown. Genealogical sources/sites did not yield complete details as to birth and death dates. (Based on author's research)

**Rear Admiral
Richard
Kempenfelt**
(1715-1782)

Mary Newton
(1689-?)
Married
Henry Rodney
(1681-1737)

**Admiral
Lord Rodney**
(1718-1792)

aged twenty-nine, of St Benet Fink parish – probably the mercer's fourth son of that name – married a Margaret Gascoigne of Romford, Essex.[13]

It was probably no accident that captains named Joseph Hunt and Edward Gascoigne enjoyed Rodney's favour. In 1757 Rodney became captain of the brand new Third Rate *Dublin* (74), which in 1758 served on the North American Station. The following year, when preparing to command a small squadron on blockade duty off France, he wrote to the Admiralty from Portsmouth requesting permission to take Hunt, 'late of the *Dublin*' and 'now at this port', with him 'as a volunteer lieutenant when I sail, as he is a person I can depend upon, when sent on any material service.' The instantaneous reply advised that Hunt (a lieutenant since 1756) 'is appointed commander of the *Mortar* bomb vessel at Deptford' and that Rodney should 'hasten him' to the Admiralty to collect his commission.

On 6 January 1761 as acting captain of the Sixth Rate *Unicorn* (28) (whose usual captain was ill), Hunt was wounded in the thigh during a two-hour contest off the Breton coast with the French Sixth Rate *Vestale* (30), taken into the Royal Navy as the Sixth Rate HMS *Flora* (32). Stoically enduring the amputation of his leg, and chiding the surgeon for paying more attention to him than to injured 'common sailors', he survived for about an hour after the French ship surrendered, having urged his first lieutenant never to strike. His last will and testament, made on 18 January 1760, referred to 'Christ my blessed redeemer', which hints that he was probably more than ordinarily religious. He left all he had to his mother Margaret. The will was witnessed by an Elizabeth Mason and a William Newton, both bearing surnames linked to the Hunts and Rodneys.

Also from Portsmouth in 1759 Rodney wrote to the Admiralty requesting that Gascoigne (a lieutenant of 1742 made commander in 1755) be allowed to volunteer to go to sea with him on a voluntary basis. The request was successful. Posted in February 1760, Gascoigne became captain of *Dublin*; he died in December 1764.[14] It would be interesting to know more about his ties to Rodney, and thus to Kempenfelt. And, needless to say, it would be instructive to know how those admirals viewed one another. Unless and until sources surface providing evidence to the contrary, it seems reasonable to conclude that the two were not close.

Rear Admiral Kempenfelt, see colour plate 6

A Dead Captain and a Sunken Ship: The Fates of Sir Jacob Wheate and HMS *Cerberus* in Bermuda

Judith E Pearson

In 2008 archaeologists from the Bermuda National Trust, St George's Archaeological Research Project and Boston University spent six weeks excavating the foundations of the historic St Peter's Church in the UNESCO World Heritage Site and Historic Preservation Area in St George's parish, Bermuda. The church is the oldest continually used Anglican church in the western hemisphere. It was commissioned in 1612 and most of the present structure dates to 1713.[1] Since it was first constructed, the church has seen numerous expansions and renovations.[2]

St Peter's Church, in St George's, Bermuda. (Author's photo)

Reverend David Raths and his church council had invited the archaeological team, led by Dr Brent Fortenberry, to explore the archaeological and architectural history of the church. The purpose of the study was to gather information about the structure and architectural details of the original foundation and to make a record of the memorials in the surrounding churchyard. Digging under the floorboards near the altar, the researchers were astonished to find human remains!

The researchers found the skeletal remains of two individuals, along with bits of wood and coffin nails, indicating that these two bodies had been encased in coffins that had long since rotted away.[3] No records of any interments under the floorboards existed. However, two metal coffin plates identified the remains.

One coffin plate identified Governor George James Bruere Sr, Bermuda's longest serving governor, appointed by the Crown, who served from 1764 until his death from yellow fever in 1780. The coffin plate reads: 'His Excellency, George James Bruere, Governor of Bermuda and Lieu Colo in his Majesty's Service OB The 10 Sept 1780, AE 59 Years.'[4] Bruere was a controversial figure in his day because his tenure took place during the American War of Independence, when political and economic tensions on the island ran high and Bermuda was caught up in the crossfire between two warring nations.[5] Perhaps for this reason, Bruere's body was interred in secret (to avoid desecration of his grave), under St Peter's Church. Perhaps the hiding place was temporary until his remains could be shipped back to England.[6] Perhaps he had received a proper burial and his coffin had been placed, temporarily – and forgotten, underneath the church floor when a new extension was added to the church in 1815.[7] Nevertheless, in June 2009 he was given a proper burial and 're-entombed' in St Peter's Church churchyard.[8]

The other coffin plate identified Captain Sir Jacob Wheate, Royal Navy. He died in 1783 in St George's of yellow fever. The coffin plate reads: 'Sir Jacob Wheate BART, Commander of his Majesty's Ship *Cerberus* OBT The 12 February 1783'.[9] These remains were 'truncated by a 1950s retaining wall'.[10] Nine days after Wheate's death, *Cerberus*, the ship he commanded, sank off the coast of Bermuda.[11]

Coffin plate of Captain Sir Jacob Wheate.
(Courtesy of Bermuda National Museum)

Jacob Wheate died at the age of thirty-eight. Perhaps because he died relatively young or because he had not seen major combat, the full story of his naval service (what is known from available information), and the fate of his ship has not been told, especially to a wider audience beyond Bermuda. This article will piece together existing details about his life in the Royal Navy and the place of *Cerberus* in naval history. Readers will learn how it was that Wheate's last days placed him in Bermuda near the end of the American War of Independence and how it was that *Cerberus* was one of many vessels that met their end on the treacherous reefs surrounding the tiny island of Bermuda.

Captain Sir Jacob Wheate RN

Jacob Wheate was born on 20 September 1745, the second son of Sir George Wheate, 3rd Baronet, of Glympton, Oxfordshire, and his wife Avice Acworth, the daughter of Sir Jacob Acworth, Surveyor of the Navy from 1715 to 1749. The family initially lived in Holborn, London, and thereafter settled in Lechlade, Gloucestershire. On 26 January 1760 at the age of fourteen or fifteen, Jacob Wheate inherited the family baronetcy upon the death of his older brother, George. Having earlier joined the Royal Navy, Jacob was commissioned a lieutenant on 20 June 1765.[12]

Wheate family blazon. The colours are green and yellow. (Wikipedia)

In August 1779 Wheate was first lieutenant of the Third Rate *Marlborough* (74), under the command of Captain Taylor Penny during a near-battle that became known as the Channel Fleet Retreat.[13] On 12 April of that year, France and Spain had entered into an alliance to bring Britain to her knees and take her overseas colonies. The plan was to gain control of the English Channel to facilitate a crossing by a combined army of over thirty thousand soldiers and some four hundred transports. Britain was at a considerable disadvantage. Her at-home army was only 52,600 personnel, over half of whom were militia. With twenty ships of the line serving in the Leeward Islands, Britain had barely thirty ships of the line in home waters. The majority of these ships were short-handed and poorly manned.

The Admiralty had recalled the 64-year-old Admiral Charles Hardy from the governorship of Greenwich Hospital to defend Britain's shores. As Commander-in-Chief of the Channel Fleet, Hardy hoisted his flag aboard the First Rate *Victory* (100) under Captain Henry Colins. Captain Richard Kempenfelt was his captain of the fleet. Hardy's initial instructions were to blockade Brest before the French fleet, led by Comte d'Orvilliers, could put to sea. However, Hardy met with repeated delays, because he lacked crews to man his ships and due to poor weather conditions. He also had to dispatch several of his ships of the line, under the command of Vice Admiral Darby, to escort the North American-bound convoy beyond the southern coast of Ireland. By 10 June, when Darby returned, the French had been out of Brest for six days and were sailing for the coast of Spain for a rendezvous with the Spanish.

On 16 June Hardy set sail from Spithead with twenty-eight ships of the line and several frigates. On that same day, Spain formally declared war on Britain. Commanded by Don Luis de Cordova, the Spanish fleet soon sailed from Cadiz and joined the French on 2 July. Within a few days, Hardy received intelligence that the combined fleet had been seen off Cape Finisterre, Ushant and Ferrol. The combined fleet's plan was to take control of the Channel to facilitate the capture of the Isle of Wight as a base from which to assault and destroy the principal British naval base at Portsmouth.

On 5 July westerly winds forced Hardy's fleet to seek refuge at Torbay. By 9 July, an invasion was imminent. Britain's coastal towns prepared their defences. Civilians made ready to evacuate. Hardy again received orders to put to sea on 14 July. After battling contrary winds for eleven days, Hardy returned to Torbay to await additional orders. During the delay, he welcomed the arrival of convoys from the Leeward Islands and Jamaica, adding eight more ships to his force. Increasingly, however, his crews suffered from sickness and inadequate provisions.

By 12 August, the British fleet took a position off the Scilly Isles. By 14 August, the French and Spanish were closing in on Britain's coast. On 15 August HM Ships *Marlborough*, *Ramillies* (74), *Isis* (50), and the sloop *Cormorant* (14) fell in with the combined fleet some forty miles southeast of the Scilly Isles. The British ships barely escaped. Sir Jacob Wheate was dispatched to Plymouth aboard *Cormorant* with news of the attack and the position of the combined fleet. Reaching port on 16 August he then travelled over land to inform the Admiralty, Lord Sandwich. This author could not find any information about whether Wheate returned to *Marlborough*.

As events progressed, the combined fleet appeared off Plymouth. Plymouth activated its militia, armed the dockyards, and ordered the garrison to action stations. The allies enjoyed their first success with the capture of the Third Rate HMS *Ardent* (64). Her commander, Captain Philip Boteler, was later dismissed from service for surrendering too readily; even though his ship had been commissioned only one week, the ship's company included four hundred pressed men, and many seamen had displayed mutinous intentions due to want of clothing.

Positioned off Plymouth, d'Orvilliers received sudden and unexpected orders to land the army at Falmouth instead. He delayed action, questioning the order. While he awaited a reply, a gale blew his fleet out of the Channel and out to sea. The French commander, however, was determined to take the battle to the British. Receiving intelligence that the combined fleet was headed his way, Hardy decided to sail up the Channel, rather than meet the enemy head on. His strategy was to keep his force intact, avoid engagement, replenish his ships, and fight the enemy in home waters.

In the meantime, conflicts arose between the French and Spanish. With the prospect of the approaching autumn and its foul weather, sickness among the French seamen, and diminishing provisions, the allies withdrew on 3 September and headed for home. By 7 September, news of the French retreat had reached the Admiralty. Opinion varied as to Hardy's actions: to some he had shown wisdom; to others he had shown cowardice.[14] In any case, the battle was averted.

On 15 November 1779 Wheate received promotion to commander and became commanding officer of HM Sloop *Ostrich* (14). He was employed in the Downs and the Thames Estuary prior to taking a convoy out to New York in 1781 and returning home in May 1782. He was posted captain on 2 April 1782. He briefly took command of the Fourth Rate *Portland* (50) and was then transferred to the Fifth Rate frigate *Cerberus* (32).[15] He joined Captain Samuel Reeve's flying squadron of four sail of the line and three frigates in the Western Approaches and the Bay of Biscay. On 25 October 1782 he seized the Spanish privateer *San Christobel*, and by the end of the year was employed in North American waters, as the American War of Independence was grinding to a close.

In November 1782 the British and Americans signed preliminary articles of peace. In December 1782 Wheate married the American-born Maria Shaw in New York. She was regarded as one of the belles of New York, albeit she was not yet sixteen. Future US president John Quincy Adams spoke derisively about the marriage, due to the age difference between the newly-weds. Adams portrayed Wheate as much older than he actually was. The marriage became the subject of much gossip, and someone composed a poem that criticised Shaw's rush to marry a wealthy older man.[16]

Lieutenant Commander H G Middleton, former Colonial Archivist for Bermuda, published an article in 1967 in the *Bermuda Historical Quarterly* on the loss of HMS *Cerberus*.[17] He speculated that Wheate and his ship were almost certainly stationed out of New York in late 1782. In early 1783, on 21 January, while cruising off Bermuda, *Cerberus* captured *Flaam Amiericking* of Ostend, then a part of Austria–Netherlands. The crew was, presumably, sailing in alliance with the French. A prize crew took *Flaam Amiericking* to New York. It is likely that shortly afterward, *Cerberus* put into Bermuda for replenishment.

On 12 February 1783 Wheate died of yellow fever, in St George's parish, where he was buried on 14 February 1783.[18] In his will, Wheate gave his address as Lechlade, Gloucestershire. Upon his death, the family baronetcy passed to his younger brother, the Reverend Sir John Thomas Wheate.[19]

Just nine days after Wheate's death, his ship *Cerberus* was wrecked upon striking rocks while leaving Castle Harbour, the main entry to St George. The ship was under the command of Lieutenant Thomas Parkinson: more about *Cerberus*'s sinking below.

On 26 April 1788 Wheate's widow married the future Admiral Hon Sir Alexander Forrester Inglis Cochrane, by whom she had three sons and two daughters. Cochrane's naval service carried him into the Napoleonic Wars and the War of 1812. He was knighted into the Order of the Bath in 1806. In 1814 he became vice admiral and Commander-in-Chief of the North American Station, led the naval forces during the attacks on Washington and New Orleans, was promoted to admiral in 1819 and became Commander-in-Chief of the Plymouth naval base.[20]

HMS *Cerberus*

Cerberus is the Greek name of the three-headed, serpent-tailed dog that guards the gates of Hades. *Cerberus* was an *Active*-class, Fifth Rate frigate built by Randall at Rotherhithe Thames shipyard and launched 15 July 1779.[21] She was the second frigate to carry the name, after the first was destroyed at Newport, Rhode Island, the previous year to prevent capture by the French who were supporting the Continentals in the American War of Independence.

In her brief four years of service, *Cerberus* had only one engagement. In 1781, under the command of Captain Robert Man, while cruising off Finisterre, she captured the Spanish Sixth Rate frigate, *Grana* (30), which was purchased into the Royal Navy. Captain Sir Jacob Wheate succeeded Captain Man in 1782.

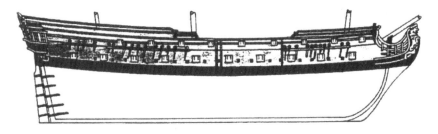

Hull of a Fifth Rate frigate of the eighteenth century. Source: Wayne Walker, p31; E H H Archibald, *The Wooden Fighting Ship in the Royal Navy* (1968), p51. (Courtesy of Bermuda National Museum)

When Wheate died, command of *Cerberus* fell to Lieutenant Thomas Parkinson, who prepared the ship to leave Castle Harbour on 21 February, after four days of waiting for a favourable wind. At 9am, the pilot came on board and ordered the ship to be unmoored. At 10.30am the ship was underway. Sometime after 11am the ship struck on the rocks in the narrow channel leading out of the harbour. Parkinson did everything he could to lighten the load and save the ship. His crew cut off the masts and jettisoned the cannons and carronades and wooden boxes of musket shot. When all hope was lost, Parkinson ordered the crew to abandon the ship as she filled with water. Troops on Castle Island saw the event and immediately dispatched small boats to rescue those in peril. As a result, not a single man was lost.[22]

In the subsequent days, the crew returned to the sinking ship to salvage cannons, carronades, gun carriages and 'sundry articles'. Much of the foregoing information was recorded in a court martial aboard the Third Rate *Dictator* (64) at the Nore on 18 October 1783 and based on testimony by the ship's gunner, Hewman Shrewsbury.[23] The court was unanimous in their opinion that the crew and the officers were not culpable for the loss of the ship and were to be

The Bermudas, or Summer's Islands, by C Lemprière, 1788, showing Castle Harbour on the eastern side of Bermuda, in the upper right of the chart. (Courtesy of Bermuda National Museum)

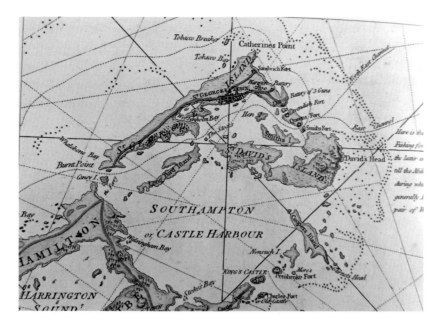

The Bermudas, or Summer's Islands, by C Lemprière, 1788, showing Castle Harbour on the eastern side of Bermuda, in the upper right of the chart. (Courtesy of Bermuda National Museum)

acquitted. Sad to say, the officers of *Cerberus* were not present to hear the verdict.

After the sinking of *Cerberus*, the ship's company was returned to England aboard the Sixth Rate frigates *Vestal* (28) and *Astraea* (32).[24] The officers were ordered back to New York aboard HM Sloop *Mentor* (18), formerly a Massachusetts privateer, *Aurora*, captured in 1781 by the Third Rate HMS *Royal Oak* (74).[25] *Mentor* left Bermuda on 16 March. She never made it to New York. *Mentor* went down in a violent gale, with the loss of all aboard (over three hundred men).[26]

One of those lost aboard *Mentor* was Lieutenant Slack of the Royal Engineers, who was responsible for the Royal Defence Works of Bermuda. His successor, Lieutenant Andrew Durnford, headed an effort to recover the remaining artillery of *Cerberus* to add to defence works around Bermuda.[27] The effort was part of his project to fortify the island, identify safe harbours and passages for large ships, and to establish locations for garrisons.[28]

Commercial salvage crews also plundered the wreck for profit, which was a common practice. In April 1783 Governor William Brown (Bruere's successor), fortified by an Act of Parliament, empowered magistrates to award compensation (one-fourth to one-half the value) to those 'who had saved sundry stores from the wreck'.[29]

As a result of *Cerberus*'s loss, the Admiralty issued orders forbidding Royal Navy vessels from using Castle Harbour, despite its advantages as a well-sheltered, deep-water anchorage.[30] The loss of Castle Harbour was a blow to the Royal Navy, because, with the signing of the Treaty of Paris, Britain lost all naval bases on the North American coast, except Halifax, Nova Scotia. In Bermuda, naval vessels shifted operations to Murray's Anchorage west of St George's Island. In 1788, Richard, later Viscount, Howe of the Admiralty ordered a survey to chart Bermuda's reef system and locate safe access to anchorages. He chose Lieutenant Thomas Hurd for the enormous task.[31]

Hurd spent nine years (1789–97) surveying Bermuda's treacherous reefs.[32] As a result of his work, he located and charted a navigable channel, The Narrows, which allowed for passage from the east end of Bermuda to the west. Ultimately, the Royal Navy base at Bermuda would be built on Ireland Island in the 1800s.[33] Hurd rose to the rank of captain and became the second Hydrographer of the Royal Navy.

Aftermath

Bermuda has 230 square miles of offshore reefs, ten times the physical land area. To divers, Bermuda is the 'Shipwreck Island' of the Western Atlantic. More than three hundred ships have wrecked and/or sunk around the island since the sixteenth century, with thirteen official major shipwrecks since 1940 alone. Remnants of Spanish naos, English galleons, French frigates, American schooners, brigantines, paddle steamers, steamships, and gunboats litter Bermuda's ocean floor.[34] Among them, *Cerberus* now lies in 30ft of water off Castle Island. Divers have designated her as the 'Musket Ball Wreck' because of the lead musket shot scattered over the wreck site. Since the 1950s, divers have investigated and mapped the site, bringing up artefacts such as lead shot, cannonballs, and a pewter plate. They have identified cast iron ballast pigs and fragments of copper sheathing on the ocean floor.[35]

Since *Cerberus*'s sinking, additional ships have carried the name. A third *Cerberus* was a 32-gun Fifth Rate frigate launched in 1794 and sold in 1814 after service in the Great Anglo-French Wars (1793–1815). The fourth *Cerberus* was a 10-gun gun-brig that HMS *Viper* captured at Mauritius from the French in 1800. She was wrecked in 1804. The fifth HMS *Cerberus* was a 46-gun Fifth Rate frigate launched in 1827 and broken up by 1866. HNLMS *Cerberus*, the first ironclad built in the Netherlands, served in the Royal Netherlands Navy in 1860s.[36]

Her Majesty's Victorian Ship HMVS *Cerberus* was built in 1867 and sent to Australia in 1871 to strengthen the colony's defences and to guard Port Philip

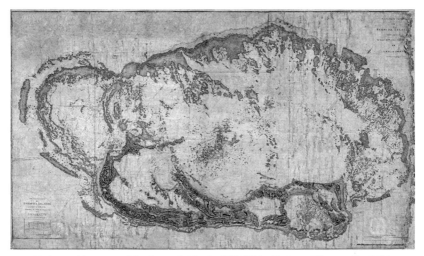

Hydrographic survey of the Bermuda Islands, 1789–97, by Lieutenant Thomas Hurd, RN.
The chart shows the dangerous reefs and shoals surrounding Bermuda.
(Courtesy of Bermuda National Museum)

Bay. HMVS *Cerberus* was among the first of England's steam-driven, ironclad ships with their armature in turrets. In 1911, with the Australian Federation, she became HMAS *Cerberus*. She was renamed *Platypus II* in 1921 and sold as scrap in 1924.[37]

As for Captain Sir Jacob Wheate, his name might have been left in the dust of history, were it not for the discovery of his remains, along with those of Governor Bruere, under the floorboards of St Peter's Church in 2008. It was only due to a coffin plate that researchers could identify the remains. Why Wheate's remains were placed under the church remains a mystery. Prior to 2008, existing records indicated he was buried in the Governor's Garden at St George's 'where a headstone once marked the spot.'[38]

In 2008, after discovery, Wheate's remains were returned to their place under the floorboards of St Peter's. In 2011 the Bermuda National Trust in conjunction with St Peter's Church and Dr Brent Fortenberry of Boston University[39] (the archaeologist who headed the 2008 excavation) accessed Wheate's remains a second time with yet another exploration under the church. The archaeological team found additional, unidentified human remains. Dr Fortenberry arranged for bioarchaeologist, Ms Ellen Chapman, then a doctoral student from the College of William and Mary, to examine Wheate's remains. After three days of studying them, she determined that Sir Jacob was around 5ft 3in in height, and had dental cavities and slight arthritis.[40]

Following the examination, Wheate's remains were again placed under St Peter's Church in the hope that a proper churchyard burial would be arranged at a later date.[41] In 2012, a local resident, retired Royal Navy captain, Alan Brooks, inquired as to the status of the proposed burial. Referring to Wheate's remains, Reverend David Raths replied via email:

> Brent Fortenberry has sent a report … on the human remains recovered from under the floor of St Peter's Church in the area under the coffin plate of Sir Jacob Wheate. Our expectation, that, as was the case the Governor Bruere, we would find at least a significant portion of Sir Jacob's remains proved to be too optimistic. In fact, very little of what can possibly be his remains has been recovered. Brent's suggestion is that we quietly return all these remains, now identified as belonging to three different individuals, to their final resting place under the floor. Until such time as more of Sir Jacob's remains might be recovered, it would not be appropriate, or even truthful, to re-inter him and we will have to leave him, and the unknown others, where they were found.[42]

Captain Sir Jacob Wheate's coffin plate is now on display in a glass case in the rectory of St Peter's Church, St George's, Bermuda.

The author thanks Dr Deborah Atwood and Ms Chynna Trott, curators of the Bermuda National Museum for their assistance in obtaining illustrations and background material. Many thanks to Ms Gillian Outerbridge, Parish Administrator of St Peter's Church, for her assistance in finding Reverend Rath's 2012 email and in reaching him where he is retired in Canada.

Duke of Clarence Swords

Mark Barton

Many readers will be aware of presentation swords being used as rewards for naval and military officers in the Napoleonic era, with those awarded by the Patriotic Fund at Lloyd's[1] being well documented. Another set is not well known and no full list has ever been published for it. That set consists of those awarded by Prince William, the third son of George III, who became the Duke of Clarence and later William IV. These cast interesting insights into how rewards were used to influence officers in the Royal Navy during the Georgian era.

The sons of George III followed what is now perceived to be a traditional noble employment pattern with George, the heir, as Prince of Wales; Frederick, the Duke of York, closely involved with the army; and the third son William, Duke of Clarence, serving with the Royal Navy. It was unexpected at that time that the Prince of Wales, the firstborn child and his brother, Frederick, would both predecease Clarence and that the third son would become king.

Whether inspired by his elder brother's interest, or whether he realised from his service how much they were appreciated, the Duke of Clarence was at the forefront of giving presentation swords, initially ones with a coffin pommel. However, following the introduction of a naval pattern sword in 1805, the Duke of Clarence appears to have soon used the official pattern, initially the 1805 and then the 1827; forty-three such swords have been identified, with three whose recipients are unknown.[2]

No full list or criteria for the awards has been identified. This article endeavours to address that deficit. However, without direct documentary evidence it is only possible to work backwards from objects, paintings and comments made by others on individual swords to bring the account together. The swords are found in museums, private collections (usually seen as auctioned) and family ownership. One came to light through a portrait of Vice Admiral Andrew Pellet Green as an illustration shown in this journal.[3] Therefore the table of known swords at the end of this article is almost certainly not complete but is the first ever published.

When identifying a sword from a painting the researcher must look for the distinctive cartouche on the grip. Fighting swords tend to be held so they add to the martial image, whereas presentation swords are displayed to show them

British School, Rear Admiral Lord Adolphus FitzClarence GCH ADC RN (1802–1856), as a young naval officer, circa 1823 and 1824. Oil painting on canvas by anonymous artist. This portrait shows an 1805 pattern Duke of Clarence sword. (Licensed for *Trafalgar Chronicle* from National Trust collections library, #1000263/ CMS_PCF_1449352)

Admiral Sir Thomas Masterman Hardy, oil painting by Richard Evans (1784–1871). This portrait shows the 1827 pattern Duke of Clarence sword. (© National Maritime Museum, Greenwich, London) off, as can be seen in the illustrations of FitzClarence and Hardy (shown here), where the cartouches are made clearly visible. A few of these swords indicate the recipient's achievement and some have the recipient's coat of arms. Such swords seem to have been generally given to naval officers when both friendship and heroic deeds led to the presentation.

George III's family interest in swords and armour
During his reign, George III and his sons started appearing in uniform in public and in portraits with swords. The wearing of uniforms with swords by the males of the royal household became a common practice after the outbreak of the Anglo-French wars (1793–1815).[4] Whether the wars led to the prevalence of wearing swords as a symbol of martial vigour, or whether this was triggered by other factors can only be conjecture, but it appears that all George III's sons were interested in swords.[5]

In the early 1800s the Prince of Wales started ordering expensive and elegant small swords to give to members of his household. It is estimated he bought sixty made by John Prosser.[6] Prosser was not the only supplier; at least one sword was made by Osborn and Gunby[7] and one by Thomas Price given to one of the Prince's brothers.[8] It is known the Prince bought pieces from Brunn for the dedicated armour display room he built at his residence, Carlton House.[9] He also presented swords to the Earl of Yarmouth in 1811,[10] Major Wright of the York Hussars, and Captain Aylmer in 1815.[11] Additionally, the Prince of Wales received two elaborate Indian swords originally captured by Lord Cornwallis. They were acquired by Sir John Craddock and presented to the Prince in 1811.[12]

The King owned the Creese (now spelt kris) of the Rajah of Assam, which had been brought back by Cornwallis. It was subsequently acquired by Lord Wellesley, who presented it to the King in 1804.

There is another sword (this one from Thomas Price) from the Prince Regent to his brother, the Duke of Cambridge, in 1816 for his wedding.[13] The Duke of Sussex gave at least one sword to Captain Thomas Pickstock, commander of the Sixth Rate HMS *Herald* (20), for action against French forces in the Bay of Naples. How much this presentation was influenced by Sussex being in the vicinity of the action is not known.[14] His interest in his regiment's swords seems similar to that of the Prince of Wales, who was involved with Loyal Northern Britons, a militia regiment that had very distinctive broadswords. Prince William Frederick, the King's nephew and son-in-law, had a sword in the style of the new City of London swords made in 1801[15] and Prince Frederick, the Duke of York, commissioned his own elaborate sword.[16]

Prince William's naval service

Prince William joined the Royal Navy at the age of thirteen, in 1778, and as a midshipman was present at the Battle of Cape St Vincent (1780). His early career seems to have been fairly typical, although a tutor went with him, and once he became a lieutenant, his promotion was extremely rapid. He is reported to have made good friends with other officers; in particular, Richard Keats (later Admiral Sir Richard Keats), who was lieutenant onboard the Second Rate *Prince George* (90) where the prince served as a midshipman, and with Nelson, under whom he served when in command of the Sixth Rate *Pegasus* (28) as a lieutenant in 1786.

Indeed, Prince William gave the bride, Frances Nesbit, away at Nelson's wedding and remained a close friend after Nelson was living with Emma Hamilton. By then, the prince was also living with his long-term mistress, Mrs Dora Jordan.[17] The prince took command of the Fifth Rate *Andromeda* (32) in 1788 and then command of the Third Rate *Valiant* (74) the following year, when he was also made Duke of Clarence. In 1790 William ceased his active naval service and became Rear Admiral of the Blue[18] but returned to serve as Lord High Admiral from 1827 to 1828.

Prince William's first swords

Pre-1805 there was no naval pattern sword; the choice was the officer's. The Duke of Clarence's own sword, held by the National Army Museum, is not of a typical naval style, although if the one shown in the painting of him by Francesco Bartolozzi and Paul Sandby is correct, then he had a more common naval style earlier in his career.[19]

What led the duke to present swords is unknown. Thomas Pocock, his biographer, noted that from an early stage the duke was willing to support new ideas,[20] and while Lord High Admiral in 1827 he was particularly interested in modifying naval uniforms.[21] It has been argued[22] that he collected swords, but no evidence has been found to support this. Similarly, he was reputed to have taken a personal interest in the adoption of the new pattern naval sword in 1827,[23] but documentary evidence has not yet been identified. It is known that he took a personal interest in the adoption of a new naval cutlass[24] when Harry Angelo, the naval instructor in cutlass, suggested improvements. The four patterns made for testing were sent to both the duke and the Board of Ordnance, who differed in their preference. In the end, neither style was ordered due to a surplus of cutlasses from the Napoleonic War.

From the known examples, the duke usually seems to have had his swords made by John Prosser or Samuel Brunn, both London-based. Brunn held the

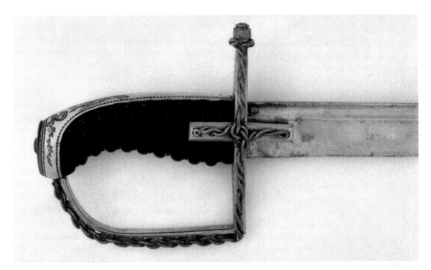

Above: Duke of Clarence's personal fighting sword. (National Army Museum, 1765-10-205-1)

Right: Prince William, print by Paul Sandy based on a painting by Benjamin West, published 15 January 1782. This portrait shows him as a midshipman, but with a different sword to that held by the National Army Museum. (© National Maritime Museum, Greenwich, London, PAH5531)

royal warrant as sword cutler to the Prince of Wales from 1800 to 1820, when he ceased business. The John Prossers (both senior and junior) were prolific sword manufacturers particularly at the upper end, and had warrants from George III, George IV, Queen Victoria and His Royal Highness Lord High Admiral (ie, the Duke of Clarence).[25]

The first sword he is known to have given was in 1786 to Lieutenant Walter Locke.[26] Lieutenant Locke served on the Fifth Rate *Hebe* (38) alongside Prince William the previous year, and the gift was an oval side ring sword which was a common style favoured by naval officers at the time. It has considerable silver gilt, so was a level above most officers' swords.

The coffin hilt swords

Maybe it was his personal choice of weapon that led the duke initially to award coffin pommel swords, which were atypical for naval officers. They were more common with the army. Regiments such as the Prince of Wales Irish Foot and some Light Dragoon regiments had the same distinctive pommel that gives the sword its name.

The City of London followed the duke's practice by gifting swords in 1797.[27] In the same year, London merchants gave presentation swords to several junior officers for dealing with the Nore mutiny. It is known that the duke presented swords to Admirals Collingwood, Duckworth, Durham, Nelson, and the Earl St Vincent. It is likely Durham was the first to receive his for the capture of the French Fifth Rate frigate *Loire* (40) in 1798 when he was still a captain (1780 to 1799). Duckworth's, Collingwood's and Durham's coffin hilt swords are documented. Three more coffin hilts known to exist have unknown recipients.

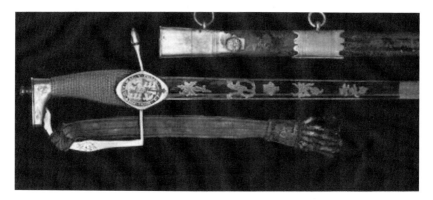

Unknown recipient's Duke of Clarence pommel sword.
(Courtesy of Bonhams, Lot 212, 29 April 2010)

The inscription on Duckworth's sword says it was given for the Battle of St Domingo (1806), so it would seem that Duckworth received his sword and that the duke continued giving out the coffin hilt swords for a short while after the 1805 pattern was introduced.

The 1805 pattern swords

The duke awarded twenty-two known 1805 pattern swords, with two recipients not known. The Earl of Northesk was one recipient. His inclusion should not be a surprise, as it features his coat of arms after the inclusion of Trafalgar. He probably received it after Duckworth received his sword, as St Domingo was January 1806.

Two more recipients served at Trafalgar. They were Captain (later Admiral Sir) William Hargood, who had previously served with Clarence and Captain (later Admiral Sir) Henry Blackwood who commanded the Fifth Rate *Euryalus* (36) at Trafalgar. Blackwood likely came to the duke's attention for looking after the heads of the other royal families of Europe when they visited England following the defeat of Napoleon. For this later event he was created a baronet.

It is unclear why the duke adopted the new naval pattern for his swords. Neither the City of London nor the Patriotic Fund did, and the Patriotic Fund even wrote to the Admiralty to make sure they could continue to give their style of sword. Admiral Sir Frederick Maitland received a sword from the Patriotic Fund for his heroic actions when he commanded the Fifth Rate (formerly *La Loire*) *Loire* (40) in 1805, the capture of the privateer *Esperanza*, the storming of the fort in the Bay of Camarinas, and his gallant conduct at Muros. His other mark of fame was that Napoleon surrendered to him.

The other surprising bestowal that is not a coffin hilt is the 1805 sword awarded to Captain (later Admiral Sir) Thomas Baker who received it for the capture of the French Fifth Rate frigate *Didon* (38) in August 1805.

Why two admirals, Sir Charles Rowley and Sir Samuel Warren, received these swords is opaque; their careers were successful but not particularly heroic. However, both had royal connections. Rowley was five years younger, but probably met Prince William when they were both midshipmen, as they were in the same squadron. Later, aged sixteen, Charles joined *Pegasus* when she was commanded by William, who made him master's mate.[28] Warren was a protégé of Stopford and went on to command the royal yacht while Clarence was Lord High Admiral.

Three more recipients shared the duke's position as the third son in a family and had gone to sea. Lord William Fitzroy was third son of the Duke of Grafton, Robert Stopford was third son of the 2nd Earl of Courtown, and Thomas Byam Martin was the third son of a baronetcy. Fitzroy was involved in various actions, including Cape Ortegal, but was dismissed by court martial for fraud and tyranny in 1810. However, his royal links ensured he was restored to his rank almost immediately by the Prince Regent, and made a Companion of the Order of the Bath in 1815, although he had no further active appointments. Stopford was a post captain by the time the Napoleonic War started; his sword was probably awarded for the Battle of St Domingo in 1806, as that is when he received a naval gold medal and was wounded in the battle. He opted to take a vase rather than the sword from the Patriotic Fund, possibly indicating he had another sword. Byam Martin's link was more personal. His first sea experience was on *Pegasus* under Prince William and they became friends and remained in close contact; indeed, for many years the prince courted Byam's sister.[29] He had a successful career, rising to Admiral of the Fleet. He managed the ships for the Russian emperor's visit under Clarence in 1814 and became Comptroller of the Navy in 1816, a post he held until 1831. What is surprising is despite the volume of his surviving papers, they make no mention of when the gift was bestowed, although there are several letters referring to his award of the Swedish Order of the Sword in 1808, a snuff box from the Emperor of Russia and a plate he received prior to 1815.[30]

Two others who served with the duke probably received theirs for being his friends. Admiral Sir Edward Thornbrough was captain of the Fifth Rate *Hebe* (38) when the prince was one of his lieutenants. Thornbrough was an admiral by 1805 but was generally ashore with stints at sea running blockade. He had no major actions to his credit.

William Hargood was first lieutenant to the duke when the duke commanded *Pegasus* and the Fifth Rate *Andromeda* (32). Hargood's sword may have been the result of his actions as captain of the Third Rate *Belleisle* (74) at Trafalgar. He subsequently commanded the Channel Islands Squadron as an admiral and retired in 1815.

Admiral Sir Augustus Clifford was another naval officer from the nobility. As the recognised but illegitimate son of the Duke of Devonshire, Devonshire's patronage ensured Clifford was a post captain by 1812 and in the subsequent peace he served as an attendant to Clarence when Clarence was Lord High Admiral.

Why Admiral Sir Thomas Ussher received his sword is unclear. He was involved in many heroic cutting-out operations during the French Revolutionary War. Although these actions left him with several wounds, he continued at sea because he was unable to get a pension. In recognition of his service he was made a Companion of the Bath in 1815, and finally, that year, awarded a pension for his wounds. Whether something in this campaign for his pension came to the notice of the duke, or whether there are other so far unfound

Duke of Clarence crest on an 1805 naval sword handle. (Courtesy of Chris Allen)

connections is unclear. In 1827 Ussher found a position in the royal household serving as equerry to the duke's mother.

Admiral van Capellan's receipt of a sword[31] was unexpected. He was a Dutch admiral who spent the Napoleonic War in Britain as an exile. But after

Napoleon's defeat, he was restored to the new Royal Netherlands Navy. He participated in the Bombardment of Algiers, alongside Pellew, who ironically didn't receive a sword for the battle. In 1816 Capellan was given an honorary knighthood. He retired from the Dutch navy to become a Dutch civil servant.

The double awards of 1805 and 1827

At least six recipients received both an 1805 and 1827 pattern swords.

Both of Admiral George Cockburn's swords survive. He most likely received his 1805 sword for his commanding of Royal Navy operations in the Chesapeake Bay during the War of 1812, particularly for the burning of Washington. His later portrait by George Lucas shows him with his 1827 pattern Duke of Clarence sword,[32] whereas his 1817 portrait by John James Halls with Washington burning in the background shows him with a standard 1805 pattern naval sword, indicating the first was probably given shortly afterwards, especially as he left active service in 1818 to become a politician. His 1820 portrait by Beechey shows him with the sword he received from Nelson.[33]

Captain Robert Cavendish Spencer's awards are slightly surprising. He had a reasonable career, but no stand-out events prior to 1827. However, his father, the 2nd Earl Spencer, was an important politician who served as Home Secretary in 1806/7. Thus one possibility is that the duke gave the sword to encourage the Spencer family to support him in his aspirations for a more active role in the navy; later in his career Robert did exactly that. Alternatively, Robert and the duke may have had a personal friendship, as in August 1827 Robert was made the duke's private secretary and groom of the bedchamber, for the period while the duke was Lord High Admiral. Spencer also worked with the duke on naval reform. Robert died in late 1830; he had just been recalled to Britain, for serving at sea in the Mediterranean. He was to become surveyor-general of ordnance and, with the position, Spencer was responsible for cutlasses, as well as cannon. He and the duke may have shared the interest in swords.

The swords gifted to Lord Adolphus FitzClarence are the clearest example of personal links. FitzClarence was the duke's illegitimate, but recognised, son whose naval service was largely after the wars finished. His portraits show how such paintings can give proof of sword type and ownership. The sword in his first portrait clearly has an 1805 pattern. However, the sword held by the National Maritime Museum has an 1827 pattern. While the whereabouts of the 1805 sword are unknown, it was probably presented when he became a lieutenant in 1821, as prior to then he would not have been entitled to wear that style. Flag Captain, then Captain (later Admiral Sir) Andrew Pellet Green, who was entrusted with FitzClarence's training as a midshipman in 1818 was also a recipient of a sword.[34]

It is not known whether some recipients returned their earlier swords or kept both, but it was probably the latter case. Each officer of the 10th Light Dragoons (who became Hussars in 1806) received swords in 1792 from their colonel-in-chief, the Prince of Wales, who even paid for their replacement swords when the pattern changed in 1808. The first swords were supposed to be returned due to a regimental scandal in 1814 relating to officers attempting to undermine their commanding officer, followed by the Prince of Wales insisting that all those who participated were to be removed from the regiment.[35] This return of swords was not because of the changeover of sword pattern. It is clear not all swords were returned or replaced, as they have been seen in auction,[36] and therefore it is conjecture that some officers ignored the instruction.

There is strong evidence that, despite the personal links, the swords of Pellet Green (his 1827 pattern is a standard purchase),[37] Hargood (his portrait from 1835 shows his 1805 Duke of Clarence sword)[38] and Baker (whose post 1827 portrait shows a standard purchase)[39] all almost certainly were not returned or replaced.

The 1827 pattern swords

The year 1827 saw both the introduction of a new pattern naval sword, coinciding with the Duke of Clarence being appointed Lord High Admiral, which placed him in the navy without giving him the operational command that he really wanted. There were attempts by King George IV and First Lord of the Admiralty to ensure he was limited in what he could change.

Thus he seems to have concentrated on uniforms. He differed with the government over whether Admiral Codrington was right to have engaged the Ottomans in the battle at Navarino (1827); he thought this would improve Britain's position and had possibly encouraged Admiral Codrington to undertake the battle. In 1827 he arranged a pageant at sea (an 1820s version of 'Meet the Navy') and in 1828 he arranged a second pageant, but managed to get the fleet to sail without any admiral embarked, enabling him to take command. The duke was made to resign from the navy for this.[40]

Introducing the new sword pattern, the duke gave swords to those involved in naval decision-making; recipients were both the officers on the Naval Board, Admirals Cockburn and Sir William Hope, as well as Admiral Sir Edward Owen, who was surveyor general of the ordnance. The duke presented additional swords to Admiral Thomas Hardy who led the pageant; Admiral Codrington who won the Battle of Navarino; one of the leading captains in the battle, Thomas Fellowes (later admiral); his old friend Byam Martin, who was serving as Comptroller of the Navy; the captain of the royal yacht, Captain Sir William Hoste; his groom of the bedchamber/private secretary, Captain Robert Spencer, and his serving son FitzClarence.

Hardy and Codrington would have been reasonable candidates to have received an 1805 pattern for their roles at Trafalgar. In a rare instance, Pocock cites a letter confirming that the Duke of Clarence sent a sword to Codrington.[41] In his portrait by Richard Evans in 1834 when he assumed the governorship of Greenwich, Admiral Hardy has the 1827 sword rather than his presentation sword for Trafalgar from the City of London. It is surprising that the sword does not feature in Admiral Thomas Fellowes's portrait by Henry Wyatt (in naval uniform) around 1836.[42] It was perhaps a sign of wanting to reconcile with Sir William Hope that the duke gave him a sword, as when Hope had served under the prince in *Pegasus*, they had dramatically and publicly fallen out.

It should not be surprising that Admiral Sir Richard Keats finally appears in this list following his friendship with the duke mentioned earlier. He had a successful career, being knighted and becoming an admiral in 1807. He retired from the sea in 1812 due to ill health, and became commodore-governor of Newfoundland. He appears not to have owned an 1805 sword as his portrait by John Jackson painted in 1817 shows him seemingly with every mark of approbation he could wear, but no special sword.[43] Therefore it is likely the sword was a later form of recognition. As Keats was governor of Greenwich Hospital from 1821, a post he held to his death in 1834, he would have been interacting with the duke as Lord High Admiral. Unless an 1805 pattern was given earlier, then the sword was probably presented in 1827 when the new pattern came out. This supports the theory that the Duke of Clarence was particularly interested in the introduction of this new pattern of naval sword.

William IV awards
Two swords were definitely presented after William became king in 1830. These follow the official pattern of the services. These are two mameluke swords, illustrating the pattern for generals in 1831, not being adopted for admirals until 1842. The first is unusual in having a polished ebony grip, instead of a white ivory grip. This blade states 'Presented by King William the Fourth to His Aide De Camp Col William Wemyss of Wemyss Castle 1831.'[44] The last sword the author is aware of that William presented was the one to Lord Hill as commander-in-chief of the army in 1834.[45]

It would appear that Admiral Gore's 1827 pattern sword was from this period and was likely awarded when he took command of the East Indies and China Station in 1831.

Lieutenant Colonel Cooper's sword with the guard having in it both Cooper's and the Duke of Clarence's crests. (*Courtesy of private collection*)

A sword of unknown date

Another sword of unknown date was awarded to Lieutenant Colonel Cooper, who became groom of the bedchamber in 1812 and remained in post until he died in 1828. It is a 1796 heavy cavalry pattern sword.[46]

Surprising exclusions

It is surprising that other officers are not on the list as having received swords. Admiral Pellew has already been mentioned, but one would have expected the inclusion of Robert Digby, who was his first captain, and Thomas Foley, who was the other lieutenant in *Prince George* alongside Keats, who also mentored him and became a lifelong friend.[47] However, the Digby family does not have a sword on display alongside the other marks of approbation that he received. Similarly, from Byam Martin's letters it is clear that Admiral Saumarez did not receive a sword, even though he was part of a corresponding social group of friends with Martin, Keats and Thorborough, all of whom did receive swords.[48] Because Locke received a sword, one might have expected the other midshipmen from *Pegasus* to feature, but (later Captain) Pitt Burnaby Greene, (later Admiral) John Smollet and (later Admiral Sir) Francis Laforey do not. Similarly, (later Admiral Hon Sir) Arthur Legge does not and (later Admiral) Robert Oliver does not from his time on *Hebe*, although Martin, Rowley and Stopford do.[49] Of course, some of these swords might have been presented and have not survived or not been found.

Conclusion

It is clear the Duke of Clarence (William IV) was keen to recognise naval officers, especially those whom he knew personally, with a mark of appreciation. From their appearance in portraits, it is clear such recognition was appreciated by the recipients. Unusual for presentation swords of the period, they are not ostentatious and are, once the navy adopted an official pattern for swords in 1805, standard service pattern swords with just a distinct mark made on them, so that those who know, know.

List of known Duke of Clarence/William IV Presentation Swords

Recipient	Sword type	Most likely date of gift	Most likely reason
Lieutenant Walter Locke	Oval side ring	1786	Lieutenants together on *Hebe*
Admiral Sir John Duckworth	Coffin hilt	1806	St Domingo
Admiral Lord Horatio Nelson	Coffin hilt	Pre 1805	Personal friend
Admiral Earl St Vincent	Coffin hilt	Possible 1797	Battle of St Vincent
Admiral Philip Durham	Coffin hilt	1798	Capture of *Loire*
Admiral Cuthbert Collingwood	Coffin hilt	1805	Trafalgar
Admiral Sir Henry Blackwood	1805	c1814	Escorting foreign heads of state
Admiral Sir Thomas Baker	1805	1805	Capture of *Didon*
Admiral Sir George Cockburn	1805	1818	For burning Washington
	1827	1827	Board member with Prince William
Admiral Sir Augustus Clifford	1805	Unclear	Personal friend

Recipient	Sword type	Most likely date of gift	Most likely reason
Lord Adolphus FitzClarence	1805	1821	His son
	1827	1827	His son
Lord William Fitzroy	1805	1805 to 1810	Personal connections, 3rd son of Duke of Grafton
Admiral Sir John Gore	1805	1818–21	Admiral at the Nore
	1827	1827 or 1831	Either new pattern or on taking command of the China Station
Sir William Hargood	1805	1805	Trafalgar, but also personal friend
Captain Sir William Hoste	1805	1811 to 1815	Battle of Lissa
	1827	1827	Command of royal yacht
Admiral Sir Byam Martin	1805	Probably 1816 to 1826	Personal friend, served at sea together
	1827	1827	Personal friend
Admiral Sir Frederick Lewis Maitland	1805	1805	Single ship actions
Admiral William Carnegie, 7th Earl of Northesk	1805	1805	Trafalgar
Admiral Sir Andrew Pellet Green	1805	1818	Looked after FitzClarence
Admiral Sir Charles Rowley	1805	Unclear	Personal friend
Captain Robert Cavendish Spencer	1805	1805–26	Family connections
	1827	1827	Groom of the bedchamber
Admiral Sir Robert Stopford	1805	1806	Battle of St Domingo but also midshipman with the prince
Admiral Sir Edward Thornborough	1805	Unclear	The prince's captain while training
Admiral Sir Thomas Ussher	1805	1815	With award of his pension for wounds
Admiral Theodorus van Capellen	1805	1816	Bombardment of Algiers
Admiral Sir Samuel Warren	1805		Presumed personal friend
Admiral Sir Edward Codrington	1827	1827	Battle of Navarino
Admiral Sir Thomas Fellowes	1827	1827	Battle of Navarino
Admiral Sir Thomas Hardy	1827	1827	Led Prince William's pageant
Admiral Sir Henry Hope	1827	1827	Board member with Prince William
Admiral Sir Richard Keats	1827	1827	Governor of Greenwich and friend
Admiral Sir Edward Owen	1827	1827	Brought in new naval sword

Recipient	Sword type	Most likely date of gift	Most likely reason
Lieutenant Colonel Cooper	1796 heavy cavalry	Post 1812	Groom of the bedchamber
Col William Wemyss	Mameluke	1831	Aide-de-camp to William IV
Lord Rowland Hill	Mameluke	1832	Army commander-in-chief from 1828

In three instances the recipient is unknown: at least one coffin hilt (and potentially two more) and two 1805s, one of which passed through Bonhams but bore an unrecognised coat of arms.

Acknowledgement: I am particularly indebted to Chris Allen, an arms valuer who has worked for several major auction houses and has noted all of these that he has seen.

HM Schooner *Whiting* After Her Capture in 1812: The Cartagena Privateer *San Francisco de Paula*

George R Bandurek

This paper examines answers to the question 'What happened next?' in the story of HMS *Whiting*, a Bermuda-built schooner. Events up to 22 August 1812 can be found in a range of sources but they do not say what happened after her capture by the French privateer *Diligent* at that date.

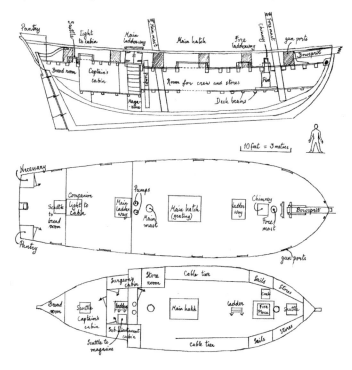

Author's cutaway drawing of *Whiting* based on Admiralty plans ZAZ6116 and ZAZ6117 at the National Maritime Museum, Greenwich, London.

Whiting was the subject of lengthy court proceedings in America because she was sold to the United Provinces of Granada and her new captain engaged in piracy. The court records provide us with her new name and details of the first few months of her new history. Her further successes as a privateer were documented in the *Jamaica Royal Gazette*. Her career was brought to a close when, in October 1813, she was captured by HMS *Forester* in an action described in detail in *Forester*'s logbooks. Comparisons with the logbooks show that the accounts in the *Gazette* and *Lloyd's List* contain errors.

HM Schooner *Whiting*

Whiting was one of twelve schooners built in Bermuda in 1804 as a dispatch vessel with a crew of twenty men and boys. A sub lieutenant wrote in his log in 1806 that *Whiting* was armed with two 12pdr carronades and two 6pdr cannons.[1]

In her first year of service, *Whiting* was used to press men illegally from Nova Scotia and pass them on to other ships in the North American Station. Keith Mercer gives a comprehensive account of this period.[2] In 1809 she was fitted to carry rockets and took part in the Battle of Basque Roads on the Biscay coast of France. She is probably best remembered for being the first British vessel to be captured in the War of 1812, though the American court ordered her release. Her freedom did not last long: the French privateer *Diligent* captured *Whiting* off the Virginia coast on 22 August 1812.[3]

The sequence of events following the capture by *Diligent* would have included judgement by a prize court and sale to a new owner. If we want to follow *Whiting*'s fate we need to find some document that joins her old and new identities.

San Francisco de Paula

We have comprehensive documentation from the New York State courts concerning a case Hallett vs Novion. Summaries and analyses of the initial court proceedings[4] and subsequent appeals to the New York Supreme Court[5] and Court of Errors[6] are available on the internet. The court proceedings tell us that:

> The schooner *Whiting* went to New Bern, North Carolina (see map of Virginia and North Carolina).
>
> By the end of 1812 or early 1813 she had moved to Washington, North Carolina.
>
> A man named Novion was agent for the owners.

Map of Virginia and North Carolina by Mitchell S August, 1860, based on one held by the Library of Congress (loc government item lva0000076).

The proceedings do not say when *Whiting* went to New Bern or who took her there: it might have been Grassin (*Diligent*'s captain) or a new owner, or Novion. There is a lengthy discussion in the documents about Novion's role and he might have been the owner himself rather than just an agent. In either case, he arranged for a ship's carpenter to undertake repairs to *Whiting* in Washington, North Carolina.

On 2 February 1813 Novion is said to have sold *Whiting* to Don Juan Pedro Laborda for $4,000, though this was contradicted in other, later evidence. Laborda then travelled to Cartagena, in present-day Colombia, which was rebelling from Spanish rule and trying to establish itself as an independent republic. The city could not afford a navy but relied on private enterprise: it would issue what was known locally as a *patente de corso* (letter of marque) to a ship, which was then legally allowed to prey on the nation's enemies.

Laborda obtained the money in Cartagena to pay for the ship, as well as a *patente de corso* allowing him to attack and capture Spanish ships. He had to put down a bond of $8,000 as security for the letter of marque that was granted to him and his schooner, *San Francisco de Paula*, commanded by Don Lewis Auris, to cruise against the vessels and property of the Spanish nation and her dependencies. It directed him to deliver said prizes to ports within the state of Cartagena, and that he should not dispose of them till the lawfulness of the prize be declared in due form. This is the first mention of the schooner as *San Francisco de Paula*.

When Laborda returned to Washington he passed the letter of marque to Luis Aury (or Louis Auris in one of a number of other variants of the name), who became *Whiting*'s captain. Aury already had a reputation as a successful French privateer and had probably been approached previously by Laborda or Novion or another character, Don Pedro Gual, whose name also appears on the letter of marque. Gual was a statesman and politician from Caracas and was in America from late 1812, taking part in discussions with President Madison and Secretary of State James Monroe on the recognition of the republic of Cartagena and the supply of arms. Morales wrote that Gual travelled back to Cartagena on *Whiting* when she left Washington.[7] Gual went on to have a successful political career in Cartagena and Venezuela.[8]

Laborda also instructed Novion to attend to fitting out the schooner, which according to Falconer meant:[9] 'The act of providing a ship with a sufficient number of men, to navigate and arm her for attack or defence; also to furnish her with proper masts, sails, yards, ammunition, artillery, cordage, anchors and other naval furniture; together with sufficient provisions for the ship's company.' The legal arguments claim that the fitting-out was illegal and in direct violation of the Act of Congress of 5 June 1794.

Map of the Kingdom of New Granada, showing the United Provinces. Author's drawing based on Milenioscuro, *Atlas básico de historia de Colombia*. (Primera república, CC BY-SA 3.0, 2012)

The official documentation that allowed *Whiting* to leave Washington for Cartagena was completed in March or April when she was 'cleared out' by the collector, Thomas H Blount: 'The *Whiting* left Washington in the beginning of April 1813 and while inside of Ocracock bar a commission was produced and read and the schooner was then called the *San Francisco de Paula* ... the Carthagena colors were then hoisted that the crew signed articles for the cruise.' Ocracock (now Ocracoke) is the exit from Pamlico Sound into the Atlantic. It is in American territorial waters and

Cartagena flag. Author's drawing based on several that can be found on the internet. The drawing depicts the contemporary flag of the period, which became obsolete.

161

would have been the last chance for a sailor to refuse to stay on the renamed, repurposed, departing schooner.

The key information here is the undeniable link between the schooner formerly known as *Whiting* and the same vessel under her new name: we must now follow the history of *San Francisco de Paula*, a privateer belonging to the United Provinces of Granada, otherwise simply called Cartagena.

Privateer successes on the first cruise

San Francisco de Paula sailed for Cartagena and took the opportunity to capture two ships on the way. The first of these received a passing mention in the Hallett vs Novion court proceedings which confirm that she was sent into Cartagena. Her name is unknown and the author has not found it in other searches: 'a Spanish vessel which was taken by the San Francisco de Paula on this cruise was sent into Carthagena and there condemned and sold and the prize money distributed among the captors.'

The second capture involves a wonderfully convoluted story which reveals the tribulations of travelling at sea. It also confirms that Luis Aury had the instincts of a pirate, even though he carried a letter of marque. The summary below is based on the Hallett vs Novion court proceedings.[10]

A brig called the *Jane*, owned by Hallett, sailed from the USA to Laguira, arriving in May 1812 with a cargo of flour. (Laguira is now known as La Guaira and is the port for Caracas in Venezuela.) The first mate on *Jane* was Charles Rise.

Jane changed her name to *Teneriffe* and adopted false Spanish papers before sailing for Porto Cavello (Cabello) in January 1813. This was done because England was now at war with the US, and she would have been prey to English ships. Rise was now the master of the brig.

On 8 January 1813 *Teneriffe* was stopped by an American privateer called the *Rosamund* and released without much delay.

On 9 January 1813 *Teneriffe* was stopped by HM Sloop *Fawn* (18) and sent into Porto Cavello with a British midshipman in charge of the prize crew. She had to pay $500 to be released.

Teneriffe changed her name to *La Hija* and retained false Spanish papers, though in the name of a different owner.

On 2 April 1813 *La Hija* (formerly *Teneriffe*, formerly *Jane*) left Porto Cavello for New York.

La Hija was taken once again by *Fawn* and carried to Curaçao, though she was soon released and continued her journey.

It was either on 20 or 26 April 1813 that *La Hija* was chased by *San*

Francisco de Paula. Different commentaries on the legal proceedings are responsible for the different dates.

La Hija was captured by *San Francisco de Paula*, even though her master, Rise, said that the 'Spanish' papers were false and that she was really American.

The court proceedings present conflicting evidence here. Novion, speaking for the captors, and three Americans in the crew said that 'the capture was made under Carthagena colors'.

In his own deposition to the court, Rise stated that the privateer at first had no flag, then raised American colours. *La Hija* raised Spanish colours, whereupon the privateer changed her colours to French. He said that he did not know the name or nationality of the captor and was told that 'he might inform his owner when he got to New York that he had been captured by a French pirate.' The court believed Novion and the American witnesses and accepted that a Carthagena privateer had captured what it believed to be a Spanish ship.

The captors now put a prize crew aboard *La Hija*, consisting of Lieutenant Ferrand and five men, and sent them off to the USA, not Cartagena. Ferrand stopped at the island of Santo Domingo (west Hispaniola, now Haiti) where Rise and the majority of the original crew were put ashore and left to make their own way home. Ferrand renamed the prize as *San Antonio* and 'endeavored to disguise the brig by painting her'. He created another set of false papers and changed his own name to Don Pedro Gonzales. The likely reason for the deception was that a prize court in Cartagena would disallow the capture on the basis that *La Hija* was not Spanish, and consequently Aury would lose his prize. William Johnson's commentary from 1819 describes the episode well:

> That the conduct of the privateer … was irregular and fraudulent, cannot be doubted. She was directed by her very commission to bring her prizes within the state of Carthagena, and not to dispose of them until the lawfulness of the prize had been declared. The commander of the privateer was no doubt soon satisfied, that the brig, though under the disguise of a Spanish vessel, was not really Spanish property, and fearing the test of a judicial inquiry, he took the mean and piratical course of disguising the prize, and appropriating her under fraudulent pretences.

Events continued to unfold in America:

> *San Antonio* (formerly *La Hija*, formerly *Teneriffe*, formerly *Jane*) arrived at Beaufort, North Carolina, in May 1813, claiming to have come from

Campeachy (Campeche in the Yucatan peninsula, Mexico).

Gonzales (really Ferrand) asked Francis La Motte, a merchant in New Bern, North Carolina, to take charge of the brig and her cargo.

Two or three days later, Novion arrived at New Bern and claimed that the brig and cargo belonged to him because it had been taken by his privateer, *Whiting*.

Gonzales then showed La Motte a letter from Luis Aury which confirmed that Novion was the owner. (This contradicts an earlier statement that Novion had sold the schooner to Laborda in February.)

Novion instructed La Motte to purchase and load a new cargo into *San Antonio*.

Aury's cunning plan unravelled when Rise and the original crew of *Jane* returned to Beaufort, recognised their ship, and informed the owner, Hallett, who started legal proceedings.

The case first went to court in 1816. The judgement of the District Court was that the prize should be restored to Hallett, who was awarded $1,000 in damages. The case then went to the New York Supreme Court on appeal, and the judgement was again in favour of the owner. The captors were told to pay him $29,687.80. Novion then took the case to another level of appeal, this time to the Court of Errors, in January 1819. He engaged Aaron Burr (the man who shot Hamilton in a duel) as his lawyer. The 'decision of the court was pronounced in an elaborate opinion', which determined that this case was outside the jurisdiction of the courts that had looked at it and should have gone to an admiralty court instead. Novion was awarded $233.24 in costs. Luis Aury and Novion kept their prize, even though they had not followed the instructions in the patent to bring prizes to Cartagena, making this an act of piracy, not privateering. It is not known whether the authorities in Cartagena ever found out.

Sojourn in Cartagena

San Francisco de Paula arrived in Cartagena in May 1813. It is likely that Aury and the political leaders were involved in a range of negotiations, for by August Aury had been appointed commodore of a flotilla, in addition to his position as captain of *San Francisco de Paula*. Morales writes that the other vessels were largely former American privateers who found it easier and more lucrative to prey on Spanish ships, using a Cartagena letter of marque, than to attack well-defended British ships. On 20 November 1813 the *Jamaica Royal Gazette* referred to *San Francisco de Paula* as 'an American privateer under Carthagenian colours', so the practice appears to have been well established.[11]

The crews of the privateers were a mixture of nationalities. The *Jamaica Royal Gazette* of 9 October 1813 says about the schooner that: 'The crew of the above privateer are a very motley group, composed, it is said, of all nations, and it is supposed that several of them will prove to be runaway negroes from different islands.'

Morales references Americans, Frenchmen and Spaniards, while Trujillo[12] mentions several Frenchmen who were in the crew of *San Francisco de Paula*, but their names are not on the muster list of HM Brig *Forester* (18) in October 1813.[13]

The legal evidence named John Harris, Robert Silver and John Bastard as seamen on *San Francisco de Paula* in April 1813. However, their names do not appear on *Forester*'s muster list, so they either left the schooner before then or lied about their names when the muster was drawn up. The majority of names on the muster are Spanish, though many of the original crew are likely to have been Americans, recruited around Pamlico. It is quite plausible that some left *San Francisco de Paula* at Cartagena or some intermediate stop and joined another ship.

San Francisco de Paula sailed from Cartagena in mid August.

Privateer successes on the second cruise
Searches for our privateer are complicated by the inconsistent use of her name in contemporary reports. Apart from obvious misspellings, *San Francisco de Paula* is also referred to as the *San Francisco*, or the *Francisco de Paula*, or simply as the *Paula*. There were also other vessels which have the same or similar names, so it is easy to be confused by a false lead. That said, a fairly comprehensive history of her movements can be established. The principal source is the *Jamaica Royal Gazette* which was published weekly. Other documents fill in various gaps and are referenced below.

26 AUGUST 1813: FIRST CAPTURE
San Francisco de Paula captured a Spanish brig, the *Patriot*, to the north of Santo Domingo (Haiti) on 26 August 1813. The date is given by McCarthy with the passage as going from Newport, Rhode Island, to Santiago de Cuba.[14] The information presented below is a quotation from the *Royal Jamaica Gazette* of 9 October 1813, which differs about the route but adds other details:

The Spanish brig *Patriot*, Captain Celestino Orleiza, taken to the northward of St Domingo by the Carthagenian privateer *San Francisco de Paula*, with a cargo of flour and lumber, from Boston to Cuba, arrived at Carthagena on the 14th ult [September]. The prisoners were landed on the coast of Cuba. Only the Captain, a passenger, and a boy, arrived at Carthagena in the privateer.

By late September, *San Francisco de Paula* was 'cruising to the windward of Cumberland Harbour'. This natural harbour is now better known as Guantanamo Bay, located on the southeast tip of Cuba. She made her next captures near there or further to the south near Morant Cays, which lie southeast of Jamaica.

24 SEPTEMBER 1813: SECOND CAPTURE

San Francisco de Paula's second capture, *Brilliant Rosa*, was a Spanish ship with fifteen guns and forty men travelling from Corunna, Spain, to Veracruz, Mexico.

The majority, if not all, of the guns on *Brilliant Rosa* were probably small swivel guns with a gun crew of two or three men; larger cannon needed much larger crews and there were too few men on board. *San Francisco de Paula* had the heavier guns, but in a close-quarters action to board their target, the swivels would have been effective against Aury's men.

The crew of *San Francisco de Paula* at this time would have been about fifty-five to sixty men. This is an estimate based on the known size of her crew a week later and an assumption that between five and seven men would be put aboard any prize that they sent to Cartagena. They outnumbered *Brilliant Rosa*, but not by much.

This was, therefore, not an example where the privateer had overwhelming force. The action lasted an hour and a half, during which the captain of *Brilliant Rosa* and two of his men were killed, and six others were wounded. *Brilliant Rosa* stayed in company with *San Francisco de Paula* until the next day, presumably to make repairs so that a prize crew could sail her.

Lloyd's List for 28 December 1813 repeats the information above.

25 SEPTEMBER 1813: THIRD CAPTURE

According to the *Jamaica Royal Gazette* for 9 October and 30 November 1813, the third capture was the brig *Ciencia* with fourteen guns and twenty men under the command of Captain Longas. The guns were again probably light swivel guns. She was sailing from Bilboa or Cadiz to Havana with a 'cargo of 1600 barrels of flour, oil, olives, wine and dry goods'. Most of her crew was put aboard *Brilliant Rosa* and both vessels were sent to Cartagena.

Unfortunately for Aury, *Ciencia* was captured by the Sixth Rate frigate HMS *Sapphire* (28) on 30 October near Cartagena and was brought to Port Royal, Jamaica, arriving on 14 November. This capture was mentioned in diplomatic notes sent between Cartagena and Jamaica in late 1813 (see below).

30 SEPTEMBER 1813: FOURTH CAPTURE

The fourth capture was *Nuestra Senora de los Angelos*. According to the *Jamaica Royal Gazette* for 9 October and 30 October 1813, she was a felucca, a vessel with lateen sails. She was sailing from Guinea, West Africa, to Havana. Her cargo was primarily slaves, of whom at least eighty were brought on board *San Francisco de Paula*, together with some beef. The prize was then released and allowed to proceed, probably because Aury wanted to keep sufficient crew on his schooner to control the slaves and to capture other prizes later, rather than having to allocate crew to the captured ship. Four of the crew from *Nuestra Senora de los Angelos* removed to *San Francisco de Paula*, and it is reasonable to assume that either they wanted to join the privateer's crew or Aury wanted to use their knowledge of the slaves.

The living conditions on *San Francisco de Paula* must have been difficult even by contemporary standards. A later muster says that there were forty-five of her crew, four from *Nuestra Senora de los Angelos*, as well as eighty slaves aboard, which makes a total of 129 people. The captain had a small cabin about 7½ft long and 10ft at the widest; two officers had cabins about 6ft long and 3ft wide. The rest of the crew normally shared a hold that was about 20ft long, 11ft wide and just 4ft high. Quite how everyone fitted in is open to conjecture. It is likely that the slaves were squeezed in below and the crew stayed on deck, where they could work the ship and avoid the stench from the hold.

This capture was discussed in later years and used as evidence both for and against the illegal smuggling of slaves into Jamaica. The British abolition laws had prevented the importation of new slaves since 1807, but the abolitionists claimed that smuggling was still rife. James Stephen, in his 'Defence of the Bill for the Registration of Slaves', makes a strong case that *San Francisco de Paula* intended to land the slaves in Jamaica and make a substantial profit.[15] She was five leagues (thirty miles) to windward of Jamaica and 'in the best possible situation for running down either side of Jamaica, and landing the slaves by night at any spot where accomplices might choose to receive them'. The opposing arguments, that Jamaican slave owners were law-abiding citizens and that further Acts of Parliament were not needed, are presented in the *Colonial Journal*.[16]

Aury did not record his intentions in a conveniently revelatory letter, but the circumstances suggest that his plan was to offload the cargo of slaves as quickly as practical and sell them in Jamaica. It is possible that the four of the original crew from *Nuestra Senora de los Angelos* who joined him were complicit in this. One of them, Fernandes Hevis, was named as the supercargo, a term which meant that he was in charge of the accounts for a cargo. This supports the idea that Aury had brought them on board to help sell the slaves. Perhaps Aury thought that, having sent three prizes to Cartagena, he was now entitled to one on his private account. Whatever he intended to do, he was thwarted by the intervention of the Royal Navy.

The hunter hunted

HMS *Forester* was a brig sloop of the *Cruizer* class with an armament of sixteen 32pdr carronades and two 6pdr chase guns. Her captain was Commander Alexander Kennedy.

The events of the encounter between *Forester* and *San Francisco de Paula* were summarised in the *Royal Jamaica Gazette*, not always accurately, but the records kept by the officers of *Forester* hold more detail. The captain's log[17] and the muster book are the most useful documents, while the ship's log[18] has more sailing details. They had not been digitised at the time of writing.

The *Royal Bermuda Gazette* for 28 August to 18 September 1813 tells about

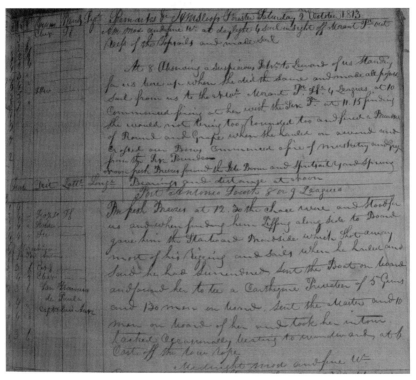

Captain's log for HMS *Forester*, 2 October 1813. (Author's photo of the captain's log, held at The National Archives, Kew, ADM 51/2376. Reproduced here with permission)

events prior to the encounter between *Forester* and *San Francisco de Paula*.[19] On 25 August *Forester* arrived in Bermuda, having delivered a convoy there from Jamaica. She had captured an American schooner, *Priscilla*, during the journey. *Forester* sailed on 16 September with a convoy for the West Indies.

On 1 October 1813 *Forester*, with her convoy, was off Port Morant, nearly home in Jamaica. But on the following day, a lookout on *Forester* sighted a 'suspicious schooner'. Captain Kennedy gave the order to chase and at 10.00am, when they were four leagues off Morant Point, 'commenced firing at her with the six pdr'.

At noon they were eight or nine leagues north of Port Antonio at the western tip of Cuba, sailing in a fresh breeze. At this point, Aury could have continued to sail his schooner close to the wind, whilst *Forester* would have had difficulty in keeping up because she was square-rigged and because her jibboom and spritsail yard were sprung (cracked). However, Aury didn't take advantage of his schooner's sailing qualities to escape and decided on a bolder tactic. He was going to board the British brig.

While there were forty-five crew on *San Francisco de Paula*, the normal complement for a *Cruizer*-class brig was 121 men and boys. Aury was taking on an experienced Royal Navy crew nearly three times the size of his own. Additionally, the disparity in armament was even greater than in crew size. Aury's schooner only had five small guns. His decision to board was certainly bold, with hindsight somewhat mistaken, and probably an act of sheer bravado. He did not stand a chance.

Captain Kennedy's log reads: 'gave him the Starboard Broadside which shot away most of his Rigging and sails. When ... hailed and said he had surrendered'. Aury's schooner was taken in tow, and on 4 October, *Forester*, her convoy and the prize arrived in Port Royal.

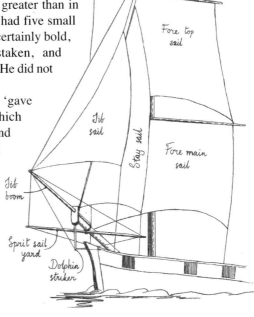

Bracing of the jibboom using the spritsail yard (the rigging is somewhat simplified). (Author's drawing, inspired by various photographs).

The *Jamaica Royal Gazette* for 4 October wrote that *Forester* and *Paula* had arrived in Port Royal. It added that the privateer had five guns (correct) and eighty men (quite wrong) and was commanded by Louis Army (close). The information from the *Gazette*, together with its errors, was repeated in *Lloyd's List* for 28 December 1813.

On 7 October Aury and his crew were sent to the prison ship *Loyalist*. They were trapped, awaiting court proceedings.

Prize court in Jamaica

Prior to Aury and his men going on trial, His Excellency the President of the State of Cartagena Manuel Rodriguez Torices sent an official despatch to Rear Admiral Brown in Jamaica on 21 October 1813, where he 'claimed the restitution of the armed schooner *San Francisco de Paula*'. A second dispatch followed on 4 November in which he presented his arguments in fulsome, flowing prose. For example, 'I found myself again under the painful necessity of repeating my official complaints of a series of hostile acts, which the interests and honour of this State, and a sacred regard to my own duty, will not permit me to pass over with indifference'. In addition to *San Francisco de Paula*, he complained about the recapture of *Ciencia* and other prizes which his privateers had already taken. The full text of the 4 November letter, in Spanish, was published in the *Gazeta de Cartagena* and copied in the *Gazeta de Caracas*.[20] An English translation is in the *Jamaica Royal Gazette* for 12 March 1814. Admiral Brown let events play themselves out in the prize court before replying.

News of the capture of *Nuestra Senora de Los Angelos* had reached the owner of the vessel, Don Philip Ravino of Saint Croix in Tenerife in the Canary Islands, who arrived in Jamaica. The original story that his ship had sailed from Guinea was now quietly hidden away because, if it were true, then the slaves on board would have been newly captured and therefore covered by the 1807 Abolition Act. They would have been condemned by the prize court and taken from their owner. The crew of *Forester* would have been awarded head money for rescuing the slaves at a rate of £40 for a male, £30 for a female and £10 for a child under age fourteen.

Slaves who were freed in this way were given the option of enlisting in the British armed forces – army or navy or marines – or of becoming apprentices for a period of fourteen years. The system was ripe for abuse and many simply stayed in a life of servitude, even though they were notionally free.

The 1807 Act did not emancipate existing slaves, and slave owners retained the right to keep their property. Don Philip Ravino made a claim to the Court of Vice Admiralty on 19 November (*Jamaica Royal Gazette* dated 20 November 1813). He said that the slaves were Creoles (born in slavery) and that he was taking them from Tenerife to Havana. The case was held over until 2 December, when seventy-eight slaves were appraised; it appears that two had died or escaped in the meantime.

Judgement was given on 10 January 1814. The judge had believed Don Philip Ravino and the slaves were restored to him, but he had to pay salvage to *Forester* because she had rescued them from a privateer. The rate for salvage was one-eighth of the value of the goods, so for the crew on *Forester* it did not make much difference which way the court decided: they would get a prize payment from either a condemnation or a restoration with salvage. Salvage was also awarded on the beef that had been taken from *Nuestra Senora de Los Angelos*. *San Francisco de Paula* was condemned and would have been sold at auction.

Several contemporary documents, such as the *Journal of the House of Commons*, provide identical tables which list slave ships the Royal Navy captured.[21] The events around *Nuestra Senora de Los Angelos* and her human cargo are given one line.

Return of all Ships or Vessels Condemned under the Acts for the Abolition of the Slave Trade (This table extracted from the *Journal of the House of Commons*)

Name of Ship	In what Colony the Proceedings took place	Date of Condemnation	Number of Creole Slaves Condemned	Alterations in the Sentence, on Appeal
San Fransisco de Paula (schooner) Aury, master	Jamaica	1814, January 10th One eighth salvage, decreed on slaves and beef	78	[N.B. 1813, Dec.2d at Jamaica 78 slaves were appraised.] No appeal

The Navy List for 1814[22] provides summaries of condemnations of prizes and uses a simple shorthand to keep the entries short.

FORRESTER, *for* San Francisco de Paula, *proceeds* of one eighth salvage on Slaves and Beef – *cond.* 10 Jan. 14 – *Agt.* Atkinson Bogle, & Co.

Admiral Brown, in his reply to the president of Cartagena on 21 January 1814, adopted a high moral tone about the procedures and legality of the actions of the Royal Navy. He wrote in conclusion: 'I enclose for your information a copy of the sentence pronounced against the *San Francisco de Paula* in the Vice Admiralty Court of this island; and as soon as the case of the *Ciencia* shall be known, I will transmit it also to your Excellency.' Admiral Brown finished his letter with good news for the president: 'I have the pleasure to inform you that I have ordered to be set at liberty several individuals, ascertained to be Carthagenians, although they were taken on board vessels brought in here and condemned as enemy's property.'

The wheels of justice had turned slowly for Aury and his crew, who had been held for over three months. Some might have been released earlier, and from the tone of the admiral's letter it is possible to interpret that some would be held for longer. The more likely outcome is that they were all released together and allowed to disperse to other ships or make their own way back to Cartagena or America.

After Jamaica

Positive identification of *San Francisco de Paula* after January 1814 has eluded the author. Records from the selling agent, Atkinson Bogle & Co, exist but only up to 1810, so we do not know who bought her.[23] There are a few tenuous clues but nothing solid about her fate.

The schooner might have been bought by the Royal Navy to resume her service, which did often happen with other recaptured vessels.[24] There was another schooner named *Whiting*, but she had entered service in January 1813 and was larger, with a complement of fifty. Her previous history is well documented and she is clearly not the same vessel.[25] If the 1804 *Whiting* was bought back, then it would have been under another name and there is no obvious record of this occurring.

San Francisco de Paula might have been purchased by agents of the Republic of Cartagena and restored to her place as part of Aury's flotilla. We know that Aury became captain of another vessel, usually referred to as the *Bellona* and occasionally as the *Velona*. *Niles Weekly Register* places him on that ship on 20 June 1814.[26] The *Jamaica Royal Gazette* puts him there at the end of the year (31 December 1814 issue). He was no longer associated with *San Francisco de Paula* and there are no mentions in several contemporary records of a privateer with that name. This absence of evidence suggests that she was no longer a Cartagena privateer.

If she kept her name after the sale then we could look for that in the records. The problems with variations of her name and with other vessels having the same or a similar name persist and are the sources of potential false leads. At least three merchant ships called *San Francisco de Paula* were captured in 1816 or 1817 and one of them could have been the final flourish of our Bermuda-built schooner.

Conclusion

In this paper, the known history of the schooner *Whiting* has been extended by a year and a half after her capture by the French. A wealth of information in original documents shows that she was successful as both a privateer and a pirate vessel. The early career of Luis Aury has also been described.

One lesson which has been reinforced is that secondary sources are not always accurate. This applies to newspapers, commentaries on court proceedings, and *Lloyd's List*, which relied on the former for its own reports.

The author's thanks go to Dr R J Parkin of Oxford University for his valuable assistance in proofreading and editing. The author also thanks Robin Mugridge for his translations of Spanish documents.

'I only wonder any civilised nation can allow them': Nelson's Actual Opinion of Privateers

Ryan C Walker

Researchers of privateers will inevitably find a Horatio Nelson statement (hereafter referred to as the Nelson Quote): 'The conduct of all privateers is, as far as I have seen, so near Piracy, that I only wonder any civilised nation can allow them.'[1] Over the centuries, the quote has taken on a life of its own, often cited by esteemed historians to indicate Nelson was against privateers.[2] Because of Nelson's reputation, historians have disproportionately applied his quotations to illustrate their opinions and validate their teachings on modern-day events and circumstances. The Nelson Quote is no exception. This article will explore Nelson's true opinion on private men-of-war by examining the original text, the context of his statement, other interactions Nelson had with privateers, and the evolution of Nelson's opinion based upon these interactions. It will clarify that Nelson's relationship with private men-of-war was far more nuanced than the manner in which this quote has previously found usage, and advocate a measured use of similar Nelsonian quotations.

Historiography

A 1898 *Puck* cartoon[3] illustrated how the privateer violated 'The spirit of the nineteenth century'. The artist conveyed the growing negative perception of privateers in individual governments and in international law. The cartoon was designed to illustrate the opinions of British naval historians and strategists such as Julian Corbett, who shifted the conversation from memorialising privateers who contributed to the

Puck: 'In the Path of the Privateer', by cartoonist Udo J Keppler, 1898.

(Library of Congress, public domain)

Britain's maritime history to justifying that privateering should be banned, because the practice was unsuitable for the modern world of diplomacy backed by a regulated military. To Corbett:

> The idea of privateering was a survival of a primitive and unscientific conception of war, which was governed mainly by a general notion of doing your enemy as much damage as possible and making reprisal for wrongs he had done you. To the same class of ideas belonged the practice of plunder and ravaging ashore ... But plunder was found to demoralise your troops and unfit them for fighting, and ravaging proved to be a less powerful means of coercing your enemy than exploiting the occupied country by means of regular requisitions for the supply of your own army and the increase of its offensive range.[4]

However, other historians of the later years of the Victorian era wrote to convince an audience sceptical that a ban forbidding commerce raiding and violation of private rights on the seas would last.[5] Historians such as Marryat, Laughton and Statham employed privateers as a historical vehicle or romanticised them, based upon their reputation in a different era.[6]

The spirit of the nineteenth century had reached Spain and the US who, despite not being signatories of the Paris Declaration Respecting Maritime Law (1856), respected the international agreement and waived their rights to use privateers in war.[7] The Nelson Quote became an easily accepted shorthand for historians seeking evidence to support their claim that contemporary British society disliked privateers, regarding them as little better than pirates. In the excellent monograph, *British Privateering Voyages of the Early Eighteenth Century*, Tim Beattie makes the case that Nelson's opinion was part of a greater trend in the gradual souring of opinion on privateers by Georgian naval officers and British society.[8] Beattie presented the Nelson Quote as primary evidence of Georgian opinion and supported this thesis by citing literary works such as Frederick Marryat's *The Privateer's Men*. Beattie somewhat misrepresents Marryat's characters; Marryat portrayed privateer captains as gentlemanly while portraying the crews as undisciplined.[9] Marryat's portrayal, and others like it, may have been influential in perpetuating a stereotype of undisciplined crews to historians such as Corbett.[10]

H C Timewell used the quote in a similar manner, though adding his opinion that the mercenary competition for prize money drove much of the mutual dislike between the public and private men-of-war.[11] Timewell's contribution has merit, but ignored that the effort to award prize money to navies had shifted to incentives associated with performance of duty by this period and was generally a benefit to senior officers.[12] Graham Bower represents a midpoint between Marryat, Laughton, Statham, Timewell and Beattie. In an article read before the Grotius Society of the UK in 1918, he argued that the German practice of unrestricted submarine warfare in the First World Ward was akin to the previous era of *guerre de course* – commerce raiding. To Bower, Admiral Vernon's opinion, together with that of Nelson's, represented contemporary opinion on privateers:[13] 'Your Excellency well knows that the granting of commissions to privateers is no part of my province, nor are they immediately under my control. I know too well what lawless libertines they are in all nations, and heartily wish no nation countenanced them.'[14]

Surprisingly, there is no letter in Vernon's papers that directly corresponds to this quote, indicating this may be based on edited, misquoted, or misused material.[15] Despite the lack of citation, Bower likely read this in Laughton's work, indicating Bower probably inherited this perception from Laughton, and the perception continues in research today.[16]

Nelson's letters have been the subject of a long line of excellent research, but the three primary texts this researcher examined are James Stanier Clarke and John M'Arthur's *The Life of Admiral Lord Nelson from His Manuscripts* (1809), Nicholas H Nicolas's *The Dispatches and Letters of Vice Admiral Lord Viscount Nelson* (1844/5), and Colin White's *Nelson: The New Letters* (2005). Despite this historiography, little deeper analysis of the exact context of the Nelson Quote has taken place. The following will seek to offer more thorough analysis from each source.

Original text analysis

The first question is where did the Nelson Quote originate? Beattie and Timewell were not the first to use it. They each cited another historian, while Bower and Statham elected to omit a citation, presumably reflecting its status as recognisably Nelsonian.[17] Fortunately, Laughton provided a citation to Nicolas's work.[18] If Nicolas's volumes had been the end of the hunt, fewer questions of authenticity, other than some questions on 'over-fussy Victorian punctuation', would be necessary.[19] Unfortunately, Nicolas did not have access to many of the letters that Clarke and M'Arthur had published, forcing Nicolas to rely upon Clarke and M'Arthur's collection to fill the gap, citing: 'From Clarke and M'Arthur, vol. II. p. 373.'[20] This presents some potential issues that are not easily rectified without an original letter.

It is now known that letters in Clarke and M'Arthur's collection were subjected to tampering. White wrote in 2003 that the Nelson Letters Projects and the Huntington Library found:

Clarke and M'Arthur were not content merely with omitting letters or editing them: at times, they even defaced and altered them … Some of the text was heavily scored through; new text had been added in M'Arthur's handwriting in the margins and between the lines. In places, scraps of paper bearing extracts, ripped from the heart of other letters, had been pasted to the top and bottom of the page. Apparently a number of people who lent letters to Clarke and M'Arthur had great difficulty in getting their property returned – now we know why![21]

Due to the potential distortions contained within Clarke and M'Arthur's volumes, the Nelson Quote cannot be taken as an inviolable, authentic, sweeping expression of Nelson's opinion on privateers.

Nelson's letter, according to Clarke and M'Arthur, was a reply to British minister Thomas Jackson, approximately 18 June 1804, 'respecting a Spanish Vessel detained by an English Privateer' in Civitavecchia, near Rome.[22] The letter itself is fairly vague, offering few details and confusing diction:

I have been favoured with your account of what had passed at Civita Vecchia, respecting a Spanish vessel detained by an English Privateer. The conduct of all privateers is, as far as I have seen, so near Piracy, that I only wonder any civilised nation can allow them. The lawful as well as unlawful commerce of the Neutral Flag is subject to every violation and spoliation; but I do not believe that any foreign power can make itself a judge, whether the detention be legal or not. The Spanish Consul, if he thought the conduct of the English Privateer wrong by an unjust detention, had only to apply to the Court of Vice Admiralty at Gibraltar or Malta. You know, my dear Sir, that no person in our Country can interfere with the Laws.[23]

From the first two lines, one would assume that Nelson condemned privateering. However, Nelson chose a more moderate tone in the remainder of the letter, emphasising that he knew only one side of the story. He went on to discuss the neutrality of the Papal State, emphasising the pressure the papal government was under from the French, forcing them to bend the rules of neutrality. Nelson concluded with his opinion: 'I have always directed the Neutrality of the Papal State to be attended to.'[24] From his viewpoint, he agreed with Jackson, offering a general condemnation of all privateers while simultaneously refraining from condemning this particular instance. This delicate position allowed him to vent his frustrations and avoid taking a permanent stance that could be taken out of context. It further endeared him to

Jackson, who would probably fixate on the same portion of the quote that historians have, but as Nelson gently chided him, to condemn them without further evidence would be outside of the bounds of law.

Was the letter in question one of the potentially tampered ones? Perhaps. In a previous structural analysis of Nelsonian letters, White noted: 'Nelson seldom used a full stop, let alone a colon or semi-colon; question and exclamation marks were unknown to him. He occasionally underlined, but his favourite way of emphasising words was to capitalize the first letter.'[25]

The amount of unlikely Nelsonian punctuation in the text raises questions about the authenticity, which cannot be conclusively confirmed until the original

surfaces. The major points of emphasis, besides properly capitalised words, become: *Privateer*, *Piracy*, *Neutral Flag*, *Laws*, and *Country*. The structure of the letter indicates it was possibly from two letters, combined into one, as the subjects were both privateers and the neutrality of the Papal State. Is it possible Clarke and M'Arthur were saving word count by combining elements of two separate letters sent to Jackson?

View of the Harbour, Civitavecchia. Watercolour on paper by unknown artist, published by Maillet, Paris, France, before 1744 or after 1760. (Courtesy of Rijksmuseum, Netherlands, public domain)

Nelson's response indicates he would have made as excellent a diplomat as he did an admiral. Unfortunately, the original letter has not been cited in any other collection and appears to be in an unknown collection or lost to history. Even if the letter was not tampered with, to fully understand the nature of Nelson's condemnation, one must consider the exact circumstances surrounding Civitavecchia. What made the privateer's conduct in Civitavecchia so egregious as to merit a sweeping condemnation?

The case in question
The Nelson Quote letter offers few details for understanding the case that led to the blanket condemnation. From examining the letter in Clarke and M'Arthur's work, we see five details that must be considered when looking for additional details:

> The private man-of-war was English.
> Only one private man-of-war was involved.
> The prize was a Spanish vessel.
> The encounter occurred at or near Civitavecchia on the Mediterranean (Tyrrhenian) Sea.
> The date of the encounter was before 18 June 1804, and had occurred within the previous year.

The first step is to verify whether other collections of Nelson's correspondence mentioned further details. There are other instances in which Nelson mentioned privateers but there is no indication Nelson had further discussion with Jackson or any others on this specific matter; nor is this unusual when Nelson discussed individual cases.[26] This author scoured the following databases:

> The National Archives at Kew
> *London Gazette* digitised database
> British Newspaper Online
> Prize Papers database
> *Reports of Cases Argued and Determined in the High Court of Admiralty: Commencing with the Judgments of the Right Hon. Sir William Scott Trinity Term 1811*[27]

Some instances about privateers emerged. Prize postings from the *London Gazette* provided few details and cross-referencing was necessary for greater detail. The best resources were prize appeals, in that they offered the most data on the circumstances of the captures, but were also the most limited in number.

If the case in question was illegal, one would expect the prize to have been appealed or not condemned, which was not unusual for those that violated the neutrality of the vessel and the course of action Nelson recommended.[28]

Surprisingly, in Admiralty court reports, only two cases matched the criteria. A 1915 analysis of prize appeals by H C Rothery concluded that RN vessels captured most of the Spanish prizes, indicating to him there were few English privateers prior to 1805 and only five captures attributable to them.[29] From Rothery's analysis this author found two cases that met the Civitavecchia criteria: *Dragon*'s capture of *Nostra (Neustra) Signora De Los Dolores* and *Surprize*, and *Two Brothers*' capture of *Venganza*.[30] The *Venganza* case has no information and was conducted by two privateers, disqualifying the case based on the information provided by Nelson. For the capture of *Nostra (Neustra) Signora De Los Dolores*, the only item preventing certainty is the location, though there is some damning evidence as remarked upon by Sir William Scott of the High Admiralty Court:

> THIS was the cafe of a Spanifh fhip and cargo which were captured on the 9th of Auguft 1803, by the private floop of war the Dragon, and decreed to be reftored, with cofts and damages, on the 19th of *December*, in the fame year … againft the owners of a privateer for the capture of a Spanifh veffel in time of peace. As far as I recollect the cafe, it was one of very great mif-conduct on the part of the captors, who had been guilty of a grofs violation of the law of nations.[31]

Unfortunately, this case lacks further details in the prize appeal and there is no mention of Civitavecchia or mention that the capture occurred in the Mediterranean. Further problems lie in the name of the prize taken; this is not the only prize case involving a vessel named *Nostra (Neustra) Signora De Los Dolores*. The Vice Admiralty Court in Jamaica also dealt with a *Nostra Signora De Los Dolores*, captured on 11 November 1805.[32] It is still the most likely candidate, although certainty is lacking due to the limitations of source data.

The difficulty in duplicate ship names leads to a potential alternative conclusion. It is possible that Nelson and Jackson received poor information. Another possibility stemming from its origin in Clarke and M'Arthur's text: could this have been a fabricated tale spread with details misconstrued, or juicy scuttlebutt? Clarke and M'Arthur's accounts did contain fabrications. Laughton draws attention to one of these fabrications; the 'half-burnt privateer', allegedly seen on 17 June 1805.[33] The passage, largely narrative, is constructed from little evidence and reads like a deduction from Conan Arthur Doyle's Sherlock Holmes:

[Nelson] immediately on seeing it, remarked, *They are French characters*! which probably stimulated him to a stricter observation. After an attentive examination, he said, 'I can unravel the whole: this Privateer had been chased and taken by the two ships that were seen in the W. N. W. The prize master, who had been put on board in a hurry, omitted to take with him his reckoning, there is none in the log book; and this dirty scrap of paper which none of you could make any thing of, contains his work for the number of days since the privateer last set Corvo, with an unaccounted-for run which I take to have been the chace, in his endeavour to find out his situation by back reckonings. The jackets I find to be the manufacture of France, which prove the Enemy was in possession of the Privateer; and I conclude by some mismanagement, she was run on board of afterwards by one of them and dismasted … If my explanation, gentlemen, be correct, I infer from it they are gone more to the northward, and more to the northward I will look for them.'[34]

This convoluted induction is representative of the lengths to which Clarke and M'Arthur went to aggrandise Nelson through their additional material. Laughton concluded that there was no evidence that any such event occurred.[35] The story does not appear to describe an actual event, as it was highly unlikely that anyone was transcribing Nelson's speech.

Due to the limitations of this analysis, the veracity of the case itself remains speculation and a further structural examination is necessary to understand what Nelson thought on the subject of private men-of-war.

Evolution of Nelson's opinion: encounters, professional bias, and personal bias
QUANTITATIVE OVERVIEW

Due to the malleability of the word 'privateer', it is necessary to distinguish what Nelson meant by that word. 'Privateer' as an adjective became a simulacrum, one used indiscriminately and interchangeably with other descriptors that fall under what N A M Rodger identified as a 'vague, anachronistic and contradictory language about private naval warfare.'[36] The author has referred to 'private men-of-war' when describing the vast realm of private naval warfare; when Nelson described a 'privateer' he often meant a vessel employed in *commerce-interdiction* duties, but not exclusively. Nelson frequently used British private men-of-war engaged in duties such as commerce interdiction or serving as packet ships, or even as fleet auxiliaries.

This author analysed the volumes of Clarke and M'Arthur, Nicolas and White for instances where Nelson mentioned privateers. The author then categorised these mentions based on the overall tone of the letters in which the mentions occurred. The letters may themselves have a passing reference or involve several subjects that are related:

> Clarke and M'Arthur's two volumes contained nineteen letters mentioning privateers. These letters contained thirteen distinct subjects. Nicolas's six volumes contained 140 letters mentioning privateers with twenty-three distinct subjects.
>
> White's *New Letters* contained eight letters mentioning privateers with seven distinct subjects.

In the analysis, letters were allowed to have multiple subjects, but they were divided only by the total aggregate of mentions. These were arranged into twenty-three categories with equal weight. This may not properly reflect emphasis, but does allow for quantitative analysis of Nelson's focus. It accounts for the number of letters while simultaneously allowing letters to show a wider scope than limiting them to one subject.

In Nicolas's six volumes, which had the largest aggregate mentions, to prevent double-counting of letters shared between his and Clarke and M'Arthur's volumes, the instances were divided by the aggregate of letters to get a percentage of categories seen in Table 2. His top five subjects were:

> *Particular Case(s)* 28.6 per cent: cases in which Nelson commented on privateers only in passing.
>
> *Violation(s) of Neutrality* 27.1 per cent: Nelson expressing frustration due to privateers using neutral ports that British forces were ordered not to infringe upon.
>
> *Commerce Protection* 22.9 per cent: orders from Nelson to his subordinates to protect commerce.
>
> *Orders to Act Against* 22.1 per cent: specific instances where Nelson called out prosecuting privateers as a primary mission.
>
> *Intelligence* 17.1 per cent: intelligence reports on enemy privateers' movements or known potential operating areas.

These instances represent the greater proportion of Nelson's surviving correspondence on privateers. The 'Particular Case(s)' category reflects the aggregate of cases discussed in individual letters; thus, the highest scoring individual category is actually 'Violation(s) of Neutrality'. When analysed in this context, the letter containing the Nelson Quote carries more emphasis on the Papal State's neutrality rather than a blanket condemnation of privateers;

those condemnations being a relatively rare instance in only three sweeping comments.[37] Indeed, in the Clarke and M'Arthur text, the Nelson Quote is the only instance of a blanket condemnation, indicating a quantitatively overblown discussion.[38]

QUALITATIVE OVERVIEW

The aggregate indicates the Nelson Quote was not Nelson's complete opinion on private men-of-war. The subsequent qualitative analysis of these letters will indicate Nelson's opinion was evolving. At times Nelson could appear collaborative, supportive, condemning, or annoyed.

When Nelson first fought American private men-of-war, he described their 'depredations' in passing, but also described encounters where he offered a grudging respect, such as when an unnamed American privateer avoided capture despite an hour-and-a-half battle.[39] Other foreign, private men-of-war, particularly French, were frequently the target of his ire. These instances primarily focus on his frustration with their violations of the laws of neutrality that he was charged to uphold.[40] This practice stymied the RN's effectiveness in prosecuting commerce interdictions. His frustration is evident in his defence of Lieutenant Shaw of the brig *Spider*, who allegedly violated this neutrality while engaged with a retreating French privateer.[41] White also wrote that Nelson directed his ire at Algerian and Barbary pirates who were infamous for not adhering to naval traditions and maritime law.[42]

Nelson's opinion in the 1790s was conflicted. Nelson's employment of private men-of-war was not exclusive to harassment of commerce. He was authorised to employ private men-of-war when the situation called for it. Nelson did encounter allied Austrian and Corsican privateers. Of these, the Corsican privateers likely made the strongest impression. He contracted with them to serve as fleet auxiliaries in exchange for sharing prizes.[43] The Corsicans did not follow orders well and when the opportunity came for them to shine, they disappointed greatly.[44] Nelson summarised the misunderstandings that plagued their relationship:

> Respecting the Corsican privateers, my answer was on a supposition that two of the Privateers would give up every other consideration, and absolutely put themselves under my orders: in that case, and in that case only, did I mean to alter the established rule for sharing. However, not one has obeyed, or put himself under my orders: it has been an age since I have seen any of them.[45]

The employment of the Corsican private men-of-war may have served political purposes as well. The plan appears to have been concocted by a civilian minister and Nelson to mollify Corsican authorities they depended on until moving their base of operations to Sardinia: 'Mr. Drake sees the necessity of it, and so do I, therefore I am more interested that a Privateer or two should come under my orders.'[46]

Nelson was willing to employ privateers when they were integrated into his fleet. A specific instance occurred in the Mediterranean, whose waters attracted poorly behaved privateers of all nationalities. When a Danish vessel in 1796 complained of being detained by the RN blockade of Genoa, Nelson offered to let the Corsican privateers settle the matter. Within two hours the Danish captain wrote a letter apologising and returned to the port.[47] The implied threat of allowing the unrestrained men of the Corsican privateer to settle the matter was enough to convince the neutral ship to comply with the blockade.

In multiple instances, Nelson hired private men-of-war, including packet ships, and recommended using them to interdict an enemy convoy off Naples and to take a scouting role in Civitavecchia.[48] Nelson mentions the disruption to trade, but he also sought to assist British private men-of-war who were employed in that role. In one case Nelson aided a British owner of a private man-of-war in circumventing official Corsican channels by allowing the owner to invoke his name.[49] Nelson's primary interaction with British private men-of-war was with packet ships such as the *Swift* cutter. Overall, these interactions were positive, they served a pivotal communication role and probably did not cause many diplomatic incidents by their interactions with other nationalities.[50] While the Corsican private men-of-war were a tactical disappointment, they also served an important intimidation and diplomatic role that RN ships could not always perform when constrained by international law.

In the 1800s Nelson's opinion shifted. He increasingly mentioned 'depredations' from English private men-of-war, specifically those identified as originating from Gibraltar, that caused his diplomatic exasperation.[51] He demonstrated an increasing tendency to be less friendly towards those he deemed to act as privateers. Nelson likely felt increasing resentment towards private men-of-war due to the inherent competition for prize money, the lack of control he had over their actions, and the violations of neutrality he accused them of. In a similar statement to the Nelson Quote, he proclaimed in 1801:

Respecting privateers, I own I am decidedly of opinion that with very few exceptions they are a disgrace to our country; and it would be truly honourable never to permit one after this war. Such horrid robberies have been committed by them in all parts of the world, that it is really a disgrace to the country which tolerates them; and the conduct of too many of our vice-admiralty courts has no wonder made neutral nations think of preventing such iniquitous proceedings.[52]

The very few exceptions prevent this statement from being as acerbic as the Nelson Quote, but the statement indicates a major shift in tone from his past collaborations with private men-of-war due to circumstances largely out of their control. A weary Nelson wrote in 1799: 'This letter is on the subject of our Bastia and Calvi prize-money. What I have got at present is nothing: what I have lost is, an eye, ... and my health; with the satisfaction of my ship's Leghorn company being completely ruined: so much for debtor and creditor.'[53] These professional considerations evolved into more blanket condemnations that expressed Nelson's frustration, though in only three of these instances did Nelson bemoan their flagrant violations of neutrality.

An angle that historians have under-examined is the potential for Nelson's personal feelings to have influenced his opinion of private men-of-war. Hired private men-of-war in the packet service played a vital role in ensuring the RN had communications and intelligence-sharing. When the French privateer *Espérance* captured the *Swift* cutter in April 1804, Nelson lost not only valuable intelligence, but also a picture of Emma Hamilton and sensitive personal correspondence. Marianne Czisnik uncovered the path these letters travelled to reach Napoleon Bonaparte:

> However Nelson handled the possibility of their liaison being published, his concern was based on a misconception of the workings of French politics. Without reading the dispatches or examining their contents, the French consul had sent on the letters to the Minister of the Navy, Decrès. Decrès had deemed them so important that he had merely ordered them to be collected at the post office and passed from there directly to the office of the First Consul, Napoleon Bonaparte. What Napoleon made of them remains unknown, but lacking in parliamentary control, let alone a public discourse on government policies, he clearly did not see any need to publish diplomatic details that might induce French citizens to form their own opinions.[54]

Due to the temporal proximity, it is safe to assume that Nelson had not forgotten nor forgiven this violation of privacy, projecting his anger when writing the letter containing the Nelson Quote to Jackson. A mixture of personal and professional history, frustration, anger and resentment imbued the letter containing the Nelson Quote, which is neither qualitatively nor quantitatively representative of Nelson's opinion on private men-of-war as an aggregate.

Evolution of Nelson's opinion: encounters, professional bias and personal animosity

The Nelson Quote has been taken far beyond its initial meaning and should no longer be used to justify Georgian opinion on privateers or private men-of-war. Nelson disliked private men-of-war of all nationalities employed in commerce interdiction that did not adhere to laws of neutrality, but he also supported private men-of-war engaged in supporting British operations. Nelson asked privateers to join his fleet, employed Corsican privateers as fleet auxiliaries, and frequently hired private ships to transport correspondence. The condemnation seen in the Nelson Quote should be viewed as an outlier or a mixture of professional and personal frustration, rather than Nelson's opinion on every instance of privateering during the Georgian era.

Due to Nelson's gravity, one must exercise caution when quoting him. Researchers should ask the following questions before employing Nelson quotes to prevent future misuse:

How has the quotation been employed in the past?
In what text did the quotation originally appear?
What was the exact circumstance of the quote?
In what other Nelsonian correspondence does the subject crop up; and how does it fit quantitatively and qualitatively?

These precautions may seem excessive, but seeing how easily this quote has been misinterpreted should underscore the necessity. The survival of the volume of Nelsonian literature is fortuitous and when used wisely, illuminating. Owing to the volume, historians do not have to depend on a meagre number of works to discern meaning. Individual works on Nelson can be compared against a large potential aggregate on the same subject Nelson discussed. Understanding that Nelson was an actor within his era should allow for proper use of Nelson's opinions on subjects of his period.

The tables overleaf show the volume of Nelsonian literature available on privateers. This author identified and categorised each letter according to subject matter. Some of the letters contained multiple subjects, allowing counting in more than one category. The categories are only representative of the sum total, rather than a zero-sum, one-subject-only count. The number of instances can be divided by the aggregate sum of letters surveyed, giving a percentage value from the privateer letter collection. As can be seen, only a few, relatively isolated instances contain the subcategory 'Blanket Condemnation' as in the Nelson Quote; in Nicolas's text only three of the 140 letters fall under the category for a dismal 2.1 per cent subcategory mention.

Table 1:

Nelson's mention of 'privateer' in *James Stainier Clarke and John M'Arthur's The Life of Admiral Lord Nelson, K., From His Lordship's Manuscripts* in two volumes

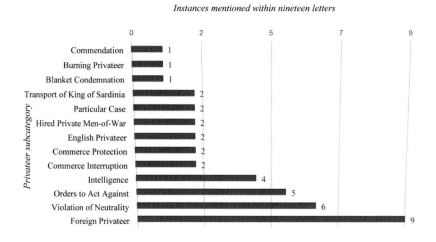

Instances mentioned within nineteen letters

Table 2:

Nelson's mention of 'privateer' in Colin White's *Nelson: The New Letters*

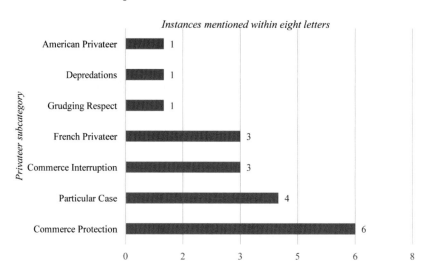

Instances mentioned within eight letters

Table 3:
Nelson's mention of 'privateer' in Nicholas Harris Nicolas's *The Dispatches and Letters of Vice Admiral Lord Viscount Nelson* in six volumes

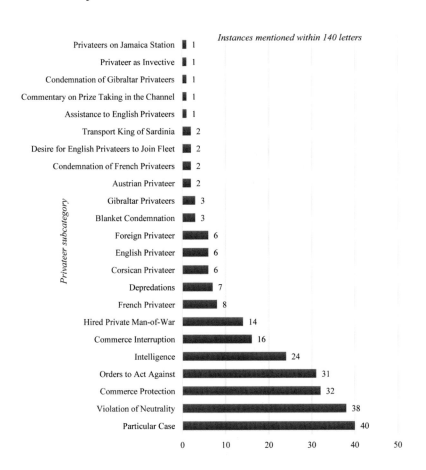

French xebec *L'Esperance* and cutter *Swift*, see colour plate 7

Contributors' Biographies

Dr George Bandurek holds a doctorate in physics from Oxford University and has now retired from a career as a consultant in problem-solving and quality engineering. He continues to use his research skills which are now focused on historical topics, often connected to modelmaking projects.

Dr Mark Barton is a recently retired Royal Navy commander who served thirty-five years as a marine engineer officer and was a former director of the Royal Naval Division at the Joint Services Command and Staff College. With a master's degree in defence studies, he completed a doctorate based on the Patriotic Fund at Lloyd's. He authored the maritime engineering element of the RN's current *Fighting Instructions*. Prior to retiring, he wrote two histories for the RN: *Royal Navy Dockyards and Bases* and *History of the Engineering Branch*, both published internally only. He has published many articles for various journals, mostly on engineering/naval architecture or in the area of his first book – *British Naval Swords and Swordsmanship*. Despite the technical aspects of these titles, it is the social history that interests him and his research continues on these topics alongside his work as a naval architect.

Dr Anthony Bruce is a former director at Universities UK and is now a higher education consultant. His first book (based on his doctorate) was on *The Purchase System in the British Army, 1660–1871* (1980). It was followed by *An Illustrated Companion to the First World War* (1998) and *The Last Crusade* (2002) on the war in Palestine, 1914–18. His *Encyclopaedia of Naval History* (1989) covers the period from the sixteenth century. Revised editions of *The Encyclopaedia* and *The Last Crusade* were published in 2020. His biography of *Lord Anson: Naval Commander and Statesman* was published in 2023. He is currently working on a study of Charles I's naval wars, 1625–29.

Andrew Field holds a graduate degree in education and history. He taught history in Suffolk county schools in England prior to retirement. With a longstanding interest in naval history, he has published the book, *Royal Navy Strategy in the Far East: Preparing for a War Against Japan*, and regularly reviews books for *Warship* and the *Naval Review*. Having lived in Eye for many years, he is familiar with Charles Cunningham's memorial and intends to develop a fuller biography of Cunningham's life and naval service.

Kenneth Flemming joined the RN in 1963 as a marine engineer at a time of modernisation and technical change. He undertook specialist training on modern diesel propulsion and mine clearance work. Joining Her Majesty's Prison Service, he served twenty years as an education officer to help prisoners develop individual learning and work skills before release. He is a former vice president, founding member and life member of The 1805 Club. He is also a past editor of the *Kedge Anchor*, the club magazine.

Captain Christer Hägg RSwN, Ret was commissioned in 1963 and began serving in destroyers before undergoing flight training. He is a graduate of the Empire Test Pilot School (UK), he was successively officer commanding patrol boat trials, staff operations officer in the Coastal Fleet and Commander First Helicopter Squadron. He has served as head of naval studies at the Swedish armed forces staff college and was naval attaché, Washington, from 1989–1992, completing his active service as flag captain of the Coastal Fleet from 1992–1994. Christer Hägg has written two books: *Fregatten Eugenies världsomsegling* (*The Frigate Eugenie's Circumnavigation*, 1999) and *Marinmälaren Jacob Hägg* (*Marine Artist Jacob Hägg*, 2003). He is one of the initiators of and a contributor to the book *The Baltic Cauldron: Two Navies and the Fight for Freedom*. Christer Hägg is a member of the Royal Swedish Society of Naval Sciences. He is also an accomplished maritime artist. See his work at ChristerHagg.com.

Captain Peter Hore RN, Rtd served in the Royal Navy from 1962–2000 as a specialist in logistics, including exchange service in the United States Navy and two tours in the NATO Standing Naval Force Atlantic. He studied at the universities of Lund and Exeter. He is a certified interpreter in Spanish and Swedish and was the joint logistics commander on Ascension Island during the 1982 Falklands War. From 1997 to 2000 he was the Head of Defence Studies (Navy) during the Strategic Defence Review and the development of British maritime doctrine. From 2000–2009 he was the CEO of the Film and Television Fund, before becoming an obituarist at the *Daily Telegraph*. He has written more than a dozen books on maritime history, biography and strategy and is one of the initiators of the book, *The Baltic Cauldron: Two Navies and the Fight for Freedom*. Peter Hore is an honorary member of the Royal Swedish Society of Naval Sciences.

Nicholas James Kaizer is a young Canadian scholar and teacher who studies the cultural history of the Royal Navy during the War of 1812. In particular, he is interested in the Anglo-Canadian responses to single-ship losses of that conflict. He has a MA from Dalhousie University and is the author of *Revenge in the Name of Honour*. He has written for *Warships: IFR*, the *Cool Canadian History* podcast, the *Napoleon Series*, the *War, Literature, and the Arts* journal, the *Trafalgar Chronicle*, and the Navy Records Society. https://nicholasjkaizer.ca/

Saikat Mondal is studying third-year history honours at Presidency University, Kolkata (Calcutta, India). He is a passionate reader of history with interests in military and economic history, a sports enthusiast, and a foodie in general.

Judith E Pearson holds a PhD in mental health counselling and is a retired licensed professional counsellor and certified master practitioner/trainer in hypnotherapy and Neuro-Linguistic Programming (NLP). She has published a book for writers: *Improve Your Writing with NLP*. Her professional background includes coaching, mental health counselling, writing, copyediting, teaching and project management. She is an active member of the Naval Order of the United States and writes for the national newsletter. She is a volunteer copyeditor for the *International Journal of Naval History*. She is a Distinguished Toastmaster with Toastmasters International. As a member of The 1805 Club, she co-edits the *Trafalgar Chronicle* with her husband, John Rodgaard (Captain, USN Ret). They live in Virginia and Florida.

Hilary L Rubinstein PhD FRHistS authored *Trafalgar Captain: Durham of the Defiance* (Stroud, Glos: Tempus, 2005) and *Catastrophe at Spithead: The Sinking of the Royal George* (Barnsley, Yorks: Seaforth Publishing, 2020). She edited *The Durham Papers* (published 2018) for the Navy Records Society. Her 'Durham's Dramas: A Trafalgar Captain at the Polls', appeared in the *Trafalgar Chronicle*, New Series, vol 6 (2021).

Andrew Venn is a young naval historian from Portsmouth, England. He holds a postgraduate degree in naval history from the University of Portsmouth and has experience working as a visitor guide onboard several museum ships, including HMS *Victory*. He is the co-author of the *Trafalgar Times*, a quarterly newsletter presenting little-known facts and under-researched topics to new audiences and enthusiasts alike. He often travels to visit museum ships and naval museums around the world and regularly enjoys researching and presenting the history of the Georgian Navy, using his youthful perspective to deliver fresh perceptions of the past.

Ryan C Walker served in the US Navy from 2014–2019, as an enlisted fire control technician aboard USS *Springfield* (SSN-761); he was honourably discharged in December 2019. Ryan graduated *summa cum laude* from Southern New Hampshire University with a BA in History. He continued his studies at the University of Portsmouth, where he received a distinction MA in naval history and hopes to pursue further studies in history. His contribution to this edition was written primarily from the research compiled while he was an MA student. His current research focus is on American submarine history (1900–1940), early development of Groton as a naval-capital town, and British private men-of-war in the North Atlantic. He currently resides in lovely Groton, Connecticut.

Notes

The Battles of Cape Finisterre, 1747

1   Michael Duffy, 'The Establishment of the Western Squadron as the Linchpin of British Naval Strategy', in M Duffy (ed), *Parameters of British Naval Power 1650–1850* (Exeter: University of Exeter Press, 1992), pp60–81; N A M Rodger, *The Insatiable Earl: A Life of John Montagu, Fourth Earl of Sandwich 1718–1792* (London: HarperCollins, 1993), p35.

2   George Anson to the Duke of Bedford, 4 November 1746, in John Russell, *Correspondence of John, Fourth Duke of Bedford, Selected from the Originals at Woburn Abbey* (London: Longman, Green, Brown and Longmans, 1842), vol I, p174.

3   Herbert W Richmond, *The Navy in the War of 1739–48* (London: Cambridge University Press, 1920), vol III, p82. See also Patricia K Crimmin, 'Anson: Cape Finisterre, 1747', in Eric Grove (ed), *Great Battles of the Royal Navy as Commemorated in the Gunroom, Britannia Royal Naval College, Dartmouth* (London: Arms and Armour, 1994), pp71–8.

4   Richmond, pp82–3.

5   British Library (BL): Anson Papers, Add MS 15,957, f172, Peter Warren to George Anson, 23 April 1747.

6   Julian S Corbett (ed), *Fighting Instructions, 1530–1816* (London: Navy Records Society, 1905), p142.

7   Richmond, p85.

8   John K Laughton, 'George Anson, Lord Anson (1697–1762)', *Dictionary of National Biography* (1885), <https://doi.org/10.1093/odnb/9780192683120.013.574>, accessed 23 December, 2022.

9   Ruddock F Mackay and Michael Duffy, *Hawke, Nelson and British Naval Leadership 1747–1805* (Woodbridge: The Boydell Press, 2009), p101.

10   Richmond, p90.

11   Andrew Lambert, *Admirals: The Naval Commanders Who Made Britain Great* (London: Faber & Faber, 2008), p133.

12   Richmond, p92.

13   Quoted in *The Naval Chronicle: Or, Voyages, Travels, Expeditions, Remarkable Exploits and Achievements, of the Most Celebrated English Navigators, Travellers, and Sea-Commanders, From the Earliest Accounts to the End of the Year 1759* (London: J Fuller, 1760), vol III, p166.

14   Julian Gwyn (ed), *The Royal Navy and North America: The Warren Papers 1736–1752* (London: Navy Records Society, 1973), xliii.

15   George Anson to the Duke of Bedford, 11 May 1747, in Russell, *Correspondence of John, Fourth Duke of Bedford*, vol I, pp214–15.

16   Julian Gwyn, *An Admiral for America: Sir Peter Warren, Vice Admiral of the Red, 1703–1752* (Gainesville: University Press of Florida, 2004), p130.

17 BL: Anson Papers, Add MS 15,955, f139, Duke of Bedford to George Anson, 16 May 1747.
18 Henry Pelham to the Duke of Bedford, 16 May 1747, in Russell, *Correspondence of John, Fourth Duke of Bedford*, vol I, p217.
19 'Further Instructions from Warren to Hawke, 8 August 1747', in Ruddock F Mackay (ed), *The Hawke Papers: A Selection 1743–1771*, Navy Records Society (Aldershot: Scolar Press, 1990), pp26–8.
20 Mackay and Duffy, p33.
21 Mackay and Duffy, pp38–9.
22 Ruddock F Mackay, *Admiral Hawke* (Oxford: Clarendon Press, 1965), p71.
23 Mackay, *Admiral Hawke*, p71.
24 Richmond, p106.
25 Edward Hawke to Thomas Corbett, 17 October 1747, in Mackay (ed), *The Hawke Papers*, p51.
26 Edward Hawke to Thomas Corbett, p54.
27 Edward Salmon, *Life of Admiral Sir Charles Saunders, KB* (London: Isaac Pitman, 1914), p60.
28 Augustus Keppel to George Anson, 26 October 1747, in Thomas Keppel, *The Life of Augustus, Viscount Keppel* (London: Henry Colburn, 1842), vol I, p113.
29 Edward Hawke to Thomas Corbett, p54.
30 'At a Council of War Held on Board His Majesty's Ship *Devonshire* at Sea', 15 October 1747, in Mackay (ed), *The Hawke Papers*, p56.
31 Mackay (ed), *The Hawke Papers*, p22.
32 Gwyn (ed), *The Royal Navy*, xliv.
33 National Maritime Museum: Sandwich Papers, SAN/V/50, p96, George Anson to Lord Sandwich, 1747/48.

Hornet versus *Peacock*: The Lost Historical Significance of the Single-Ship Actions of the War of 1812

1 Nicholas James Kaizer, '*Constitution* versus *Guerriere*: The Lost Historical Significance of the Single Ship Actions of the War of 1812', *Trafalgar Chronicle*, New Series 5, vol 7 (Barnsley: Seaforth Publishing, 2022), pp144–54.
2 Nicholas James Kaizer, *Revenge in the Name of Honour: The Royal Navy's Quest for Vengeance in the Single Ship Actions of the War of 1812* (Warwick: Helion & Company, 2020), xx.
3 Kaizer, *Revenge*, p175.
4 N A M Rodger, *The Command of the Ocean: A Naval History of Britain, 1649–1815* (New York: W W Norton, 2005), p516.
5 *Alert*'s commander gambled on a quick assault on *Essex*, hoping to disable one or two of her spars and so effect an escape. Porter misinterpreted this as a genuine attempt to attack, perhaps recalling the daring of Commander Thomas Cochrane of HMS *Speedy* in 1801. Kaizer, *Revenge*, p45.
6 Unbeknownst to him, he had just been promoted to post captain.
7 Kaizer, *Revenge*, pp46–7.
8 Theodore Roosevelt, *The Naval War of 1812 or the History of the United States Navy during the last war with Great Britain* (New York: G P Putnam's Sons, 1882), pp160–3.

9   Kevin D McCranie, *Utmost Gallantry: The US and Royal Navies at Sea in the War of 1812* (Annapolis: Naval Institute Press, 2011), p83.
10 Kaizer, *Revenge*, p91.
11 Kaizer, *Revenge*, pp131–4.
12 Kaizer, *Revenge*, p135.
13 William James, *Naval History of Great Britain: From the Declaration of War by France in 1793 to the Accession of George IV*, vol 6, reprint (London: Macmillan and Co, 1902), pp317–18; Roosevelt, *Naval War of 1812*, p216.
14 ADM 1/5440, Verdict, CM *Boxer*, The National Archives of the United Kingdom, Kew.
15 Kaizer, *Revenge*, pp98–9.
16 Commander-in-Chief of the North American Station in the first half of the War of 1812.
17 MG12 ADM1/506, Admiral's Dispatches, North America, C 12855, Commander Richard Wales to Vice Admiral Alexander Cochrane, 8 May 1814, Library and Archives Canada, Ottawa; McCranie, pp204–5.
18 ADM 1/5447, CM *Epervier*: Testimony of Commander Richard Wales, The National Archives of the United Kingdom, Kew.
19 ADM 1/5447, CM *Epervier*: Testimony of Lieutenant John Hackett, The National Archives of the United Kingdom, Kew.
20 ADM 1/5447, CM *Epervier*: Testimonies of Lt John Hackett, David Genlan, Master, William Pearson, quartermaster, The National Archives of the United Kingdom, Kew.
21 Kaizer, *Revenge*, xx–xxi.
22 Nicholas Tracy, *The Naval Chronicle: The Contemporary Record of the Royal Navy at War*, vol 1 (London: Chatham Publishing, 1998), vii.
23 'Tremlett to the Editor, 21 May 1813', *Naval Chronicle*, vol 28, p465.
24 Michael Duffy, 'The Gunnery at Trafalgar: Training, Tactics, or Temperament?', *Journal for Maritime Research*, 7:1 (2005), pp140–5.
25 Julian Gwyn, *Frigates and Foremasts: The North American Squadron in Nova Scotia Waters, 1745–1815* (Toronto and Vancouver: UBC Press, 2003), p143; Martin Bibbings, 'A Gunnery Zealot: Broke's Scientific Contribution to Naval Warfare', in Tim Voelcker (ed), *Broke of the Shannon and the War of 1812* (Barnsley: Seaforth Publishing, 2013), pp103–26; Martin Bibbings, 'The Battle', in Voelcker (ed), *Broke of the Shannon,* pp127–8; McCranie, pp150–1.
26 ' Admiral Sir John Warren, RN, Standing Order on the North American Station, Bermuda, 6 March 1813', *Naval War of 1812*, vol 2, p59.
27 Martin Bibbings, 'A Gunnery Zealot: Broke's Scientific Contribution to Naval Warfare', in Voelcker (ed), *Broke of the Shannon,* p114.
28 Duffy, p145.
29 Robert W Neeser, 'American Naval Gunnery: Past and Present', *North American Review*, 196:685 (1912), pp780–2.
30 Rodger, p516.
31 Kaizer, *Revenge*, pp95–7.

Bombay Marine, the Vanguard and Precursor of the Royal Indian Navy,

1   Charles Rathbone Low, *History of the Indian Navy (1613–1863)* (London: Richard Bentley and Son, 1877).
2   Satyindra Singh, *Under Two Ensigns: The Indian Navy, 1945–1950* (New Delhi: Oxford & IBH Publishing Company, 1986), p35.

NOTES

3 Colaba was one of the islands that is now part of Mumbai.
4 The Sidis are an ethnic group originating from East Africa and were brought to the subcontinent through the slave trade.
5 Commander K Sridharan, *A Maritime History of India* (New Delhi: Ministry of Information and Broadcasting, 1965), p100.
6 Thomas Mathews, *Dictionary of National Biography, 1676–1751*, vol 37, p44.
7 Mathews.
8 Kavalam Madhava Panikkar, *India and the Indian Ocean: An Essay on the Influence of Sea Power on Indian History* (London: G Allen & Unwin, Limited, 1962), p61.
9 This collection consists of photocopies and transcripts of East India Company papers held in India relating to the British factory in Bombay, 1755–1820, and similarly for Basra 1763–1811.
10 Low, p118.
11 Len Barnett, 'The East India Company's Marine (Indian Marine) and its Successors through to the Royal Indian Navy (1613–1947)', http://www.barnettmaritime.co.uk/mainbombay.htm (accessed 2 February 2023).
12 Satyindra.
13 Barnett.
14 Low, p176.
15 Philip MacDougall, 'British Seapower and the Mysore Wars of the Eighteenth Century', *Mariner's Mirror*, 97:4, 2013, p302.
16 Anirudh Despande, 'The Bombay Marine: Aspects of Maritime History 1650–1850', *Studies in History*, 11(2), 2016, pp289–90.
17 Despande, p281.
18 Low, p215.
19 Barnett.
20 Barnett.
21 K Sridharan, *A Maritime History of India* (New Delhi: Ministry of Information and Broadcasting, 1965), p124.

Russian Naval Power during the Eighteenth Century
1 Robert A Theobald Jr, 'Russian Navy – History and Traditions', *Naval War College Review*, vol 6, no 6, February 1954, pp25–52.
2 Robert K Massie, *Catherine the Great: Portrait of a Woman* (New York: Random House, 2011), p344.
3 Donald W Mitchell, *A History of Russian and Soviet Sea Power* (New York: MacMillan Publishing, 1974), p53.
4 Mitchell, p54.
5 Mitchell, p56.
6 Isabel de Madariaga, *Russia in the Age of Catherine the Great* (New Haven, Connecticut: Yale University Press, 1981), p209.
7 Bernard Pares, *A History of Russia* (1926; reprint Chicago: Marlboro Books, 1991), p307.
8 *The Annual Register*, 1769, 'The history of Europe', chap I, p2.
9 De Madariaga, pp209–10.
10 De Madariaga, p211.
11 George Sydenham Clarke, *Russia's Sea-Power, Past and Present* (London: John Murray, 1898), p30.

12   Clarke, p37.
13   Robert K Massie, *The Benthams in Russia, 1780–1791* (Oxford: Berg Publishers, 2005), pp216–22.
14   Clarke, p42.
15   R C Anderson, *Naval Wars in the Levant, 1559–1853* (Princeton, New Jersey: Princeton University Press, 1952), p335.
16   Anderson, p336.
17   'Russo-Swedish War of 1788– 1790 Began', Boris Yeltzen Presidential Library, online https://www.prlib.ru/en/history/619352.
18   Clarke, p40.
19   'Russo-Swedish War'.
20   A G Cross, 'Samuel Greig, Catherine the Great's Scottish Admiral', *Mariner's Mirror*, vol 60, issue 3 (Routledge: Society for Nautical Research, Taylor & Francis Group, 1974), pp251–65.
21   'Russo-Swedish War'.
22   Clarke, pp41–2.
23   Theobald, pp34–5.
24   Theobald, p35.
25   Clarke, p51.
26   Edgar Vincent, *Nelson: Love & Fame* (New Haven: Yale University Press, 2003), p300.
27   Mitchell, p110.
28   Mitchell, p111.
29   Clarke, p55.
30   Mitchell, p111.
31   Hans Christian Bjerg, *A History of the Royal Danish Navy 1510 – 2010* (The Royal Danish Navy, 2010, revised 2015), p119.
32   Mitchell, p114.
33   R M Johnston, *The Napoleonic Empire in Southern Italy and the Rise of the Secret Societies* (New York: MacMillan and Co, Ltd, 1904), p61.
34   Johnston, p68.
35   Johnston, p72.
36   Clarke, p116.
37   Clarke, p117.
38   Nicholas Tracy (ed), *The Naval Chronicle: The Contemporary Record of the Royal Navy at War*, vol IV, 1807–1810 (London: Chatham Publishing, 1999), pp62–5.
39   Clarke, pp122–4.
40   Clarke, pp126–8.
41   Clarke, pp132–3.
42   Clarke, pp137–45.

Diplomacy, Restraint and Protection: The Actions of Saumarez's Baltic Fleet 1808–1812

1   James Davey, *In Nelson's Wake: How the Royal Navy Ruled the Waves after Trafalgar* (New Haven, Connecticut: Yale University Press, 2015), p148.
2   François Crouzet, 'The British Economy at the Time of Trafalgar: Strengths and Weaknesses', in *Trafalgar in History: A Battle and its Afterlife*, David Cannadine (ed) (Basingstoke: Palgrave MacMillan, 2006), pp7–17 (p13).

3   Anthony Sullivan, *Man of War: The Fighting Life of Admiral James Saumarez: From the American Revolution to the Defeat of Napoleon* (Barnsley: Frontline Books, 2017), p154.

4   Davey, p148.

5   Sullivan, p150.

6   Sullivan, p150.

7   Martin Robson, *A History of the Royal Navy: The Napoleonic Wars* (London: I B Tauris, 2014), p152.

8   Sullivan, pp155–6.

9   Anthony Ryan, 'An Ambassador Afloat: Vice-Admiral Sir James Saumarez and the Swedish Court, 1808–1812', in *The British Navy and the Use of Naval Power in the Eighteenth Century*, Jeremy Black and Philip Woodfine (eds) (Leicester: Leicester University Press, 1998), pp237–58 (p245).

10 Robson, p154.

11 Robson, p155

12 Davey, p248.

13 N A M Rodger, *The Command of the Ocean: A Naval History of Britain; 1649–1815* (London: Penguin Books, 2005), p561.

14 Sullivan, p235.

15 Ryan, pp247–8.

16 Sullivan, p162.

17 Sullivan, p162.

18 Sullivan, pp162–5.

19 Davey, p246.

20 Robson, pp153–4.

21 Robson, pp156–7.

22 Richard Woodman (ed), *The Victory of Seapower: Winning the Napoleonic War 1806–1814* (Great Britain: Chatham Publishing 1998), p135.

23 Hans Christian Bjerg, *A History of the Royal Danish Navy, 1510–2010* (EAC Foundation 2010, reprinted and revised by the Royal Danish Navy, 2015), p121.

24 Bjerg, p121.

25 Robson, p148.

26 Davey, p155.

27 Davey, p155.

28 Robson, p148; Davey, pp155–6.

29 Robson, p148; Woodman, p118.

30 Brian Lavery, *Nelson's Victory: 250 Years of War and Peace* (Barnsley: Seaforth Publishing, 2015), p149.

31 Sullivan, p153.

32 Davey, pp243–7.

33 Rodger, p557.

34 Davey, p248.

35 Davey, pp247–8.

36 Ole Feldback, 'Denmark in the Napoleonic Wars: A Foreign Policy Survey', *Scandinavian Journal of History*, 26:2 (June 2001), pp89–101 (p95).

37 Davey, p248.

38 Feldback, p89; Davey, p248.

39 Lavery, p150.
40 Sullivan, p235.
41 Iain Ballantyne and Jonathan Eastland, *Victory: From Fighting the Armada to Trafalgar and Beyond* (Barnsley: Pen and Sword, 2013), p182.
42 Woodman, p113.

'An Officer of Great Merit': Captain Charles Cunningham and the Nore Mutiny

1 Suffolk Records Office, Ipswich UK, HA75/4/22 *The Annual Biography And Obituary* (United Kingdom, Longman, Hurst, Rees, Orme and Brome, 1835), p110.
2 Suffolk Records, *Annual Biography*, p111.
3 *Charles Cunningham*, www.wikipedia.org.
4 Suffolk Records Office, Ipswich UK, HA75/4/22 *The Papers of the Doughty Family of Theberton and Martlesham*.
5 *Charles Cunningham*.
6 *Charles Cunningham*.
7 Charles Cunningham, *A Narrative Of Occurrences That Took Place During The Mutiny At The Nore In The Months Of April, May, June 1797* (London: William Burrell, 1829, reprinted British Library Historical Print Editions, 2011), vii.
8 James Dugan, *The Great Mutiny* (London: André Deutsch, 1966), p178.
9 Dugan, pp179–80.
10 Dugan, pp21–35.
11 Geoffrey J Marcus, *Hearts of Oak: A Survey of British Sea Power in the Georgian Era* (Oxford: Oxford University Press, 1975), p110.
12 Christopher Lloyd, *The British Seaman* (United Kingdom: Collins 1968), pp200–1.
13 Dugan, pp178–80, gives a clear idea of conditions at the Nore. See also George E Manwaring & Bonamy Dobree, *Mutiny: The Floating Republic* (London: Century Hutchinson, 1987), pp122–4.
14 Manwaring & Dobree, p185.
15 National Maritime Museum, London (hereafter NMM), *The Cunningham Papers*, CUN/6 'Log Book of the *Clyde*', 1796.
16 NMM CUN//6.
17 NMM CUN//6.
18 NMM CUN//6.
19 Cunningham, *Narrative*, p16.
20 Dugan, pp207–8.
21 Cunningham, *Narrative*, pp21–2.
22 Cunningham, p28.
23 Cunningham, p30.
24 Cunningham, p32.
25 NMM CUN//6.
26 Cunningham, *Narrative*, p129.
27 Cunningham, *Narrative*, pp33–5.
28 Cunningham, pp34–5.
29 Cunningham, p37.
30 Manwaring & Dobree, p155.
31 Cunningham, p38.
32 Cunningham.

33 Manwaring & Dobree, p157.
34 Cunningham, p40.
35 Cunningham, pp44–5.
36 Cunningham, pp46–7.
37 Cunningham, p48.
38 Cunningham.
39 Cunningham, pp50–1.
40 One excellent analysis of the Navy Board's role and St Vincent's attempts at reform is in Roger Knight & Martin Wilcox, *Sustaining The Fleet 1793–1815: War, The British Navy and The Contractor State* (Woodbridge: Boydell Press 2010).
41 Knight & Wilcox, pp4–5.

Rodney and Kempenfelt: How They Were Related
1 Richard Harding and Peter LeFevre (eds), *Precursors of Nelson* (Mechanicsburg, Pennsylvania: Stackpole Books, 2000).
2 Both admirals have entries in the *Oxford Dictionary of National Biography*, hereinafter abbreviated *ODNB* (that for Kempenfelt is not wholly satisfactory); Edward Vernon to Richard Lestock, 7 April 1741, in *An Account of the Expedition to Carthagena* (London: 1743), p90.
3 See J K Laughton (ed), *Letters and Papers of Charles, Lord Barham, 1758–1813*, vol I, Navy Records Society Publications, vol 32 (1907), pp356–60.
4 David Syrett (ed), *The Rodney Papers, vol I, 1742–1763* and *The Rodney Papers, vol II, 1763–1780* (Navy Records Society Publications, vols 148 and 151); Young to Middleton, 24 July 1780, in Laughton (ed), *Letters and Papers,* p69; Rodney to Lord George Germain, 11 December 1781, referring to 'Kempenfield', in *Ninth Report of the Royal Commission on Historical Manuscripts. Part III. The Manuscripts of Mrs Stopford Sackville, of Drayton House, Northamptonshire* (London: Eyre and Spottiswood, 1884), p114; David Spinney, *Rodney* (London: Allen & Unwin, 1969); Peter Trew, *Rodney and The Breaking of the Line* (Barnsley, Pen & Sword, 2005); Christopher J Valin, *Fortune's Favorite: Sir Charles Douglas and the Breaking of the Line* (Tucson, Arizona: Fireship Press, 2009).
5 Laughton (ed), *Letters and Papers*, pp356–9; Åke Lindwall, 'The Encounter between Kempenfelt and De Guichen, December 1781', *Mariner's Mirror*, vol 87, no. 2 (2001), pp163–79; Hilary L Rubinstein, *Catastrophe at Spithead: The Sinking of the Royal George* (Barnsley: Seaforth, 2020); ancestry.co.uk.
6 Åke Lindwall, 'The Kempenfelt Family', *Mariner's Mirror*, vol 57, no. 4 (1970), pp379–83; Herbert G Wright, *Studies in Anglo-Scandinavian Relations* (Bangor, Wales: Jarvis & Foster, 1919), pp10–15 (chapter titled 'The Kempenfelt Family and English Literature'); ancestry.co.uk; findmypast.co.uk; familysearch.org. Perhaps Richard Steele was in fact the admiral's godfather, and my search for grandfather Richard a lucky red herring!
7 'The Mayors of Shrewsbury. From 1638 to 1935', *Shropshire Notes and Queries*, 6 November 1885, p193; *Derby Mercury*, 30 November 1753; John Venn and J A Venn (comps), *Alumni Cantabrigienses* (Cambridge: The University, 1922), p454.
8 Findmypast.co.uk; *The Visitation of London, Anno Domini 1633, 1634 and 1635*, vol 1, p404; John P Prendergast, *The Cromwellian Settlement of Ireland*, 2nd edn (London: Longmans, Green, Reader, & Dyer, 1870), pp411, 430, 443–8; Marriage Licence

Allegations in the Registry of the Bishop of London, Part II, 1660–1700, p2; ancestry.co.uk; 'The Mayors of Shrewsbury. From 1638 to 1935', *Shropshire Notes and Queries,* 6 November 1885, p193; *Derby Mercury*, 30 November 1753. For the Gascoignes of Yorkshire see 'The Gascoigne Family, *c*1309–1592: Gentry and Identity', Christopher Matthew Bovis, PhD thesis, University of York Centre for Medieval Studies, January 2017.

9   John Graves, *The History of Cleveland* (Carlisle: F Jollie, 1808), p22 and Appendix; *Oxford University Alumni, 1500–1886*, vol 2, p552 (on ancestry.co.uk); W A Shaw and G D Burtchaell, *The Knights of England: A complete record* (London: Sherratt & Hughes, 1906), p97.

10 Thomas Hargood, *Alumni Etonenses: Or, A Catalogue of the Provosts and Fellows of Eton College* (Birmingham: 1797), pp241–2; W Bruce Bannerman (ed), *Miscellanea Genealogica et Heraldica*, 4th Series, vol 5 (London: 1914), p235; cf William Senior, 'The Judges of the High Court of Admiralty', *Mariner's Mirror*, vol 13, no. 4 (1927), pp333–47.

11 William Hampton (rector of Worth, Sussex), quoted in John Ward, *The Lives of the Professors of Gresham College* (1740), p318; Philip Thicknesse, *Memoirs and Anecdotes* (Dublin: 1790), p131; familysearch.org.

12 Rodney's entry in the *ODNB*; familysearch.org. The former source gives mercer Henry Newton as 'of Highley, Essex', a place hard to pin down; Highley, Shropshire, was his ancestral location. For more on the clever and capable Mary Hunt, see Laura Gowing, *Ingenious Trade: Women and Work in Seventeenth Century London* (Cambridge University Press, 2022), pp27–8.

13 Ancestry.co.uk; Margaret may have been related to Rear Admiral John Gascoigne, whose will made in the 1740s when captain of HMS *Torbay* gave his locality as Stratford in the parish of West Ham, Essex (The National Archives, Kew, PROB 11/803/333, on ancestry.co.uk). Possibly the John Gascoigne baptised in Holborn, London early in 1695, he married in Aldersgate, London in 1727, and died in 1753.

14 Rodney to Clevland, 20 August 1759, *Rodney Papers*, vol I, p298; Clevland to Rodney, 24 August 1759, ibid; Rodney to John Clevland, 18 June 1759, ibid, p285; Clevland to Rodney, 20 June 1759, loc cit; see also ibid, p256; *Caledonian Mercury*, 24 January 1761. For Gascoigne's will see ancestry.co.uk.

A Dead Captain and a Sunken Ship: The Fates of Sir Jacob Wheate and HMS *Cerberus* in Bermuda

1   Amanda Dale, 'Centuries-old Remains Found Beneath Church', *The Royal Gazette*, 10 February 2011.
    https://www.royalgazette.com/other/news/article/20110210/centuries-old-remains-found-beneath-church/ (Accessed 2 February 2023). Much of the information in this newspaper article was based on an interview with Dr Brent Fortenberry.

2   Brent Fortenberry, 'Recent Excavations at St Peter's Church, St George's Bermuda', PDF placed online 26 April 2017, original in *Journal of Church Archaeology*, vol 12, 2008, pp67–72.

3   Dale.

4   Fortenberry, p70.

5   Michael Jarvis, *In the Eye of All Trade: Bermuda, Bermudians and the Maritime World 1680–1783* (Chapel Hill, North Carolina: University of North Carolina), pp385–436;

Keith Archibald Forbes, 'Bermuda's History from 1505 to 1779', at Bermuda Online.org: http://www.bermuda-online.org/history1505to1799.htm (Accessed 28 February 2023).

6   Fortenberry, p71.

7   St Peter's Church records, courtesy of Ms Gillian Outerbridge, Parish Administrator, accessed 25 February 2023.

8   St Peter's Church records.

9   Fortenberry. p72.

10   Fortenberry, p72.

11   Gordon Payne Watts, Jr, *Shipwrecked: Bermuda's Maritime Heritage* (The Old Royal Naval Dockyard, Bermuda: National Museum of Bermuda Press, 2014), p151.

12   Richard Hiscocks, 'Sir Jacob Wheate', 24 December 2016, More Than Nelson blog, https://morethannelson.com/officer/sir-jacob-wheate (Accessed 2 February 2023); ADM 6/22 Commission and Warrant Book 1779 – July 1782.

13   Richard Hiscocks, 'The Channel Fleet Retreat – August 1779', 24 November 2016. More Than Nelson blog, https://morethannelsom.com/channel-fleet-retreat-1779/ (Accessed 26 February 2023).

14   Hiscocks, 'The Channel Fleet Retreat'.

15   ADM 6/22.

16   Hiscocks,'Sir Jacob Wheate'.

17   H G Middleton, 'The Loss of HMS "Cerberus" (The Musket Shot Wreck) 1783', *Bermuda Historical Quarterly*, vol xxiv, Winter 1967, p122. Middleton cited the 'Reverend Alexander Richardson's private register of births, deaths, and marriages' as the source of his information about Wheate.

18   Middleton, p122.

19   Middleton, p126.

20   'Alexander Cochrane', Wikipedia, https://en.wikipedia.org/wiki/alexander_cochrane (Accessed 2 February 2023).

21   J J Colledge and Ben Warlow, *Ships of the Royal Navy* (London: Chatham, 2003), p64; Watts, pp163–4.

22   Wayne Walker, 'HMS *Cerberus* and The Royal Navy Dockyard', *Bermuda Journal of Archeology and Maritime History*, no. 8, (1996), pp30–40.

23   Middleton, pp122–4.

24   Watts, p164.

25   Wikipedia, 'HMS *Mentor*', https://en.wikipedia.org/wiki/HMS_Mentor (Accessed 26 February 2023). Middleton, however, wrote that *Mentor* was a former French frigate, *La Sybille*.

26   Middleton, p125.

27   Walker, p39; Middleton, p125.

28   Adrian James Webb, *Thomas Hurd, RN and His Hydrographic Survey of Bermuda (1789–97)* (Royal Naval Dockyard, Bermuda: National Museum of Bermuda Press, 2016), pp27–9.

29   Middleton, p125.

30   Walker, p33.

31   Webb, p40.

32   Webb contradicts Walker, who wrote that Hurd's survey took place from 1783 to 1794.

33   Walker, p39.

34   Shipwrecks in Bermuda: https://www.bermuda.com/shipwrecks-in-bermuda/
     (Accessed 2 February 2023).
35   Watts, pp163–4.
36   'HNLMS *Cerberus*', Wikipedia: https://en.wikipedia.org/wiki/HNLMS_Cerberus
     (Accessed 27 February 2023).
37   Royal Australian Navy, 'HMAS *Cerberus* (HMVS)', https://www.navy.gov.au/hmas-
     cerberus-hmvs (Accessed 27 February 2023).
38   Middleton, p126. Middleton added, 'no such memorial can be seen today [1967] and
     it would now be difficult, if not impossible, to determine the exact location of his
     interment.'
39   As of this writing, Dr Fortenberry is now affiliated with Tulane University.
40   'Expert Examines the 228-year-old remains of a ship's captain', *The Royal Gazette*, 2
     December 2011. https://www.royalgazette.com/other/news/article/20111202/expert-
     examines-228-year-old-remains-of-ships-captain/ (Accessed 14 February 2023).
41   'Expert Examines ...'
42   Reverend David Raths to Alan Brooks, email, 30 August 2012. Subject: 'Re-
     enterment of Sir Jacob Wheate'. Many thanks to Ms Gillian Outerbridge, Parish
     Administrator of St Peter's Church, for sending this email to me in response to my
     inquiry about the final status of Wheate's remains. Many thanks to Reverend David
     Raths (Retired) for giving permission to cite this email, via his email communication
     to me on 16 March 2023.

Duke of Clarence Swords

1   While often referred to as Lloyd's Patriotic Fund, this is a later name change from the
     Crimean War when it wished to distinguish itself from other patriotic funds.
2   An unattributed 1805 Duke of Clarence sword was sold at Bonhams, 26 May 2021, lot
     81.
3   Charles Fremantle, 'Sir Andrew Pellet Green', *Trafalgar Chronicle*, New Series 5
     (Barnsley: Seaforth Publishing, 2020), p113.
4   Examples include Beechey's portrait of the Duke of York at the Guards' Museum and
     his painting of the King reviewing his soldiers at Hyde Park, lost in the 1992 Windsor
     Castle fire. National Army Museum has another version, 1971-05-30-1; National
     Portrait Gallery holds a portrait of Duke of Clarence in naval uniform, NPG 2199;
     National Trust has one by Thomas Lawrence at Fenton House; Royal Collection has
     Prince William and Edward, Duke of Kent, RCIN403398.
5   Adam Zamoyski, *Phantom Terror* (London: William Collins, 2014), p100.
6   Gerry Marks, 'Swords of an Ancient Style', *Classic Arms & Militaria*, vol 12:1,
     Feb/Mar 2014, pp48–9.
7   Lot 32, Morphy's, 24–26 February 2017, Blade marked Osborne and Gunby of
     Birmingham and Pall Mall, so dates from 1808–1818.
8   Cowan's New York, 30 October 2018, William Koch collection, lot 453 dated in
     inscription 22 July 1816.
9   Leslie Southwick, 'New Light on the Georgian Sword and Gunmaker, Samuel Brunn',
     Journal of Arms and Armour Society, vol 23:3, March 2020, pp168–206, p186.
10   Sabre with Indian blade by Tatham.
11   Lot 374, Bonhams, 30 November 2017, made by Prosser, for teaching Austrian sword
     exercise to the Light Dragoons.

12 Queen's Librarian, *Trophies and Personal Relics of British Heroes* (London: John C Nimmo, 1896), Section VII. In 1896 in Royal Collection.

13 Leslie Southwick, 'The maker's mark of Thomas Price on British presentation swords', *Journal of the Arms and Armour Society,* vol 4:1, 2007.

14 Jersey museum. Action occurred while Duke of Sussex was visiting Naples; he asked Pickstock to visit that evening. The sword, although gifted, was not engraved until later, with the duke agreeing to the words.

15 Cowan's, New York, 30 October 18 William Koch collection, lot 454 made 'I W M a Solingen'.

16 Visible in John Jackson's 1820 painting at Bamburgh Castle.

17 Tom Pocock, *Sailor King, The Life of King William IV* (London: Sinclair-Stevenson, 1991), pp164–8.

18 While some sources say he commanded *Valiant* as a rear admiral (eg Wikipedia), the *Commissioned Sea Officers of the Royal Navy 1666–1815* (Naval Records Society), p82, gives date of promotion as 3 December 1790.

19 Engraving by Francesco Bartolozzi, and Paul Sandby, published 15 January 1782, NPG D33545.

20 Pocock, *Sailor King*, p59.

21 Pocock, *Sailor King*, p190.

22 Sim Comfort, *Naval Swords and Dirks (*London: Sim Comfort Associates, 2008), vol 1, p151.

23 Comfort, vol 3, unreferenced assertions.

24 *Minutes of Evidence taken before The Committee on Cutlasses & Cutlass Sword Bayonets supplied to the RN* (London: His Majesty's Stationery Office, 1887).

25 Richard Bezdek, *Swords and Sword Makers of England and Scotland* (US: Paladin Press, 2003), p55 and p141, respectively.

26 Recorded in W May and P Annis, *Swords for Sea Service* (London: Her Majesty's Stationery Office, 1970), vol 1, p65.

27 Admiral Jervis for the Battle of St Vincent. City of London Library Committee, *London's Roll of Fame being Complimentary Notes and Addresses from the City of London on Presentation of the Honorary Freedom of that City* (London: Cassell & Company, 1884), p75.

28 Private correspondence with family history researcher.

29 Pocock, *Sailor King*, p78.

30 *Letters of Sir Byam Martin* (Naval Record Society), vol II (1898), letters for 1808, Vol III (1900), p4 and vol III, pp247–56, respectively.

31 Held by Rijksmuseum, Holland.

32 Held at Governor's Residence, Gibraltar.

33 Painting is NMM BHC2618 and sword is NMM WPN1167.

34 Fremantle, 'Sir Andrew Pellet Green', p111.

35 Richard Dellar, *The British Cavalry Sword 1788–1912: Companion Volume* (England: Dellar, 2019), pp28–9.

36 Lot 297, Wallis & Wallis, 9 June 2015, attributed Lieutenant Rowland Edward Williams.

37 Personal visit to family collection.

38 NMM BHC2747.

39 NMM BHC2524 and sold by Sotheby's, 21 July 2003, lot 171.

40 Pocock, *Sailor King*, pp188–208.
41 Pocock, *Sailor King*, p197.
42 NMM BHC2687.
43 NMM BHC2975.
44 Sold by Michael Long, item SKU19500, still on website in September 2022.
45 NAM 1963-10-123.
46 Sold at Bonhams on 6 April 2006.
47 Pocock, *Sailor King*, p8 and p15, respectively.
48 *Letters of Sir Byam Martin*, vol 3, Letter: 9 April 1834, from Saumarez to Martin.
49 *Letters of Sir Byam Martin*, vol 1, (1902), p9 for *Hebe* and p28 for *Pegasus*.

Schooner *Whiting* after her capture in 1812: The Cartagena Privateer *San Francisco de Paula*

1   ADM 51/4518, Log book for John Roach, WHITING 1806 Apr 29 – 1806 Oct 28. Original kept at The National Archives, Kew, London.
2   Keith Mercer, 'Terror in the Countryside: HM Schooner *Whiting* in Southern Nova Scotia in 1805', *Trafalgar Chronicle*, 2009.
3   A copy of *Bowditch* exists that was given to Lieutenant Maxey by Woode Langdon of the brig *Drummond* when *Whiting* was released from the USA. It has hand-drawn annotations about the second capture. If anyone knows where to find this copy, please contact the author.
4   William Johnson, *Reports of cases argued and determined in the Supreme Court of Judicature and in the Court for the Trial of Impeachments and the Correction Errors, in the State of New York*, vol XIV, 1864, pp272–94.
5   Ralph Lockwood, *An Analytical and Practical Synopsis of all the cases argued and reversed in Law and Equity in the Court for the Correction of Errors of the State of New York from 1799 to 1847*, 1848, pp4–9.
6   Johnson, *Reports of cases argued*, vol XVI, 1819, pp327–47.
7   Edgardo Perez Morales, *No Limits to Their Sway: Cartagena's Privateers and the Masterless Caribbean* (Nashville, Tennessee: Vanderbilt University Press, 2018), p68.
8   Biografias Pedro Gual: https://www.venezuelatuya.com/biografias/gual.htm.
9   William Falconer, *Dictionary of the Marine* (London: 1784).
10 George Bandurek, 'Travels of a Merchant Brig During the War of 1812', *Kedge Anchor*, issue 57, Spring 2022, pp18–19.
11 *Jamaica Royal Gazette*: https://www.britishnewspaperarchive.co.uk/titles/royal-gazette-of-jamaica.
12 Nhora Patricia Palacios Trujillo, *Los Franceses en Colombia*, 2009, p112.
13 ADM 37/4576 Muster book HMS *Forester* 1813 Jan – 1814 Aug. Original kept at The National Archives, Kew, London.
14 FO 316/64 Foreign Office Archive. Original kept at The National Archives, Kew, London. As referenced by Matthew McCarthy, *Privateering and Piracy in the Spanish American Revolutions* (online dataset, 2012), http://www.hull.ac.uk/mhsc/piracy-mccarthy, downloaded November 2014.
15 James Stephen, *Defence of the Bill for the Registration of Slaves*, 1816, pp115–16.
16 *Colonial Journal*, vol 1, April 1816, pp223–6, published by Baldwin, Cradock and Joy. No author or editor is named.

NOTES

17 ADM 51/2376, Captain's log HMS *Forester* 1812 Aug 1 – 1816 Aug 7. Original kept at The National Archives, Kew, London.

18 ADM 53/513, Ship's log HMS *Forester* 1810 Sep 28 – 1814 Apl 29. Original kept at The National Archives, Kew, London.

19 *Royal Bermuda Gazette*, 28 August to 18 September 1813. http://bnl.contentdm.oclc.org/cdm/landingpage/collection/BermudaNP02

20 *Gazeta de Caracas*, 12 May 1814, vol 66, p253.

21 *Journal of the House of Commons*, vol 69, Session 1813 to 1814, p853 (Appendix 13, 25 July).

22 Navy List for 1814, The National Archives, Kew, p127.

23 Private communication from E Gooding, ING Group, 5 May 2020 (ownership of Atkinson Bogle & Co passed to Barings Bank and then to ING Group).

24 Rif Winfield, *British Warships in the Age of Sail 1793–1817: Design, Construction, Careers and Fates* (Barnsley, England: Seaforth Publishing, 2008), pp359–61. Four schooners of the Fish and Bird classes, like *Whiting*, were taken and then recaptured. Three (*Pike*, *Jackdaw*, *Landrail*) were returned to service in the Royal Navy, but *Flying Fish* was not. The *Adonis* class of schooners also had four recaptured, of which three were returned to service.

25 Winfield, p367.

26 *Niles Weekly Register*, 04 April 1818.

'I only wonder any civilised nation can allow them': Nelson's Actual Opinion of Privateers

1 James Stanier Clarke & John M'Arthur, *The Life of Admiral Lord Nelson from His Lordship's Manuscripts*, vol 2 (London: Bensley, 1809), p373.

2 J K Laughton, 'Privateers and Privateering in the Eighteenth Century', in *Fraser's Magazine New Series vol XXIV: From July to December 1881* (London: Longmans Green & and Co, 1881), p464; E P Statham, *Privateers and Privateering* (London: Hutchinson & Co, 1910), p12; Graham Bower, 'The Nation in Arms: Combatants and Non-Combatants', *Transactions of the Grotius Society*, vol 4 (1918), p79, accessed 23 September 2022, http://www.jstor.org/stable/743047; H C Timewell, 'Guernsey Privateers', *Mariner's Mirror*, vol 56, no 2 (1970), p216, accessed 23 September 2022, https://doi.org/10.1080/00253359.1970.10658533; David J Starkey, *British Privateering Enterprise in the Eighteenth Century* (Exeter: University of Exeter Press, 1990), p260; Mark P Donnelly and Daniel Diehl, *Pirates of Virginia: Plunder and High Adventure on the Old Dominion Coastline* (Mechanicsburg Pennsylvania: Stackpole Books, 2012), p3; Tim Beattie, *British Privateering Voyages of the Early Eighteenth Century* (Woodbridge: Boydell & Brewer, 2015), pp7–8.

3 Udo J Keppler, Artist, *Puck: In the Path of the Privateer* (New York: Keppler & Schwarzmann, 1898), accessed 8 September 2022, https://www.loc.gov/item/2012647564/.

4 J S Corbett, *Some Principles of Maritime Strategy* (London: Longmans, 2004), pp95–6.

5 Maritime League for the Resumption of Naval Rights by Great Britain, *Address to the Shipowners of Great Britain*, Pamphlets (1875), accessed 23 September 2022, https://jstor.org/stable/60236640; W Singleton, *Why Is England Defenceless?*, Pamphlets (1871), accessed 23 September 2022, https://jstor.org/stable/10.2307/60235140; Lewis Appleton, *Reform of International*

Maritime Law, Pamphlets, *Continental Herald and Swiss Times* (1874), https://jstor.org/stable/10.2307/60236496.

6   Laughton, 'Privateers', p468; Statham, *Privateers*, p365.

7   *The London Gazette*, 10 May 1898, issue 26965, https://www.thegazette. co.uk/London/issue/15280/page/875.

8   Beattie, *British Privateering Voyages*, pp7–8.

9   Frederick Marryat, *The Privateer's Man: One Hundred Years Ago* (Leipzig: Bernh Tauchnitz, 1846), pp5–7, 8–10, 22, 47–8, 106–7, 142–3, 288–95; for deeper analysis, see Ryan C Walker, 'Raising the Anchors of the Past: Re-Examination of British Private Warfare in the North Atlantic 1500–1815' (University of Portsmouth: MA Dissertation, 2022), pp70–3.

10   Corbett, *Some Principles*, pp95–6.

11   Timewell, 'Guernsey Privateers', p216.

12   Laughton, 'Privateers', p468.

13   Bower, 'The Nation in Arms', p79.

14   Laughton, 'Privateers', p468.

15   Edward Vernon, '468. Vernon to the Secretary of the Admiralty', in B McL Ranft (ed), *The Vernon Papers* (London: Navy Records Society, 1958), p532.

16   Statham, *Privateers and Privateering*, p12; Laughton, 'Privateers', p464; Douglas C Peifer, 'Maritime Commerce Warfare: The Coercive Response of the Weak?', *Naval War College Review*, vol 66, no. 2 (2013), pp85, 95, accessed 18 July 2022, http://www.jstor.org/stable/26397373; Christopher J McMahon, 'Maritime Trade Warfare: A Strategy for the Twenty-First Century?' *Naval War College Review*, vol 70, no. 3 (2017), pp14–38, accessed 18 July 2022, http://www.jstor.org/stable/26398039; Mark Cancian and Brandon Schwartz, 'Unleash the Privateers!: The United States Should Issue Letters of Marque to Fight Chinese Aggression at Sea', *Proceedings*, vol 146 (2020), accessed 18 August 2022, https://www.usni.org/magazines/proceedings/2020/april/unleash-privateers. Bower offers no citation, but the sentence is almost verbatim from Statham.

17   Statham, *Privateers*, p12; Bower, 'The Nation in Arms', p79.

18   Laughton, 'Privateers', p468; Nicholas Harris Nicolas (ed), *The Dispatches and Letters of Vice Admiral Lord Viscount Nelson with Notes*, vol 6 (London: Henry Colburn, 1846), pp79–80.

19   Colin White (ed), 'Introduction', *Nelson: The New Letters* (Woodbridge: Boydell Press, 2005), xxiii.

20   Nicolas (ed), *The Dispatches*, vol 6, p79; White, 'Introduction', *The New Letters*, xix.

21   Colin White, 'Nelson Apotheosised: The Creation of the Nelson Legend', in David Cannadine (ed), *Admiral Lord Nelson* (London: Palgrave MacMillan, 2005), p104.

22   Clarke & M'Arthur (eds), *The Life of Admiral Lord Nelson*, vol 2, p373. The modern spelling of 'Civitavecchia' is not used in the original text. For Nelson, the town was 'Civita Vecchia', which appears to have been the contemporary spelling.

23   Clarke & M'Arthur (eds), *The Life*, p373.

24   Clarke & M'Arthur (eds), *The Life*, p373.

25   White (ed), *The New Letters*, xxiii.

26   See Tables 1 & 3.

27 H C Rothery, *Prize Droits: Being a Report to HM Treasury on Droits of the Crown and of the Admiralty in Time of War*, E S Roscoe (ed), (London: Eyre and Spotiswoode Ltd, 1915).

28 Clarke & M'Arthur (eds), *The Life*, p373.

29 Rothery, *Prize Droits*, p65.

30 William Scott, 'June 28, 1813, Nostra Signora De Los Dolores: Morales', in *Reports of Cases Argued and Determined in the High Court of Admiralty: Commencing with the Judgments of the Right Hon Sir William Scott Trinity Term 1811*, John Dodson (ed), (London: A Strahan, 1815), pp290–9.

31 Scott, 'Nostra Signora De Los Dolores', pp290, 295.

32 Prize Papers Database, 'Nostra Signora de los Dolores', accessed 21 January 2023, https://portal.prizepapers.de/ship/prizepapers_ship_44ec0460-7d24-40d0-9c45-34f3d417b3e9/1/-/.

33 J K Laughton (ed), *Letters and Despatches of Horatio, Viscount Nelson: KB Duke of Bronte Vice-Admiral of the White Squadron* (London: Longmans & Green Co, 1886), pp336–7.

34 Clarke and M'Arthur (eds), *The Life*, p418.

35 Laughton (ed), *Letters and Despatches*, pp336–7.

36 N A M Rodger, 'The Law and Language of Private Naval Warfare', *Mariner's Mirror*, vol 100, no. 1 (February 2014), p5, accessed 23 September 2022, https://doi.org/10.1080/00253359.2014.866371.

37 See Table 3.

38 See Table 1.

39 White (ed), *The New Letters*, pp8, 138; Nicolas, *Dispatches*, vol 1, p6, p50.

40 See Table 3.

41 Nicolas (ed), *Dispatches*, vol 2, pp203–4.

42 White (ed), *The New Letters*, xxx.

43 Nicolas (ed), *Dispatches*, vol 2, pp203–4.

44 Nicolas (ed), *Dispatches*, vol 2, pp253–5.

45 Nicolas (ed), *Dispatches*, vol 2, p225.

46 Nicolas (ed), *Dispatches*, vol 2, pp222–3.

47 Nicolas (ed), *Dispatches*, vol 2, pp215–16.

48 Nicolas (ed), *Dispatches*, vol 2, pp228, 244.

49 Nicolas (ed), *Dispatches*, vol 1, pp306, 353, 488; vol 2, pp37, 302.

50 Nicolas (ed), *Dispatches*, vol 1, p59; vol 2, pp215–16, 222–3, 228, 232, 300–3; vol 3, p336; vol 5, p415.

51 Nicolas (ed), *Dispatches*, vol 5, p267; vol 6, pp62, 146, 226.

52 Nicolas (ed), *Dispatches*, vol 4, p395.

53 Laughton (ed), *Letters and Despatches*, p73.

54 Marianne Czisnik (ed), *Nelson's Letters to Lady Hamilton and Related Documents* (New York: Routledge, 2020), pp361–2, 575–80. Exactly what Nelson meant when he said 'picture' is unknown. Nelson frequently mentioned a picture of Emma Hamilton (pp127, 170, 440, 443) but does not elaborate. Czisnik offers in a footnote (p170): Christie's speculates here: 'a mention of Emma's picture (presumably the pastel portrait done by J H Schmidt in 1800), which hung in Nelson's Cabin'.

The 1805 Club

President: Admiral Sir Jonathon Band GCB DL
Chairman: Captain John A Rodgaard USN Ret

The 1805 Club is a registered charity no. 1071871

The 1805 Club was established in 1990, and as of 2023 celebrates its thirty-third year of dedication toward commemorating and conserving the history and heritage of the Georgian Era sailing navies, with emphasis toward the Royal Navy of the period.

No other organisation is so dedicated in its programmes of commemorative and conservation initiatives, education, publications and support to scholastic research of the Georgian era, as exhibited in such a publication as the *Trafalgar Chronicle*.

For thirty-three years, the members of The Club have demonstrated their enthusiasm for all aspects of the sailing world of the Georgian era, and through the partnership of Seaforth Publishing, the *Trafalgar Chronicle* represents such a singular endeavour.

To join The 1805 Club go to www.1805club.org
to access the membership application form.